GW00384798

Attacking Currency Trends

Founded in 1807, John Wiley & Sons is the oldest independent publishing company in the United States. With offices in North America, Europe, Australia, and Asia, Wiley is globally committed to developing and marketing print and electronic products and services for our customers' professional and personal knowledge and understanding.

The Wiley Trading series features books by traders who have survived the market's ever-changing temperament and have prospered—some by reinventing systems, others by getting back to basics. Whether you are a novice trader, a professional, or somewhere in between, these books will provide the advice and strategies needed to prosper today and well into the future.

For a list of available titles, visit our web site at www.WileyFinance.com.

Attacking Currency Trends

How to Anticipate and Trade Big Moves in the Forex Market

GREG MICHALOWSKI

WILEY

John Wiley & Sons, Inc.

Published by John Wiley & Sons, Inc., Hoboken, New Jersey.
Published simultaneously in Canada.

For general information on our other products and services or for technical support, please contact our Customer Care Department within the United States at (800) 762-2974, outside the United States at (317) 572-3993 or fax (317) 572-4002.

Wiley also publishes its books in a variety of electronic formats. Some content that appears in print may not be available in electronic books. For more information about Wiley products, visit our web site at www.wiley.com.

Library of Congress Cataloging-in-Publication Data:

Michalowski, Greg.
   Attacking currency trends : how to anticipate and trade big moves in the forex market / Greg Michalowski.
       p. cm. – (Wiley trading ; 487)
   Includes index.
   ISBN 978-0-470-87438-7 (hardback); ISBN 978-1-118-02349-5 (ebk);
   ISBN 978-1-118-02350-1 (ebk); ISBN 978-1-118-02351 (ebk)
   1. Foreign exchange market–Handbooks, manuals, etc.   2. Investments–Handbooks, manuals, etc.   3. Foreign exchange–Handbooks, manuals, etc.   I. Title.
   HG3851.M493 2011
   332.4'5–dc22

                                                                  2010051235

Printed in the United States of America

10 9 8 7 6 5 4

To Deb, Matt, Brian, and Bobby Michalowski

Contents

Acknowledgments

I will always remember something Bill Kidder said to me 25 years ago, soon after I met him for the first time. He said, "Your dad was one of my first mentors. He gave me his time and taught me a lot about the markets. He is a good man." These words are very powerful words and they stuck with me.

Bill was my first trading mentor, and the first thing he taught me, without saying, was to follow in my father's mentoring footsteps. Over the last few years of my career I have been able to pay the favor forward—to be a mentor. Although it is less personal than the mentoring I received, I do hope it has provided a benefit to your trading. Remember, however, that ultimately you will need to "fish for yourself."

Other life mentors I would like to acknowledge include my wife, Debbie; my mother and father; my sons, Matt, Brian, and Bobby; my six siblings; and all my extended family members (and it is a very large clan). I cannot thank you enough for all your support and unconditional love. Professionally I would like to acknowledge Tom Bonen, Guy Whittaker, Ted Muller, Kim Hamilton, Tom Bergen, Joe Bockier, Emil Assentato, Shawn Powell, my hardworking colleagues at FXDD. Each has helped form me over the years in some way or another and my appreciation is not forgotten. I would like to acknowledge my "trading apprentices" that ask for advice and support my efforts at FXDD. You provide joy to my life through your successes as traders. I would like to thank the respected traders that have crossed my path on the various social media sites. Even though an alias may be used and we may never physically meet, trading is not as lonely because of you. I would like to acknowledge my spiritual mentors, including the vibrant and positive St. Patrick's community. I start and end my week at St. Patrick's and it gives me the direction during all the minutes in between. Last but not least, I give thanks to the ultimate spiritual mentor, God, for giving me wisdom, the humility to accept failure, the will and desire to correct my mistakes, the opportunity to pay it forward, and all the other incredible gifts from His amazing grace.

Attacking Currency Trends

Introduction

When I was in college at Clemson University, I dreamed of a career on Wall Street. My father, Joseph Michalowski, worked on Wall Street his entire career, working his way through the ranks. There have been very few people I have met who had a professional relationship with my father who did not say, "Your father is a good man. He taught me a lot about the markets."

One of the highlights of my father's career was working at Chase Manhattan Bank. He was once put in charge of uncovering, unwinding, and being the expert during the Drysdale Government Securities crisis that shocked Wall Street in 1982. The crisis, built on a string of reverse repurchase agreements that went wrong, sent repercussions throughout Wall Street when the boutique firm defaulted on an interest payment totaling $250 million. The knock-on effect of the crisis resulted in the Federal Reserve's issuing that now all-too-familiar statement, "The Fed stands ready as a lender of last resort."

What was the catalyst for the crisis? The use of too much leverage (i.e., risk) and the lack of a plan and controls. Compare and contrast this to the 2008–2009 financial crisis where the same fundamental faults led to a near-global financial meltdown. Twenty-seven years later the lessons have not been learned.

In addition to his knowledge of interest rate products and the markets, my father was a technician, or a chartist, who would painstakingly construct by hand bar charts of bond prices on grid graph paper. At night, he would tape together the pages when the prices moved above or below the boundary of the paper, or when a new page had to be added as time progressed. He would fold his "moon charts"—as he liked to call them—as deftly as an origamist would fold a piece of paper into a swan.

During the early years of his career and without modern technology, he was able to carve a career as a technical trader by keeping analysis basic, finding good trade locations, defining risk, and trading the trend. There were no Relative Strength Indices or Stochastic Indicators. Shorter time-period moving averages could be calculated if the trader was dedicated enough, but 100 or 200 bar simple moving averages were more difficult and time consuming (if they were even done at all). Exponential moving averages could not be done without the aid of larger computer resources.

Trading technically was simpler then than most technicians find it today. Bar charts and maybe point and figure charts were used predominantly, and to bring them to life, trend lines provided the bells and whistles, defining the trend in the process. My father and most other successful traders made money by attacking the trends. My father's career on Wall Street got me interested in trading, and that became what I wanted to do.

MY JOURNEY

I started my journey as a summer intern in 1981 for an interest rate trading pioneer named William Kidder (no relation to Kidder Peabody, a prominent Wall Street firm at the time). Bill was one of the first to use mispriced interest rate futures to arbitrage the U.S. Bill and Bond markets. In 1981 he started a software company with a goal to build a menu of programs used to exploit arbitrage opportunities in the interest rate markets. The programs would run on Apple IIs, one of the first desktop computers.

Bill's software was all about finding value and defining risk. I learned through Bill that all successful traders look to find good value and to define their risk. By doing so they are able to keep their fear to a minimum and trade more profitably.

To do the computer programming, Bill hired a team of college students—mainly from Ivy League graduate schools—and promised a lecture a day, an hourly wage, and a folding chair and computer. I did not qualify as an Ivy Leaguer—being a rising junior at Clemson University (not even an Ivy League institution of the south)—but I did qualify as being the son of Joe Michalowski. I was also "hulky" enough to carry a computer to trading rooms around New York City when needed, a task I was happy to do, being the wide-eyed undergraduate in the Big Apple.

I got the break I needed, and I was working on Wall Street, taking the morning train, reading the *Wall Street Journal*, and wearing one of my three suits in the rotation. Although hired for my hulk, I ended up holding my own with the Ivy League work colleagues, and the computer lugging was replaced by programming. I also learned a tremendous amount from Bill's morning lectures on the fundamentals of the markets, trading, value, and risk. The next year I was asked back for another summer internship opportunity. I became motivated to learn more. After graduating from college in the spring of 1983, I started full time with Bill's firm, selling the software to Wall Street's interest rate arbitrageurs.

The experience of the internship and my first job gave me a foundation for the business of trading, and more importantly, it also taught me about finding value in the market and defining risk.

In 1984, one of my clients at Citibank was looking for an entry-level trader for the interest rate arbitrage desk in the bank's funding area. Since the software they were to use was the software I helped develop and now sold, I was the obvious fit for the job. Green as I was to trading, I was offered a position, and my career as a trader began.

I worked for Citibank New York for six years, initially as a trader's assistant in the bank's funding department and later making markets in short-term forward rate agreements and interest rate swaps. In 1991, I was fortunate to move to London for four more years where I helped start up Citibank's short-term interest rate derivatives desk. It was during this time that I became more interested in technical analysis. I went to seminars, read books. Computers were becoming more mainstream. As a result, getting electronic price feeds into a spreadsheet could be done easily and allowed calculating the algebraic breakevens instantaneously. More sophisticated charting programs started to surface with the ability to add indicators and draw trend lines directly on the screen.

It was during this time I was introduced to a trading concept called Market Profile^{TM}. The Market Profile taught me to recognize different market patterns (i.e., visuals) that helped me understand "exact" risk and how to anticipate trends—two seeds that my father and Bill Kidder first planted in my brain. It became the basis for the development of thinking like a *successful* trader rather than simply being a trader. It was a foundation for moving to the next step.

THE MARKET PROFILE APPROACH

Market Profile was developed by a bond trader in the Chicago futures pits named J. Peter Steidlmayer. The concept centered on breaking down the day into time periods that each lasted a half hour. The periods were lettered A, B, C, and so on. For example, the letter A would be assigned to all prices that traded in the first half hour. The price need only trade once in the A half-hour window to get assigned a spot on the profile. In the second half hour, the letter B would be assigned to all prices that traded in that period. Prices that traded in the third half hour of the day would get assigned the letter C, and so on.

A "Market Profile" would develop with the price moving vertically from high to low. If a price traded in the A and B periods, the two letters would go side by side, A first, then B. This way, rows of letters going horizontally would start to develop as the day's profile was built at each price.

There were four types of days that would develop using the Market Profile. Each day fell into one of the buckets. By recognizing the type of day, a trader could discover important clues about value, risk, trade location, and even what might happen tomorrow. As a group, they started to teach me about key aspects of becoming a more successful trader. The types were normal distribution, nontrend, double distribution, and trend days.

Normal Distribution Days

The most common type of day was a normal distribution day. These would occur approximately 70 percent of the time, and at the end of the day would look something like Figure I.1. Not surprisingly, the normal distribution day looked like a normal distribution of a bell curve.

The profile, as it was termed, showed the high volume price, or HVP for short. This was the price that traded the most over the course of the trading day. In Figure I.1, the HVP was at 101-22 or 101 and 22/32nds (bonds

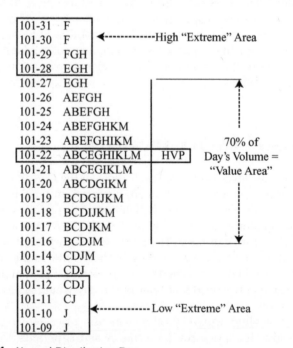

FIGURE I.1   Normal Distribution Day

and notes, which the system was developed using, trade in 32nds). The horizontal line at the end of the lettered distribution indicated that those prices were part of the value area. The value area was where 70 percent of the day's trades took place, representing roughly one standard deviation for those who might be mathematicians (I am not one, by the way). The Value Area in Figure I.1 comes in at 101-16 to 101-27.

Types of Traders   During normal distribution trading days, the average trader would mainly trade around the middle of the Value Area, making a little, losing a little—basically treading water. A mentor of mine once called these traders the "Uncle owns the firm" traders. He reasoned that they could not get fired, by virtue of blood connections. However, blood only goes so far, so they would not advance in rank within the firm either.

The ends of the trade distribution bell curve were called the extremes. There were two types of traders who traded the extremes. The first type saw the market moving lower and just knew it was going even lower. They sold the lows only to have the market bounce right back where they would then cover at the upper extreme—or highs—for a nice large trading loss. These traders were termed the "Mother owns the firm" traders, since the only way they could ever keep their job was if their mother owned the firm.

The other traders who traded the extremes were doing the exact opposite. They would be buying at the low extreme and selling at the high extreme. They understood good trade location. They understood the type of market the day was developing (i.e., range bound), and what a normal trade distribution would look like at the end of the day (yes, it does help to visualize the normal bell curve developing). They were great traders, and they were termed the "Owns the firm" traders.

There was another set of traders: the ones who traded in the middle of the day's range, but were not satisfied enough at the positive extreme to take their profit. So instead they held the position and became scared enough to get out at the losing extreme—and book a loss. Needless to say, these traders were also "bad traders" and were a hybrid between the "Uncle" and "Mother owns the firm" traders. They likely got fired at some point.

Finally, there were those who traded in the middle and were content to take a quick profit near the profit extremes. They made smallish gains and were a little better than "Uncle owns the firm" traders.

So overall, there was one group (a small percentage, mind you) that made the money by buying low and selling high at the extremes. There was another that caught part of the day's ranges and made a living, but did not get rich. There was another group of traders that broke even in the middle and two groups of traders that consistently lost money (this was the bulk of the traders).

Although very simplistic, I began to think in terms of what kind of trader I was and what kind of trader I wanted to be. It was harsh to realize that I was likely an "Uncle owns the firm" trader. Needless to say, I wanted to be a Trader who "owns the firm" (or as close to it as possible), but did not fully know how. It is one thing to say you want to be good at something, and another to understand how to do it. I started to study the Market Profile further and search for clues that it told me about the markets.

Trading Clues from Normal Distribution Days   It was thought that normal distribution days took place 70 percent of the time. The ranges differed from day to day, but the pictures ended up looking similar. Since seven out of ten days were "normal," I began to start to see and anticipate how the days might develop more clearly. Over time, I began to develop an idea of what a normal range was and began to think in terms of buying and selling near targeted extremes.

There were also some rules I learned that could be used to anticipate where the normal distribution day would peak or trough. For example, I learned that if you took the High to Low range for the first hour of trading and subtracted (or added) that value to a range extension down (or up), it would project the low price (high price) extreme for the day. Knowing this taught me how to be aggressive on breaks above or below the initial range, how to anticipate a move in the direction of the break, and target a level to take profit, or even to initiate a counter trend trade.

Because of things like rules, I was becoming a trader with a *reason for the trade* rather than a trader who traded because the price was moving higher or lower. I also learned that if I had a reason to do a trade, I also had a reason to get out of a trade if the market did not do what I expected it to do. I started defining risk. By defining risk I found fear from trading started to abate. With less fear I was able to stay in positions longer and to catch intraday trends. The pieces of being a real trader started coming together.

For example, in Figure I.2, the first hour (i.e., initial range) of trading during the A and B periods has a 16/32 range. When the initial range is breached on the downside during the C time period, the range extension rule says the market should target an extension level equal to the initial range of 16/32nds.

By following the rule for trade extensions, a short position at 98-10 would be initiated, with a target take profit level being at 97-27, 16/32nds lower. A stop for the trade would be if the price extends back above 98-14 (to 98-15), which was the low of the A period in the chart. With that stop in place, risk would be 5/32nds. The target gain would be 15/32nds if the target was reached. A risk/reward ratio of 1:3 was pretty good.

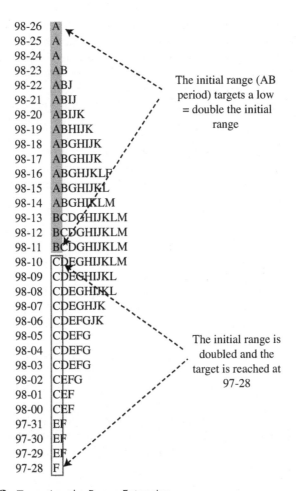

98-26	A
98-25	A
98-24	A
98-23	AB
98-22	ABJ
98-21	ABIJ
98-20	ABIJK
98-19	ABHIJK
98-18	ABGHIJK
98-17	ABGHIJK
98-16	ABGHJKLF
98-15	ABGHIJKL
98-14	ABGHIKLM
98-13	BCDGHIJKLM
98-12	BCDGHIJKLM
98-11	BCDGHIJKLM
98-10	CDEGHIJKLM
98-09	CDEGHIJKL
98-08	CDEGHIKL
98-07	CDEGHJK
98-06	CDEFGJK
98-05	CDEFG
98-04	CDEFG
98-03	CDEFG
98-02	CEFG
98-01	CEF
98-00	CEF
97-31	EF
97-30	EF
97-29	EF
97-28	F

The initial range (AB period) targets a low = double the initial range

The initial range is doubled and the target is reached at 97-28

FIGURE I.2 Targeting the Range Extension

The "If . . . Should" Rule   This process of trading was the foundation for what I now call the "If . . . Should" rule. The "If . . . Should" rule says: "If the market does XYZ, the market should do ABC. If it does not do what it is supposed to do (i.e., ABC), then *get out*." We will discuss the "If . . . Should" rule further in Chapter 4.

The "If . . . Should" rule in relation to this example would say something like this: "*If* the market is a normal distribution day and the price moves below the initial trading range (first hour of trading), the market *should* double the initial trading range in the direction of the extension. If it does not do what it is supposed to do, then *get out*."

In the example, the price extended the range lower and did not go to the 98-15 stop level. The market *did* what it was supposed to do.

Over time, I found that I could easily define my risk. This was very important to me as it reduced my fear. I could also define logical profit targets. They became more defined during normal distribution days. I started to find that I was selling and buying more extremes at levels that made sense. My trade location was improving, and my trading profits improved with the better trade location.

I know real estate professionals say the three most important things in real estate buying are Location, Location, Location. In trading, maybe it's not three times location, but having good location is definitely a big relief.

Nontrend Days

Of course, the market does not trade normally all the time. There were three other types of day formations I learned using the Market Profile concepts, and each gave me a further understanding about risk, the potential for reward, and even anticipating a trend.

One was a nontrend day. A nontrend day was a variation of the normal distribution day, but in this case, the day had an abnormally narrow low-to-high trading range and low volume. The profile of a nontrend day would look like Figure I.3.

Nontrend days did not provide much in the way of profit potential—in fact, they could be downright frustrating for the impatient young trader. However, I learned that the rewards of nontrend days were not from what happened that day, but for the potential for the subsequent day(s). The reason is that nontrend days tended to signify a balanced market with neither buyers nor sellers in control.

The good news for traders is that nontrend markets tend not to last long. Often, either the buyers or sellers look to take control and move the market away, either higher or lower. The reason is that trading markets

```
101-25   A
101-24   ABCGM
101-23   ABCEFGHIKM              Nontrend Day
101-22   ABCDEFGHIKLM  |HVP      Low volume
101-21   ABCDEFGIKL              Narrow range
101-20   ABCDEGIKM
101-19   BCDGIJKM
101-18   B
```

FIGURE I.3   Nontrend Day

are there to facilitate trade in a direction, up or down. If a market ceases to trade due to nontrend activity, why have a market?

Eventually, the traders in that market get antsy and look for reasons to move the market away from the current level. Often that move is exaggerated in the direction of the break (i.e., a trend-type move). The market becomes like a spring—coiling but ready to uncoil at the slightest nudge by aggressive buyers or aggressive sellers.

For me, the picture of a nontrend day and the understanding of what it signifies was an important "aha" moment for my trading success, and I use it to this day. Although I do not use the Market Profile for currency trading (it is not suited for a 24-hour currency market), the concept of nontrend days remains a very important leading indicator for catching a trend move.

Traders who can *anticipate* a trend type move are more *prepared* to trade the trend move. Nontrend days were one of the first clues that helped me increase trend trading success simply because I could better anticipate when a trend move might be forthcoming.

Later in the book I discuss in more detail the clues from nontrending markets and how they tend to be precursors for attacking currency trends.

Double Distribution Days

Another formation that was developed using the Market Profile was a double distribution day. This day formation created two separate normal distributions that trended up or down. The move was a more powerful trend type directional move with larger ranges. The two distributions often shared an extreme in the middle of a day when the market transitioned from one normal area to a higher or lower *new* normal area. Moves like this were typically initiated by some news that forced the market higher or lower to the new range.

In Figure I.4, the shared extreme occurs during the G period. The example illustrates a typical double distribution day where the price trends higher from a low normal distribution area to a higher normal distribution area.

The double distribution day gave me the visual to find exact levels to lean against that helped define risk of the trade. By defining risk clearly, I had more confidence and with it, less fear.

For example, in Figure I.4, the A to F periods were characterized by a narrow, nontrend-like trading range (low was 101-00 to 101-12). In the G period, the market broke to the new upside, the move left a string of single letters—or "single prints"—up to a new high of 101-24 in that period, with the 101-13 level being the lowest single print in that sequence.

Those single prints became levels to lean against on corrective moves back down, with the 101-14 being the lowest level the market could go

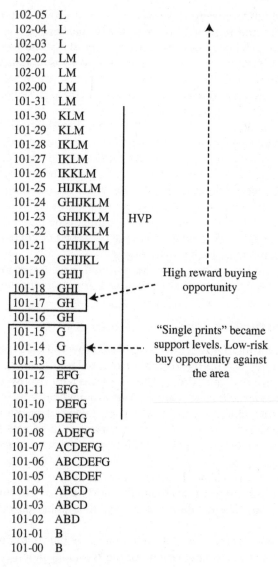

FIGURE I.4 Double Distribution Day

down to in a subsequent half-hour period that would keep the single print string intact.

The Market Profile rules believed that "*If* the market was forming a double distribution day, the market *should* have left single letter prints in its wake. If it did not, it was *not* a double distribution day and therefore don't expect further momentum in the direction of the break." (Note the "If . . . Should" rule.)

As with normal distribution days and nontrend days, the double distribution day was another type of trading day that gave clear clues that could be used to reap good profits with little risk.

The ability to visualize trades, understand risks, and target profits are all important prerequisites for trading successfully. Understanding the characteristics of the double distribution days was another way to put the odds of trading success more firmly in my favor.

Trend Days

The final distribution that Market Profile developed that helped me lay the foundation for becoming a successful trader was the trend day distribution. This was the most powerful of market movements and provided the greatest profit potential to me as a trader. In a trend day distribution, which was estimated to occur on 10 percent of the days, the market moved directionally up or down, leaving multiple single prints in its wake. Figure I.5 is a Market Profile of a typical trend day distribution.

Characteristics that made trend days most profitable were:

- The high-to-low ranges were much larger than on normal days, providing greater profit potential.
- The market stepped higher in a consistent fashion, with each half-hour period having a higher high along the way.
- The steps had spurts where the Market Profile would leave a series of single prints (similar to the double distribution day) along the way. These single prints could be used to lean against when initiating or adding to a trading position. They also could be used to define risk by providing a stop loss if the market reversed.
- They often came after a nontrend day or after a period where the market stayed in an abnormally narrow trading range.

In Figure I.5, at C, E, and J, traders could buy against the single prints, with a stop if the price filled in the single prints. Being aware of the profit potential of a trend day and being able to anticipate the moves greatly increased the odds of success in the favor of the trader while keeping the risk to a minimum. Even though the trend day was a one-way street with little in the way of risk, the hardest thing to do was to stay on the trend. However, following the clues and the rules from the single prints at C, E, and J provided the road map for a potentially big trade.

The lessons the Market Profile gave me early in my career were the basis for my trading today. Although I do not use the method to trade

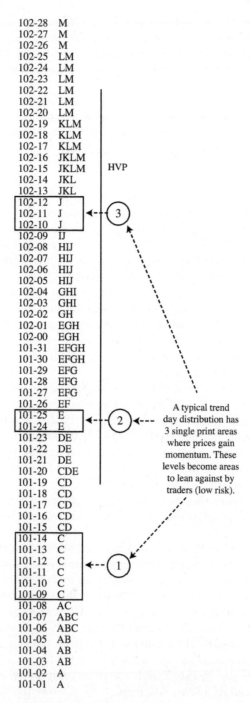

FIGURE 1.5 Trend Day Distribution

currencies (it does not work well with a 24-hour market), the concepts I learned in those informative years from the Market Profile are still very relevant. The difference comes in the tools I use.

IT'S A PROCESS

In this book I will look to take progressive steps forward from forming a foundation for success to showing you how to attack trends. The basis of the steps comes from two sources. One is from my 16 years of experience trading on behalf of major global financial institutions. What you have read so far was just a small piece of some of the things that helped build my foundation as a trader, and I thank those firms and the people at those firms who allowed me to develop those skills.

The second basis for the steps outlined in this book has come over the past 10 years of my career. Over these years, I have been fortunate to work for a retail currency brokerage company, FXDD, since the day of its inception. Through those years, the hats I have worn at the various stages (and often simultaneously) have incorporated everything from customer support, risk management, sales, trading, software testing, and interface design. I prepared the firm's first customer agreements and account opening procedures. I even designed and programmed the firm's first web site. Being so involved is an advantage. I know the retail currency trading business.

The last 10 years have also taken me on the other side of the fence, as I like to tell our customers. That side is from the perspective of the *market maker*, not the *market taker*.

Market Maker versus Market Taker

For a market maker, positions are assumed and managed from the trading side. We have tens of thousands of customers logged into our trading system at any one time, and each is given a two-way bid-and-ask price in 20 different currency pairs. Those prices are live and dealable, 24 hours a day, five and a half days a week.

The benefit to the market maker is that there is a bid-to-ask spread that gives an advantage with a critical mass of traders dealing at the same time. That is, if one trader is hitting a market maker's bid in the EURUSD, another may be dealing off the ask price at nearly the exact same moment. With tens of thousands of customers, this forms the basis of a business where profits are made by virtue of facilitating trade for a large number of traders dealing off a bid-to-ask spread.

In contrast, the first 16 years of my career I spent as a *market taker*. I primarily dealt off market makers' prices when trading and had to pay away the bid-to-ask spread (i.e., sell at the bid and buy at the ask). Although there were some customer flows, the positions were self-induced and dependent on my trading acumen. If I made money, it was because I had the right position.

Most people who are reading this book are likely market takers (it is written for your benefit, not the market makers'). You decide if you want to be long or short, where your stop loss is, perhaps where you will target a profit. You initiate everything, and you also are solely responsible for your profit and loss. Although you may know others in the market and have knowledge of how they are doing, they likely represent a statistically insignificant sample of the market.

For myself, however, in the role of market maker, I have been able to see what a statistically significant sample of retail traders (again, the number reaches tens of thousands) do right and what they tend to do wrong. I also get to see what types of markets the traders trade poorly. This is valuable information to know, especially when trying to fix a problem or even write a book.

I liken myself to the golf professional at my local public golf course. Let me explain.

I love the game of golf but find the game challenging, to say the least. Priorities in life (i.e., children, family, work, writing a book) also keep me from playing with any regularity. Nevertheless, I do want to improve, so from time to time I may take a golf lesson from a trained golf professional.

What normally happens in a lesson is that the golf pro will take me out to a driving range where he will throw a dozen or so balls down on the grass. He will then ask me to take the club I am most comfortable swinging and, without giving any instruction, will have me hit the balls. Invariably, the first few will be straight down the middle, the customary 150 yards. However, fear soon enters my brain and the pulls and the slices, the fat shots and thin shots, start to rear their ugly heads.

When all the balls have been hit, I don't turn to the pro and say, "What am I doing right?" Instead, I am more likely to turn to him and say "What am I doing wrong?"

The golf pro, by virtue of the fact that he has likely hit thousands of balls more than me, has had many more hours of instruction, and has played many more holes in his life, understands the importance of a proper grip and fundamentals of a swing and is far more qualified to tell me what to do to make myself a more successful golfer.

So I listen to what he has to say. It is not my position to tell him what I am doing wrong, but for him to tell me what I am doing wrong. From there it is up to my skill and ability to fix it. In other words, he can teach me to fish, but I still have to do the fishing.

I am your golf pro for trading. You are reading this book because you need a lesson. There is something in your trading swing that is just not right. As a result, you have instilled your confidence in me and specifically in this book.

That is what I do in my job, and what I will look to accomplish in this book. I can see your swing in a trading context. I have been involved with financial markets for 26 years. I have experienced failure and success. I have been influenced and mentored by fellow pros who have provided me with wisdom of the trading swing. Most importantly, I have seen what types of markets most retail traders trade well and what types they trade poorly.

It's now up to you to listen to what I have to say, believe in it, and apply it.

THE JOURNEY AHEAD

So what types of markets do retail traders do poorly in?

Whenever I speak, whether it is at a company-sponsored event or perhaps a trader's convention, I will quiz the audience with this question. Specifically, I will ask, "In what type of market do retail traders make the most money?"

I give them two simple choices:

1. A trending market where the price is directional up or down for an extended period of time, or
2. A nontrending market where the market is moving up and down in a choppy fashion.

Invariably, by a wide margin, the answer is that retail traders do best in a trending market. Wrong! Retail traders tend to do poorly fairly consistently in trending markets.

This book will look to address this fault in your trading and will outline how you can better anticipate and attack the trend in currencies. I will look to move via a step-by-step approach. I want the book to be easy to read—to progress in a logical manner. I want you to say, "That makes sense" and "That does too." I want you to say, "I have experienced that fear." I want you to learn and trust me like I trust my golf instructor, not because I am the best trader in the world (who is?), but because I have the right combination of trading experience, of experience watching retail traders, of the nuances of the currency market that can help swing the trading results in your favor.

The journey will start in Part I: The Foundation for Success. It is my firm belief that retail currency traders ignore this part altogether, and in the end, it leads to their failure. Be warned.

Part I will start with a look at the characteristics of the retail currency trader and then outline the attributes of successful currency traders. The first two chapters are intended to outline the good, bad, and ugly of traders and are meant to open the eyes to what has to be fixed and what needs to be done to move toward success. From there the book will transition into the mission statement, which is the big-picture goal for all currency traders. The game plan will follow with an understanding of what needs to be done to accomplish the mission. Next will come a chapter on the rules that will need to be followed in order to have a chance of satisfying the game plan. Finally, the currency trader's foundation will be complete with an introduction to the technical trading tools for our mission and why they were chosen (and why others were not!).

In Part II of the book, Tools and Strategies, I will transition into the technical tools that I use to anticipate and trade the trends. There will be three main charting tools used, each helping to anticipate, define, and stay on the trend. There will also be three time periods I will look at: a short-term, intermediate-term, and long-term time period. You will learn why successful currency traders look at all three time periods equally and trade using all three. I will give you a hint—you don't need to be a position trader to trade using the daily chart.

I will discuss ways you can anticipate a trend and through the process be better prepared to be greedy (yes, *greedy*!) with your profits. I will outline those precise moments when the trends may be transitioning into nontrends and what to do during these periods.

I will use plenty of examples to show how trading successfully does not have to be overly complicated. In fact, it can be quite simple. By "simple" I do not mean it is easy—as in easy to make money. Instead, what I mean is it can be very straightforward and logical. There will be no need for advanced technical trading knowledge. There will be no secret formulas or "Green for Buy, Red for Sell" boxes. If you are looking for the black box of trading that will guarantee you will double your money in weeks, thank you for buying the book, but it is likely to disappoint. I will be teaching you a new way to think about the market and, in the process, provide you with the tools to apply the sound trading strategies.

Throughout the book I will use what I hope are familiar analogies, like the golf pro analogy used earlier. I will also use observations from being a father of three boys (24, 21, and 13), a husband of 25 years, a brother with six siblings, from parents who provided a foundation for living life. You might be surprised how trading can be a microcosm of life. People learn from comparing other aspects of life to trading.

I will utilize my belief that there is a right and wrong fork in the road for a lot of things, including trading. The wrong road is often the easiest to take, but is often the sucker play. That is one reason why trading is not so easy. I hope that my observations will help paint the picture more clearly and make the book a little more than your run-of-the-mill book on trading.

I will incorporate unique terms like "the If . . . Should rule," "Three's a Crowd," "Trading between the Goal Posts," the "Bullish or Bearish Highway," and others. These may not mean a thing now, but my goal is for them to be part of your trading vocabulary in the future.

Through it all, I will focus on attacking currency trends. Are you ready?

The Foundation for Success

A house needs to be built on a strong foundation. Otherwise, there is a risk that the house will fall down in a storm. A successful trader has a strong trading foundation. Otherwise, the risk is the trader's account will blow up in a volatile market.

The currency market is characterized—rightly or wrongly—by volatility. I think what people might mean when they say this is that currencies can go up and they can go down. The evening news will say, "The dollar is strong" or "The dollar is weak." That may sound volatile to a stock investor who is used to buying and holding because over time stocks go higher. However, is that theory still necessarily true, especially in a country like the United States, which has seen stock prices move up and down over the last 10 or so years? If you listen now, the stock market is characterized as being "more volatile" as well.

To me, volatility means that the price can trend one way and then trend the other way. Those trend changes can wreak havoc if a trader does not have a firm foundation for the risk. It is not good enough to buy and hold, because the reversals in trends can be storms that cause total failure. Many traders blame the failures from large losses on volatility. They may blame them on the institutional traders or "big boys" whom they believe cause that volatility, that change in trend. I like to think the blame lies with a faulty trading foundation. A foundation that is not strong enough to weather the trend storms.

Part I of this book builds that foundation for your currency trading so you have a chance during the storms. In fact, if the foundation is truly solid, the storms should not have an effect at all. You should be able to stand strong, just like the big boys.

Chapter 1 is an introduction to the characteristics of the retail currency trader and will address why trend trading is so difficult for most traders. Just because it is difficult does not mean you cannot do it. It means you may have to change, though. So be prepared for some soul searching in that chapter. In Chapter 2, I discuss those attributes that are needed to be a successful currency trader. There are six of them, and they build on each other. If you skip one, you will most likely fail; your foundation will crumble. From there, I progress to the trader's mission statement in Chapter 3. When I ask retail traders whether they have a mission statement, 99 percent of them say no. Do you have one? You need one. Without one, that storm will knock you out. I will give you a mission statement in Chapter 3. Chapter 4 outlines the game plan for satisfying our mission statement. What do you have to focus on to win the game—to satisfy the mission? If there is a game plan, that implies a game of some sorts. All games have rules that provide control. Successful traders need to follow rules so they too can have better control over their trading. Those rules are outlined in Chapter 5. Finally, Part I ends with a look at the tools needed in the trader's toolbox. Not just any tool is allowed; some tools can be counterproductive. They do more harm than good. I will warn you of what tools are not welcomed, but more importantly tell you which ones will help you with your mission and game plan.

I have the opportunity to talk to many retail traders. Many times the story starts with "I blew up and . . ." What they really often mean to say is that their foundation wasn't in place, a storm came along, and the account blew up. Don't ignore the storm warnings. A storm is indeed approaching. So firm up that foundation before it is too late.

CHAPTER 1

Stereotyping the Retail Currency Trader

S tereotyping people is something I do not feel comfortable doing. It mainly comes from being wrong in the past about people whom I bucketed as being one way, only to find out they were not at all what I thought.

My biggest blunder occurred when I was offered a job at Citibank in London in 1991. I remember my wife and I being warned that the British were hard to get to know. They liked to keep to themselves. We would be better off living in an expatriate community and for our young sons to go to the American school.

When my wife and I went over to look for a place to live, we were sure we should live where the American school was located and settle in what we thought was our comfort zone—in a place where we would be happiest.

We arrived in London in early February 1991 and faced something we were very accustomed to—snow. It was the blizzard of 1991, and although the eight or so inches did not approach the snowfalls we experienced in the northeast United States, it crippled the city. Despite the distractions from shoveling out the family car, going sledding with their children, and stocking up on supplies, my new work colleagues made a special effort to immediately welcome me.

My wife and I both realized our preconceived thoughts about the people we would meet in our new home—our new country—bore no resemblance to the people we met. It was then we realized we did not want to live overseas in an American enclave. We wanted to do the total opposite and embrace living with the British people, sending our young children to British schools and respecting and learning about their customs and

21

traditions. We wanted to call cookies *biscuits* and french fries *chips*, do without American football and learn about British football, and figure out what a cricket score really meant.

We spent four years in the U.K. and met many wonderful British people. I wonder what it would have been like if we had kept our misguided stereotypical thoughts and moved into the American community. I am sure the experience would have been less memorable and rewarding.

Since that experience, my family and I have always welcomed a new adventure where the idea of change takes you forward—not backward. We may now be back to calling chips *fries* and biscuits *cookies*, but I still say "Cheers." I realized that introspection and change can often be a good thing.

So with my confession out of the way, it is with some apprehension that I have to stereotype retail currency traders. However, it is also done with more than 10 years of knowledge from monitoring retail currency traders, and from my share of trading blunders, that I try to right some of the wrongs before they send you down trading paths that will cost you money.

For some of you, the characteristics may strike a chord after your own self-analysis. I hope it helps force a change. For others, you may have already come to the realization and changed. For still others, you may look to stay the same. For those who may be reluctant, I only ask that you take a serious look at yourself and consider a change. You might like what you eventually see.

THEY THINK TRADING CURRENCIES IS EASY

I often have retail traders come to me at trade shows or other events, put a chart in front of me, and say, "All I have to do is flip a coin. If the flip says 'buy,' either I will be right, and the price will go up, or I will be wrong, and the price will go down. I am willing to take that bet."

I have to stop them and tell them if it were so easy, this room would be empty, and everyone would be trading rather than looking for the next answer to the age-old question of how to trade successfully.

Nevertheless, on the surface it does seem easy. There is a price for the euro versus the U.S. dollar (conventionally displayed as EURUSD), say 1.3512, and that price is either going up or going down. If the event of the next price movement were isolated, and not dependent on any outside forces like fundamental analysis or technical analysis, a trader could flip a coin to determine whether he or she should be bullish and buy, or be bearish and sell.

Currency pairs like the EURUSD, GBPUSD, USDJPY, USDCHF, USDCAD, AUDUSD, and NZDUSD are quoted in the market in terms of how much of the base currency it would take to buy one unit of the counter currency. The base currency is the first currency in the currency pair, and is represented by a universally derived three character "name." EUR is short for the euro, USD is short for the U.S. dollar, GBP is short for the British pound, JPY is short for the Japanese yen, CHF is short for the Swiss franc, CAD is short for the Canadian dollar, AUD is short for the Australian dollar, and NZD is short for the New Zealand dollar. These currencies make up the major currencies. The combinations of any one of the major currencies to the U.S. dollar make up the major currency pairs.

The major currency pairs are quoted for trading in a consistent, universally accepted convention. For example, the EURUSD currency pair has the euro as the base currency and the U.S. dollar as the counter currency. The convention is that the value of the base currency remains constant at 1.0000. The value of the counter currency is floating. As a result, a price of 1.3512 would imply that 1.3512 U.S. dollars are equivalent to 1.0000 euro. If a trader thought the euro was going to appreciate versus the U.S. dollar, he would buy the EURUSD. If the price of the EURUSD went higher, say to 1.3525, he could sell the 1.0000 euro for that higher value of 1.3525 U.S. dollars. When this happens, the euro is said to be strengthening and the dollar is said to be weakening. Note that one currency in a currency pair is always getting stronger while the other currency is getting weaker. If another trader thought the euro was going to depreciate versus the U.S. dollar, she would sell the EURUSD. If the EURUSD did fall to 1.3500, the trader could buy back the euros she sold at the cheaper price of 1.3500 U.S. dollars for the same 1.0000 euro.

The pricing convention versus the U.S. dollar is the same for the EUR, GBP, AUD, and NZD. That is, it is in terms of how many dollars it would take to equal 1.0000 units of the foreign currency.

The JPY, CHF, and CAD pricing conventions are reversed versus the U.S. dollar. For these currency pairs, the USD is the base currency (i.e., USDJPY, USDCAD, and USDCHF) and the foreign currency is the counter currency. As a result, the price of the currency pair is in terms of how many foreign currency units it would take to buy or sell 1.0000 U.S. dollar.

If, for example, the USDCHF was at 1.0112, it would take 1.0112 Swiss francs to buy (or sell) 1.0000 U.S. dollars. If the USDCHF went up, the dollar would have said to strengthen. If the price went down, the dollar would have weakened.

TABLE 1.1 Bid-to-Ask Spread Matters

Buy Price –	Sell Price =	Loss on Trade
1.31512 –	1.3510 =	– 2 pips

However, what is important to realize is that the 50-50 probability of the price moving higher or lower is for the next price change *only*, which is typically a one-pip move (a pip is the minimum a currency pair can fluctuate). That is, if the price is at 1.3512, there is a 50-50 chance the next price move will tick up to 1.3513 or down to 1.3511.

If there were no bid-to-ask spread, the 50-50 probability of making a pip or losing a pip from a standing start would be correct (all things being equal). However, in currency trading (and all trading for that matter), there is a bid-to-ask spread that skews the odds for success slightly against the trader. This spread is the property of the market makers or brokers who quote the market prices 24 hours a day, 5 days a week.

For example, the EURUSD, which is the most liquid currency pair, tends to trade at around a two-pip bid-to-ask spread. Assume the current price in the market is 1.3510 Bid/1.3512 Ask (see Table 1.1). If a trader flips a coin that has "buy" written on one side and "sell" on the other, and the random flip says to "buy," the trader would need to buy at the ask price of 1.3512.

If the deal were immediately liquidated, the best the trader could do would be to sell at the bid price of 1.3510. If this were done, the trader would incur a two-pip loss on his long position.

Taking a two-pip loss is not the definition of successful trading. A trader needs to make a profit to be successful. So where would his long position be profitable?

To make a profit of one pip, the trader would need the bid price to move up to 1.3513. This would be the minimum price that would guarantee the trader a profit. If the market bid-to-ask price is 1.3510/1.3512 when the trade is initiated, three successive price moves up would be needed to make a profit (see Table 1.2). That is not as easy as a 50-50 proposition from a standing start. Table 1.2 outlines those moves.

What about the Trading Losses?

Let's take this example a step further. Assume the trader flips the coin and has a rule that as soon as he makes a one-pip profit, he closes the position. We have seen the trader has to have the price move three pips to make that one-pip profit.

TABLE 1.2 EURUSD P/L Profile for a Three-Pip Move in the Trade's Favor

Bid	Ask	Profit/Loss
1.3510	1.3512	–2-pip loss
1.3511	1.3513	–1-pip loss
1.3512	1.3514	0-pip loss
1.3513	1.3515	+1-pip gain

What about the stop loss? The same trader cannot just flip the coin, go long or buy, and if the price goes down, not have a stop loss price that limits the loss by squaring the position.

So let's assume that if the profit requires a three-pip move in the direction of the trade to take a profit, the trader will tolerate a similar three-pip move in the opposite direction of the trade before stopping the position out. Since there is a bid-to-ask spread in currency pair prices, and traders need to buy at the ask price and sell at the bid, the three-pip move in the opposite direction would create the loss profile shown in Table 1.3, assuming a purchase at 1.3512.

Initially, as soon as the trade is executed, the trader can sell at 1.3510 and incur a two-pip loss. Should the price move down one pip, it would bring the price down to 1.3509. A two-pip decline moves the price to 1.3508, and a three-pip move results in being stopped out by selling at 1.3507. For the same three-pip move in the opposite direction, the trader stands to lose five pips on his trade. The trader buys at 1.3512 and sells at 1.3507. Yikes. A three-pip move in the trader's direction equals a one-pip gain, while a three-pip move against the trader leads to a five-pip loss.

How Would the Best Scalper in the World Do?

Let's say a trader was right an amazing 84 percent of the time with his coin-flip strategy whereby he either let the market move three pips in his favor and booked a one-pip profit or let it move three pips against him

TABLE 1.3 EURUSD P/L Profile for a Three-Pip Move against the Trade

Bid	Ask	Profit/Loss
1.3510	1.3512	–2-pip loss
1.3509	1.3511	–3-pip loss
1.3508	1.3510	–4-pip loss
1.3507	1.3509	–5-pip loss

and booked a five-pip loss. That success rate is obviously well above the average for traders. On the 84 trading wins, the cumulative wins would result in 84 pips of profit (84 trades × 1 pip gain = 84 pips).

The losses for the remaining 16 trades would cumulate to minus 80 pips (16 trades × −5 pips = −80 pips).

A win/loss rate of 84 percent would be needed to eke out a four-pip gain. You are not exactly lighting the world on fire with those results.

Ironically, a lot of retail currency traders look to trade, or incorporate trading systems, whereby they rely on this pip-type strategy. After a while, they wonder why it all ends in tears with losses in their accounts. Sure they get a rush from the win/loss percentage—who wouldn't want to boast about being profitable 84 percent of the time at their next neighborhood cocktail party—but in this game called currency trading, it is not necessarily the win/loss percentage that wins the championships. It is the quality of the wins that really matters.

To prove it, take a win/loss percentage of just .400 with 40 wins and 60 losses over our fictitious 100-trade season. On the 40 wins, assume we require an eight-pip gain. Given our two-pip bid-to-ask spread, this would require a ten-pip move. That is, if you buy at 1.3412 ask price, you need for the ask price to go to 1.3422 to sell at the 1.3420 bid price for our eight-pip gain.

On the 60 losses assume we maintain our five-pip loss. So,

$$40 \text{ wins} \times 8 \text{ pip gain} = +320\text{-pip gain}$$

$$60 \text{ losses} \times -5 \text{ pip loss} = (300)\text{-pip loss}$$

$$\text{Net Gain} = +20 \text{ pips}$$

By my math, the trader who comes in last in most sports leagues with a .400 win/loss percentage wins the trading league when compared to the .840 win/loss percentage trader. In fact, his net gain is five times more with a 20-pip gain versus 4 pips. It isn't just about wins and losses in currency trading.

You Have to Work at It

The message from the example is this: The profitable trader has to make eight pips, not just one. How do you do that? By working at it. By trading smart. By having a mission statement and goals for achieving that mission statement. By following rules. By looking for and anticipating trends that make the eight-pip hurdle easier.

But the first thing you need to understand is trading is not easy. It takes effort. It is more than an auto-execute program that wins 84 percent of the time. It's not only about the wins in currency trading, but about the quality of the wins and about limiting those darn losses. Eighty-four wins and 16 losses would win any league in any sport. In currency trading it does not come close.

This simplified example illustrates the hurdle that traders have to overcome to make money. Traders who simply take the approach that trading is a 50-50 proposition and assume that trading is easy will soon find out that the bid-to-ask hurdle skews the odds against them. As a result, to be successful, traders need to do more. They need to look at the market with a more intelligent and logical focus and in the process skew the odds of success back in their favor by trading trends.

Look at yourself in the mirror. What do you see? A trader who thinks trading is as easy as making a pip or two, or a trader who realizes that to be successful it will require some work. It requires catching the trends. What is your bias? How do you trade? Maybe you should rethink your strategy.

THEY HAVE TOO MUCH FEAR

Another characteristic I often find among retail currency traders is they assume they will have little or no fear of trading. It may be a "macho" thing to think this way, but I can tell you it is simply not true.

Most retail traders have fear, whether they realize it or not, and ironically, fear does not simply manifest itself in terms of losing money. It also is prevalent when most traders are winning. In fact, it is the *fear of success*—as I like to call it—or fear from profits that leads to retail traders not being able to remain on a trend for an extended period of time. This idea will be further explored in Chapter 2 and throughout the book as we build toward the theme of attacking the currency trends.

I can say that traders all have some fear. The fear is partly a result of the thought that the market price will move opposite to the trader's position. What most retail traders don't realize is the inherent fear they will have simply from the volatile price action.

As even the most novice of currency traders realize, prices do not always move in a consistent direction in the currency market. That is, prices move sporadically at times. In a normal market the price may go from 1.3512 to 1.3511, to 1.3510, back to 1.3511, up to 1.3512, back down to 1.3511, and 1.3510, and 1.3509, and back up to 1.3511, and 1.3512, and 1.3513 all in the time span of less than a minute.

With this sporadic volatile movement, it is no wonder the trader immediately hits the bid at 1.3513 and books a one-pip profit when given the first opportunity for a positive gain. Most new retail traders' minds are not ready for so many events in such a short time period.

Trading Is Like Roulette on Steroids

I like to parallel trading ideas with analogies that most people can relate to. The best way to teach a new concept or to change a thought pattern is to relate the concept to something more universally known and accepted.

With the volatility of the currency market moving actively with many price changes over the course of a minute, hour, day, or longer, I liken the market movements in this fast-paced world to what it would be like playing a fictional game of "roulette on steroids." The analogy to roulette is not meant to compare trading to gambling. Gambling is a game of chance and luck. Trading successfully is much more calculated. It takes much more knowledge. We learned that two pages ago.

Let's assume bets of red for bearish or black for bullish are the only options on our fictional roulette wheel. You analyze the market and choose black because you think the market price will go higher. The croupier spins the wheel and the ball lands in a black or bullish slot immediately (our wheel does not need the time to settle in a slot). In currency terms, the price moves up a pip because black is a bullish move.

Now instead of the waiting for the pit crew to pay off the winners and for you to place your next bet, the croupier spins the wheel again, and you are forced to keep the same black or bullish bet on the table. The next spin is made automatically within seconds of the last. This time, within a second or so, it comes up red or bearish. The price moves back down a pip.

The pit crew takes your chip and automatically your bet is reestablished on black again. The wheel keeps on spinning and spinning as if it were hyped up on some sort of performance-enhancing steroid drug. On each spin either you win one unit or you lose one unit.

In the real world, a start-to-finish roulette bet might take a few minutes from the time a bet can be placed to when the ball settles in a black or red slot on the wheel. In between you are having a drink, chatting with the other people, having a good time. In currency trading there may be 30 "spins" or market price changes in that few-minute time period. There are usually no people with you, and I certainly would not recommend drinking anything other than a nonalcoholic beverage while trading.

I am not a big gambler, but if I go to Las Vegas and have a choice to sit at a blackjack table that has five players or one where it would be just me and the dealer, I choose the one with the five other players. Why? Fewer hands are dealt with more people. Fewer hands slows down the potential for loss. With fewer hands and a more drawn-out game, I will have less fear.

Most retail traders when they start trading—and even after they have done it for a while—are not ready for the frequent price action, and their lack of preparedness manifests itself through increased fear. What does fear do to your trading? It often leads to trading errors.

Think of the initial and largest hill on a roller coaster. It causes the most fear. Each "tic-tic-tic" as the rollercoaster climbs intensifies that fear. It is the same when the currency market is "tic-tic-ticking," or more appropriately, "pip-pip-pipping." Fear intensifies. You need to control it.

Know What Causes Your Fear

Fear is an emotion that traders need to control but most cannot or don't know how to. Most traders do not understand fully what causes the fear. Not knowing what causes fear makes figuring out ways to control it difficult, if not impossible.

Understanding that currency trading is like roulette on steroids is a step in the direction of understanding, facing, and controlling one aspect of traders' fear. If you know that the market will fluctuate and not just go up in a straight line or down in a straight line, you are more able to face those gyrations with less fear. In other words, you will not be as scared of the first hill on the roller coaster.

The fact is that most retail traders have fear, and that fear will lead to closing out positions too quickly. It will lead to overleveraged positions. It will lead to ignoring stop levels. It will lead to losses.

In this book, I will look to show how fear can be defined and, more importantly, controlled. Hopefully by the end, you will be able to look at yourself and honestly say "Fear? What fear?" rather than pretend you don't have any.

THEY LOSE MONEY

I like to tell retail traders that there tends to be a bell curve of results when it comes to trading, just like there is a bell curve when it comes to other businesses or skills.

For example, most people know that opening a restaurant is risky. Common benchmark studies show that 60 percent fail within three years from opening. That number may be rising as a result of the harsh recession of 2009 and the tighter credit conditions from banks.

For demonstration purposes, let's assume 68 percent of restaurants fail over a certain time period (say three years). For those who have a rudimentary knowledge of statistics, that percentage represents a single standard deviation of a normal distribution.

The second standard deviation encompasses those restaurants that stay in business with some just barely surviving, while others do better. That pool of restaurants, if it is a normal distribution, makes up the next 27 percent, with 13.5 percent making, as an example, 1 to 8 percent profit and the other 13.5 percent making 8 to 15 percent.

Finally, the third standard deviation of the bell curve consists of 2.5 percent who make 15 to 25 percent and 2.5 percent who make more than 25 percent on average over three years. This pool contains the restaurants that hit the home runs in the culinary world, get four and five stars, and are packed night in and night out, recession or no recession.

The restaurants get to their respective buckets on the bell curve not by luck, not by hit-or-miss, but by running their business like a business in all aspects. This includes things like the restaurant's location, the decorations, the kitchen facilities, the personnel and customer service, the menu choices, the food suppliers, the pricing, and of course the most important aspect, the expertise in food preparation. All of the pieces come together to make the restaurant a success.

A similar story and distribution can be made with currency traders. It should be no secret that the biggest group of traders will not be able to make money trading currencies. The reasons can vary, but in Chapter 2, I will outline the "Six Attributes of Successful Traders." Lacking any one of the attributes is reason enough for potential failure.

If I were to bucket retail currency traders over the course of one month, there is likely a group of 68 percent or so who lose money. The next 27 percent of traders could be broken into 13.5 percent who make 1 to 3 percent and 13.5 percent who make 3 to 6 percent. On the far extremes are the 2.5 percent who make 6 to 10 percent and finally 2.5 percent who hit the home runs and make more than 10 percent.

The buckets are likely to include different traders each month. This will tend to make the numbers skew even more to the negative over an extended period of time. That is, someone who made a small percentage one month could lose a greater percentage the next month and be down overall.

I know I am not being too positive, but just like facing the fear of trading will make you aware of it, knowing the challenge of the profit/loss curve should be an encouragement to make yourself better.

What part of the bell curve of traders did you fit into last month? Were you in the fat part that lost money or were you in a group that made money? How about the month before? Can you consistently be in the groups that make money? Do you have an idea of how to get there, like your favorite restaurant knows how to survive through the worst recession in decades?

Knowing that traders in the fat part of the bell curve lose money trading currencies gives you two choices right now. One is to put the book down, close your trading account, and find something else to do with your time and money. I do thank you for buying the book, however.

The second option is to not give up, but at the very least complete this book, take heed of what it has to say, and put the effort toward becoming successful by paying attention to the details, like the successful restaurant owner pays attention to all those things that make her restaurant a success.

This includes knowing the attributes of successful traders, having a mission statement, having a game plan to succeed in the mission statement, following the rules of the game, picking the right tools to be successful with the game plan, and finally, and most importantly, finding the ways to attack currency trends as they ultimately will make you the most money. If you can attack the trends and avoid trading on the wrong side of the trends, which causes the people in the fat part of the bell curve to Fail—fail with a capital F—you will move forward with a good chance of being one of the four- or five-star traders.

Can I guarantee you success? No. No one can give a 100 percent guarantee of success. However, you will take steps forward, be more aware of what needs to be done, and hopefully by the end of the book, you will have the skills and knowledge to be able to trade with more of a purpose and with the chance for greater success.

Most retail currency traders lose money, but so do most restaurants. Do you want to do the things like your favorite restaurant owner does, or do you want to quit or be satisfied with failure? That is what you are facing. The choice is yours.

THEY ARE TOO FUNDAMENTAL (NOT TECHNICAL ENOUGH)

In the world of trading there are two types of trading analysis. The first is fundamental analysis, and the second is technical analysis. Fundamental analysis for currencies involves the study of influences that affect the price of a currency pair over a time period. The main fundamental influences include:

- Economic statistics
- Political policy and influences

- Central bank policy
- Intermarket relationships and influences
- Natural currency influences or uses

Fundamental analysis takes a collection of influences and throws them in a pot, and through cause and effect analysis, the trader creates a bias for the directional move of a security, or in our case a currency price.

For example, a currency trader might take a fundamental view that the price of the Australian dollar versus the U.S. dollar (AUDUSD) would go up because Australia's recent economic data is strong, central bank policy is being tightened, the country is running a trade surplus, and fiscal policy is under control. All of these fundamental reasons should cause a currency to be in demand and therefore rise. In comparison, the United States is mired in a recession with sluggish economic data, is running an increasing trade deficit, has rates at or near zero, and has a deteriorating fiscal position. All these fundamental influences should lessen the demand for the U.S. dollar. The divergence of the fundamental news should improve the value of the AUDUSD.

The other type of analysis used by currency traders is technical analysis. Technical analysis is the study of the historic prices of a traded instrument, in the form of a chart. Trend lines that connect lows and/or highs in a chart are one technical tool traders use to determine a bullish or bearish bias. Technical analysis also involves the study of mathematically derived indicators using historical prices. Calculated values such as Fibonacci retracements, moving averages, and the Relative Strength Index give directional bullish or bearish biases for traded instruments such as currencies. Technical traders use technical analysis to predict or anticipate price direction, to reaffirm a price trend, and to define risk.

Most traders have a bias toward using either fundamental analysis or technical analysis. To say that it is not good to have knowledge of both would be wrong. I use both fundamental and technical analysis each and every day. However, the one I will always base trading decisions on is technical analysis.

I tend to use fundamental analysis to support technical analysis and quite frankly I (and everyone) sound smarter when talking about the fundamentals that effect currency rates. This is why the people you will see on business television will talk fundamental analysis 99 percent of the time.

Can you imagine if CNBC's Larry Kudlow stopped talking about free market capitalism and instead spoke about the how the price broke a Fibonacci level? What if Ben Bernanke went in front of Congress and said how the stock market was oversold on a RSI basis and was due for a correction. Better yet, imagine if you and your spouse were invited to a dinner party with new neighbors. After the host asked you what you thought of "the market," you went into a monologue on how the price moved above the Ichimoku Cloud, or how the hammer formation on the candlestick chart points toward a strong rebound—both technical tools. Most dinner hosts would think twice about the next invite. People sound smart knowing why the market did what it did from a fundamental perspective.

However, when trading, the fact is that if I had to do without either technical analysis or fundamental analysis, I would gladly rid myself of all fundamental analysis—and learn to keep my mouth shut at the dinner parties. The majority of retail currency traders are not willing to make this leap. There is something in the mind that says to retail traders "I need to sound smart" and find and use the fundamental reason before trading. Do me and yourself a favor and *change*.

Why do I use technical analysis over fundamental analysis? There is one simple reason. Technical analysis can always tell you what the "full" fundamental story is saying, whereas someone's specific fundamental analysis can run counter to what the technical charts are saying.

For example, if the dollar falls, oil prices should rise. The fundamental reason is that oil is denominated in U.S. dollars, so oil producers will need to demand a higher price to achieve the same revenue. As a result, the market will price in less supply in order to push up the price. Yet there are instances when the dollar can rise with higher oil prices. Government budget deficits in the United States can be surging, which should also be bearish for the U.S. dollar, yet the currency can instead appreciate. Unemployment can decrease in Canada, which from a fundamental perspective should lead to higher rates and a higher Canadian dollar, yet the Canadian dollar can instead decline. Portugal, Ireland, and Greece might be in the midst of a sovereign debt crisis that should lessen the demand for capital inflows into those European Union (EU) countries and therefore decrease the value of the euro, yet the EURUSD can instead strengthen. The U.K. election of 2009 ended in a hung parliament, which fundamental analysis would suggest would cause a lower pound, yet the GBPUSD rose. Australia may tighten rates, which from a fundamental perspective would be bullish for the Australian dollar, yet the AUDUSD can trade in a trading range or correct lower.

These fundamental events all have occurred in recent trading history, yet the fundamental story did not follow the expected price movement—at least for a time period. Sure, they may right themselves eventually, but they may not before you take a trading loss and exit your position. Most retail traders cannot stand the fear of waiting for "eventually" to happen, and this often leads to the retail trader panicking. In addition, there is also the chance that the fundamental analysis is wrong and the price simply trends the other way. What I like to say is that fundamental analysis can be ambiguous at times. That is, the market price can go in the opposite direction of what is fundamentally expected from the news or events.

By using the proper technical tools, however, the fear of waiting for the market to turn likely can be avoided. We will learn what tools to use, why, and how to take the clues from them, so you don't have to wait for the market price (if it does) to support your fundamental analysis.

Making the technicals king, with the ultimate say in your positions, will allow you to trade the fundamentals only when the technical charts say you should trade—and not before it's time. It will also allow you to avoid the ambiguity that fundamental analysis can cause.

Are there technical tools that I do not recommend? Yes! Quite frankly there are some technical tools—and widely accepted technical tools as well—that I will not use or suggest you use. The reason is that they can be as ambiguous as fundamentals at times. Ambiguity begets fear. I will warn you of those technical tools as the book progresses.

Admittedly, technical analysis can be boring and a buzz-kill at dinner parties. However, if the goal is to make the most money you can as a retail currency trader and keep fear to a minimum, save the Larry Kudlow story for the dinner party, and focus on the technicals for your trading. Too many retail traders focus too much on the fundamental analysis and not enough on the technicals. Make a change!

There is a saying in golf that you "drive for show but putt for dough," meaning that those who are great putters on the greens will often beat those who can pound the ball 300 yards down the fairway. The fact is, 99 percent of the golfers out there would choose a 300-yard drive over five fewer three-putts per round. In the world of trading, the analogy is the same. That is, 99 percent of the traders out there will justify a losing position by talking about the fundamentals, when if they simply focused on the technical charts, they would beat the heck out of the fundamental trader.

So start believing in "fundamentals for show and technicals for dough." It will save you money and also make you more money.

THEY DON'T KNOW ENOUGH ABOUT KEY FUNDAMENTAL REQUIREMENTS

How can I say retail traders are too fundamental and then say they don't know enough about fundamentals? Hear me out before you close the book.

The distinction is that I firmly believe traders should not base trading decisions on the fundamentals, but they should not be totally blind to fundamentals, either. For example, not knowing that U.S. unemployment figures are due for release at 8:30 AM EST is an example of being totally blind to the fundamentals and irresponsible as a trader. If risk is increased, traders should be aware of that risk and, if need be, refrain from trading until more normal risk levels return.

Technicals will tell the true market bias story all the time, but there are fundamentals that certainly can help the retail currency trader judge risk, prevent stupid trades, and give a bullish or bearish bias for a trend type move. In the next section I will give a broad stroke lesson on fundamental influences and point out some influences that retail traders should be aware of and prepared for.

Economic Statistics

Each month a collection of economic statistics are compiled by each country or region (such as the Eurozone). The values, which are normally published on a month on month (MoM) and year on year (YoY) basis, are released according to a specific schedule. The important thing to note is there is a calendar of economic releases.

In the United States, economic statistics are generally released at 8:30 AM, 9:15 AM, or 10:00 AM EST. There can be some minor exceptions. In other countries and the Eurozone the releases are also generally released at set times. In the U.K. and Eurozone, for instance, the normal times for release are at 9:00 to 10:00 AM GMT.

The statistics are compiled from various sources. For example, the U.S. Bureau of Labor Statistics (www.bls.gov) compiles the weekly and monthly U.S. Unemployment statistics. The U.S. Commerce Department (www.commerce.gov) will release statistics like Retail Sales, Durable Goods Orders, GDP, and the U.S. Trade Balance.

In the Eurozone, Eurostat (http://epp.eurostat.ec.europa.eu) releases most of the statistics for the EU.

Each country's statistics can be found online. Some can be found at the central bank's site. Others are found elsewhere. Below are the main country websites that show key economic statistics. Bookmark them on your computer and visit them. They are good sources to see how macroeconomic trends for a country are shaping up. However, do not base trading decisions solely on the data.

- Japan: www.stat.go.jp/english/index.htm
- U.K.: www.statistics.gov.uk
- Switzerland: www.bfs.admin.ch/bfs/portal/en/index.html
- Canada: www.statcan.gc.ca
- Australia: www.abs.gov.au/
- New Zealand: www.treasury.govt.nz/
- United States: www.bls.gov and www.commerce.gov
- Eurozone: http://epp.eurostat.ec.europa.eu

Daily Economic Releases

The majority of the global economic releases are compiled on a monthly basis, but there are some that are quarterly releases, like GDP, and a few that are weekly, like the U.S. Initial Claims for Unemployment.

Most of the releases are lagged. For example, the U.S. Retail Sales release would be the change for the month preceding the release date. Most of the releases are revised and seasonally adjusted. The seasonal adjustments can also be revised each year, which can make the original number a shadow of its original self. Does that matter for your trading? Not really, as trading is about what we know now versus expectations. If the fundamentals paint a different picture of today six months from now, it does not matter.

It's important for retail traders to know that major news services will often have an estimate of the daily releases compiled from surveys of chief economists from global banks. The economists employ statistical modeling in their analysis and are well versed in the nuances of the data.

Most traders will use the estimates as the benchmark to base bullish or bearish sentiment after data is released. That is, if the U.S. Nonfarm Payroll change in jobs is expected or forecast to show a gain of 100,000 jobs and the actual data shows a gain of 150,000 jobs, that number is stronger than expectations and the market should act accordingly. I would anticipate that the dollar should get stronger. The fundamentals from the data don't necessarily guarantee a move in the anticipated direction as there are other influences for direction other than the economic number. Plus, one never knows if the number was fully discounted by the market already.

Most retail currency brokers will review the key economic events and releases each day on their websites (I know I do). In addition, most will also have a calendar of economic releases along with the estimates from a survey of economists.

There is often also a level of importance noted for each release. Some use colors with red being most important, orange being next in importance, to yellow being not important at all. Others may use a number system or other symbol designation that determines a rank of importance. Figure 1.1 is an example of such a web site, www.fxddondemand.com.

In Figure 1.1, take note of the level of "Importance." The importance is a proxy for risk. The greater the importance, the greater the risk, both before (as positions are squared) and after the release.

The "Forecast" in Figure 1.1 is the next most important piece in an economic calendar. The forecast is generally what the market will base the relative strength or weakness on after the fundamental data is known.

The bigger the deviation of the "Actual" value from the "Forecast," and the greater the importance, the larger the likely jump or fall in price. This

Date	Time	Currency	Importance	Event	Actual	Forecast	Previous	
Apr 28	07:00	USD	▼	MBA Mortgage Applications	-2.90%		13.60%	⊕
	08:50	EUR	▼▼	German CPI (MoM) P	-0.10%	0.10%	0.50%	⊕
	10:30	USD	▼	Crude Oil Inventories	1.90M		1.90M	⊕
	14:15	USD	▼▼▼	Interest Rate Decision	0.25%	0.25%	0.25%	⊖

> Global Economic Calendar (GMT -5:00) Date Range ▾ Filter Results ▾
> Adjust Timezone

Interest Rate Decision   🖶 Print

Actual 0.25%
Forecast 0.25%
Previous 0.25%

The Federal Open Market Committee (FOMC) decision on short term interest rate. The decision on where to set interest rates depends mostly on growth outlook and inflation. The primary objective of the central bank is to achieve price stability. High interest rates attract foreigners looking for the best "risk-free" return on their money, which can dramatically increases demand for the nation's currency.
A higher than expected rate is positive/bullish for the USD, while a lower than expected rate is negative/bearish for the USD.

| Details | Chart | History |

Importance: High
Source Of Report: Federal Reserve
Release URL: http://www.federalreserve.gov/

	14:15	USD	▼▼▼	FOMC Statement				⊕
	17:00	NZD	▼▼▼	Interest Rate Decision		2.50%	2.50%	⊕
	17:00	NZD	▼▼▼	RBNZ Rate Statement				⊕
	18:45	NZD	▼▼	Trade Balance		372.00M	321.00M	⊕
	20:00	AUD	▼	CB Leading Index (MoM)			-0.20%	⊕

FIGURE 1.1 Example of Economic Calendar
Source: www.fxddondemand.com.

is termed *event risk*. In addition, the volatility generally increases after an important economic release. That is, the price can move sharply higher, then come down sharply, before rising again. This is what I term *volatility risk*. The bid-to-ask spreads for the currency pairs can also widen due to a reluctance to quote with the increased uncertainty. This is called *liquidity risk*. Finally, it is not unusual for the price to gap. When a gap occurs, the trader is often exposed to slippage. The term *slippage* refers to the difference between an order price—like a stop loss order—and the actual fill or trade execution price. Traders, not brokers, are responsible for slippage risk because a stop order simply triggers a market order. If the price gaps through a stop order, the next price where the market trades is the fill price. It can be materially different from the order price, especially if the data is a surprise. This is another risk that traders should be aware of through the more important economic releases such as GDP, unemployment, and inflation. With all these added risks, doesn't it make sense to be aware of those that are most important? I would think so.

Should traders be paranoid about all economic releases? I think there are times when taking on the risk is justified and other times when it is not. For example, if you have an unrealized gain on a position and the economic and technical bias is in the direction of your position, it can make good sense to keep the position through the increased risk.

Traders need to weigh the risk more carefully when trading through the more important economic releases. In most cases the risk and reward is the same or similar, but the magnitude of risk is often larger than what is customary during normal market conditions. That is, instead of 25 pips of risk, the risk could be two, three, or even more times the market exposure.

What tends to happen is the ego of having a position through the more important economic numbers is too overwhelming for a lot of retail traders, and large trading mistakes can be made.

In general, what I like to tell retail traders is that trading should not be based on luck, but on risk management. In all my years of trading I had no sound reason to deviate from what the survey of economists' forecasts had projected, and I can tell you that 99.9 percent of retail traders will not have an empirically sound reason to doubt any forecast either.

Therefore, any retail trader who has the ego to go long the U.S. dollar versus the Japanese yen (USDJPY) just prior to U.S. Nonfarm Payroll because he thinks it will show a strong +250,000 jobs when the survey of economists says it will be +75,000 is just betting black on the roulette wheel.

Economic statistics help move markets, and traders look for those movements especially when trading trends. However, it is important to weigh the relative risks from the data before trading.

Too many retail currency traders consider the risk in normal times equal to risk through an important economic release. It is not.

My suggestion is to change. Do the smart trades. Don't gamble needlessly unless there are a number of winning chips in front of you, and it makes sense from a technical and fundamental perspective. But whatever you do, don't let your ego get in the way of sound trading decisions and cloud your judgment.

Political Influences

Politics is also a fundamental influence that traders should have some knowledge of. The balance of power via the election process and fiscal policy decisions enacted by governments are both potential political influences on the value of a currency pair.

The U.K. general election in 2010 is one example, as the shifts in power had an influence on the currency rates before and after the election. There were several instances where surprise weekend polls sent the GBPUSD to a gapped Sunday opening. Be aware of the political risks during elections, especially over weekends. It will help you avoid the big surprises on the new week's opening.

The Greek debt crisis of 2010 is another recent politically initiated influence that had a major impact on the value of the EURUSD as the crisis unfolded. In the short term, the fluidity of the news kept a negative bias on the euro. However, it also increased volatility risk for the currency as political comments from Greek, German, ECB, EU, and IMF officials kept traders guessing.

There are many instances where market sentiment can focus on the political influences on currency rates. Generally speaking, the bias from politics on a currency rate tends to be more negative than positive for the currency in focus. Perhaps it is the cynicism that the market has toward politics in general. After all, politicians tend to be political.

However, when politics are the fundamental focus, there also tends to be room for increased volatility because people who are in charge of the crisis are there to solve the problems. As a result, their efforts can lead to sharp reversals of the seemingly obvious trend. For example, while Greece was in crisis and the euro was being sold, it ultimately was an injection of aid from the European Central Bank (ECB) and the International Monetary Fund that quickly turned the market around. Retail traders should be aware of these politically motivated moments to anticipate the increased risk and volatility from the solutions. Don't be too married to the position; be aware and be prepared for quick changes.

Another temptation for retail traders is to make a directional currency play on a fundamental political idea that is not a major focus now. Betting that the dollar will be fundamentally weak because Social Security will go broke is not what a retail currency trader should focus trading decisions on today. Betting that the EU will fall apart and the EURUSD will go to parity is also not what a retail trader should be concerned about. It may be the case in the long run, but as John Maynard Keynes once said, "In the long run we are all dead." Therefore, the retail traders should keep focusing on the short run first, and if the bias is so overwhelmingly bearish or bullish, they can be sure that the charts and the political fundamentals will be saying the same thing for a long time and they will ride that trend.

Central Bank Influences

Central bank influences include interest rate changes, comments from key central bank figures like the chairman of the Federal Reserve, Ben Bernanke, or the president of the ECB, Jean-Claude Trichet, and direct currency intervention.

In the 2008–2010 period, the central banks of the world also became more entrenched in other nontraditional stimulative measures, including the use of quantitative easing whereby purchases of financial instruments were done as a way to add liquidity into the economy. The reserve requirement rate is also a new rate that will likely become more important, especially in the United States, when monetary policy starts to be reversed from easing to tightening. In fact, it is likely to be the new "change in interest rates" for the Federal Reserve Bank, when they do look to be less accommodative.

These fundamental influences from the central banks have effects on currency rates in the short term and as a result, being aware of when they occur and the potential impact is an important requirement for retail currency traders.

Changes of Interest Rate Policy   Global central banks control interest rate policy by lowering or raising a short-term interest rate, which is the rate that money is targeted to be borrowed and lent in the interbank market for one day, or what is called overnight. The raising or lowering of this rate is thought to control other interest rates along the yield curve. As such, changes in interest rate policy are thought to stimulate or restrict economic activity, which in turn influences currency rates.

The central bank interest rate decisions are generally made after scheduled central bank meetings. This, however, is not always the case because sometimes the immediacy of a change demands action before a scheduled meeting in order to allay market fears. Usually, however, these changes are well anticipated by the market and often spoken about by economists and market analysts. That is, they are not a surprise.

Generally speaking, a rise in interest rates should lead to a higher currency value, while lowering interest rates should lead to a lower currency value.

Rising interest rates imply a strong economy. A strong economy is often synonymous with a strong currency. One way to slow a strong economy is to make exports more expensive abroad in an attempt to slow sales overseas. The rising domestic currency does this because foreign importers have to pay more for the exporter's currency in order to buy the exports. They will look for cheaper alternative—perhaps within their own countries.

Rising interest rates also imply an elevation of inflation risk. If inflation is expected to rise, a higher currency should lower the cost of imports and in turn lower import inflation down the road.

Finally, rising interest rates are thought to be an attraction to capital as global investors look to benefit from *carry profits*. Carry profits involve buying, or being long the higher yielding currency and short the lower yielding currency. The carry trade has been influential in recent years.

The opposite dynamics should occur if a central bank lowers interest rates due to a slowing economy. That is, the currency should fall. A falling currency makes exports more competitive abroad, which should stimulate economic activity. The United States used a weaker dollar in 2008 and 2009 to keep the economy on life support while domestic consumption declined.

With inflation likely on the decline, a lower currency should increase the cost of imports, and this should keep deflationary forces from taking hold. Finally, a declining currency should dissuade capital investment because investors earn less from the carry trade by being long a lower yielding currency.

When rates are first changed, retail traders often neglect to anticipate the potential for future changes. When rates are changed from declining to rising, or vice versa, that trend will likely remain for an extended period of time. This should lead to a trend-type move for the currency. Traders should be biased for a trend move, especially if the change is one of the earlier changes and if the market has not fully discounted the move already.

However, as each successive change is made in interest rates, the impact from the changes can lose its directional momentum for the currency. This is simply because the impact of the currency and interest rate change starts to be felt in the economy. That is, if rates are being raised, the currency should increase. Eventually, the higher currency will slow exports. The higher rate should also slow economic growth. Eventually, the central bank will need to look toward steady policy and perhaps reversing rates.

Finally, retail traders should be aware that a raising or lowering of interest rates loses its currency significance if the change is done in conjunction with other countries doing the same thing. That is, if interest rates are being lowered in the United States while they are being lowered in the Eurozone, as happened during the global market meltdown in the 2008–2009 period, the market will likely focus on other fundamentals because there is no interest rate advantage as a result of the interest rate differential changing.

Changing interest rates is like changing a ship's course on the open seas. It takes a while to do, but once it is done, it tends to continue in the direction for a while. Retail traders should not be surprised by this and get caught trading against the trend—especially when the ship has just turned around.

Comments from Central Bank Officials   Central bankers will often speak publicly, and when they speak the market listens. They might be required by law to speak in front of government officials to explain their policy actions. They might give speeches at economic forums or roundtables. They might make public comments after interest rate decisions, either in the form of a press release or, with some banks like the ECB, during a full press conference. Obviously, central bankers' comments can have an impact on currency rates.

Like with government statistics, there is a schedule of speaking engagements published for key central bankers. Retail traders should all know the schedule. The significance of the comments can generally be tied to where the economy is in the business cycle and the topic of the comments. If the market perceives the economy is at a turning point, the risk from the comments increases in significance. If, however, comments are made during the normal midcycle period, they often tend to sound like comments made previously and are less important.

As mentioned, most interest rate decisions from central banks usually come with published comments. In recent times, the comments have come under microscopic scrutiny from financial wordsmiths who dissect—sometimes word for word—what is released and what it implies about future monetary policy action.

The U.S. Federal Reserve purposely worded comments that rates would remain low for an "extended period of time" during 2009 and 2010 (and likely into 2011 too). This was done to assure the market that a tightening was not imminent even if the economy improved.

The Bank of Canada used a more direct approach. In its comments starting after its April 2009 meeting, bankers said the overnight rate "can be expected to remain at its current level until the end of the second quarter of 2010." Rates stayed the same until the second quarter of 2010.

One problem retail traders experience with comments from central bank officials is they often do not have access to the comments—especially those from interviews. The cost of real-time headline news is often prohibitive for retail traders. This is a risk traders face and quite frankly nothing can be done. However, like economic releases, moves may be anticipated by knowing the schedule and taking into consideration any risk. A surprise comment with no warning obviously cannot be anticipated but it will be reflected in the market move, often within seconds.

I find it beneficial to get a feel for what the central bankers are thinking by reading their speech transcripts. Below are the names and websites of the major global central banks where speeches from central bankers typically can be found.

- Federal Reserve Bank (Fed): www.federalreserve.gov/
- ECB: www.ecb.int/home/html/index.en.html
- Bank of England (BOE): www.bankofengland.co.uk/
- Swiss National Bank (SNB): www.snb.ch/
- Bank of Canada (BOC): www.bank-banque-canada.ca/en/index.html
- Reserve Bank of New Zealand (RBNZ): www.rbnz.govt.nz/
- Reserve Bank of Australia (RBA): www.rba.gov.au/
- Bank of Japan (BOJ): www.boj.or.jp/en/

Central Bank Intervention

Central banks generally try not to interfere with market forces. However, there are instances where they feel compelled to reverse the trend of their currency so as to prevent adverse economic impact from the move. To do this, the central banks will intervene directly in the interbank market by buying or selling in order to influence the direction of their currency.

The most notable intervention in recent history was the periodic intervention from the Swiss National Bank to lower the value of its currency in 2009–2010. The reason for the intervention was that the higher currency was thought to be slowing export growth at a time when the domestic economy was sputtering. In addition, the higher currency was also dampening the cost of imports at a time when inflation was slowing. A similar move by the Bank of Japan was also taken in 2010 as it too worried about the impact of inflation (or deflation) and growth.

On March 12, 2009, the SNB tested the market's desire to sell in the face of warnings and intervened in the market, buying EURCHF at the 1.4765 level. The action led to a whopping 565-pip move higher in one day, with little relief.

The Bank of Japan intervened on September 15, 2010 for the first time in six years and the USDJPY soared from 82.87 to 85.90. Moves like this can be dangerous for unsuspecting currency traders.

The good news about central bank intervention is that it does not happen very often, and at times the central bank may give verbal warnings. The bad news is that it is hard to time intervention, and if you are on the wrong side of the trade, the losses can be significant.

Common sense says to heed central bank intervention warnings and consider the risks too great to even trade the currency, no matter the profit potential. The reason is that you never know when the intervention will take place and the central bank may watch the currency drift down (or up) and intervene when the market is least expecting it, maximizing the impact.

Currency traders always have options to trade high-risk currency pairs or more stable currency pairs. If risks are elevated from potential intervention, I strongly suggest either don't trade the pair or lower the trading amounts, but never trade against the central banks' warnings when intervention is possible. Also, after intervention be aware that there can be large corrections as traders on the right side take profits. Intervention risk is often not a good time to trade. Use common sense and let the allure pass until more normal markets with less risk prevail.

Intermarket Influences

Intermarket influences such as stock markets and prices of commodities such as gold, copper, silver, and oil can affect the value of currencies. Generally speaking, the commodity prices of gold, copper, silver, and oil will have an influence on the commodity currencies. These include the Australian and Canadian dollars and to a lesser extent the New Zealand dollar. Needless to say, these countries are reliant on the exporting of commodities and therefore their currency value becomes tied to them. If prices trend up, the commodity currencies tend to go up. If prices of commodities are going down, the commodity currencies tend to go down.

The stock market is another intermarket influence on currencies, but it can vary. At times a robust stock market can mean a stronger currency and a weaker stock market a lower currency. In recent times, however, a stronger stock market, often led by the U.S. stock market, led to a flight into what became considered risky currencies. Risky pairs included anything with yen, such as USDJPY, GBPJPY, EURJPY, CHFJPY, and AUDJPY. The British pound; euro; and commodity currencies like the Australian, Canadian and New Zealand dollars also tended to benefit from the move into risky currencies.

Conversely, a decline in the stock market led to a flight into quality, with quality defined as anything with the Japanese yen, Swiss franc, and U.S. dollar, in that order. The other currencies all declined, including the euro, pound sterling, Canadian dollar, Australian dollar, and New Zealand dollar.

Although it is nice to know the relationship—especially in a trend-type market in commodities—retail currency traders should remember they are trading currencies and not commodities or stocks. The stock, commodity, and currency markets can have their own quirks and corrections, and there may be other influences that may diverge from the expected relationship. For example, oil prices can decline and should lead to a higher USDCAD (lower Canadian dollar). However, it does not always happen.

I think it may help retail traders' results if they are more aware of intermarket relationships, but should this be the main focus for trading currencies? *No.* Don't make the intermarket relationships your focus.

Traditional Foreign Exchange Influences

There are natural foreign exchange uses that affect the value of currency rates. For example, Coca-Cola is a multinational corporation that may look to remit foreign currency back to the United States periodically. Japanese exporters to the United States are known to sell the USDJPY pair periodically to remit funds back to Japan. Other natural foreign exchange uses occur from mergers and acquisitions. A Canadian company may purchase a U.S. company (or vice versa) and affect the value of the USDCAD exchange rate when the payments are made to complete the purchase and sale. Options expirations where the value of a currency is near a strike price can cause a currency pair to move as traders defend the levels. These are some examples of the traditional influences on currency rates. Can a retail trader anticipate these fundamental influences? No. There is little the trader can do with respect to anticipating them without insider knowledge.

In summary, fundamental influences are many (I just reviewed a small list), and combined they are thought to influence the direction of a currency pair's value. For retail traders, knowing the key things that can move rates is a comfort or can influence a bias (in conjunction with technical analysis), but this knowledge can also steer traders in the wrong direction.

Be aware of the key fundamental influences, understand how they affect risk, and then trade accordingly. If the risk is too high because of the threat of intervention, then don't trade. If the risk from an economic statistic is too great, don't trade.

Understand that your assessment of fundamentals may not be what is driving the market. For example, you may have all the reasons in the world to expect that the USDCAD should go up, but because of a big merger, it goes down. The only protection is the technicals in this instance; this is why I favor them over fundamentals.

However, if you can get an edge and the edge comes from a deeper understanding of fundamentals, make that extra effort, learn, and reap the rewards.

THEY FAIL TO ANTICIPATE TRENDS

The final thing that most retails traders don't do is anticipate trends. Anticipating a trend is not all that revolutionary. It does not necessarily mean you need a magical crystal ball. After all, most successful businesses, whether they are large or small, anticipate trends.

Google anticipated the need for an efficient search engine and also anticipated that businesses would pay to have sponsored links to their sites. Facebook anticipated the need for a social networking site. Amazon anticipated a need to download books online and manufactured the Kindle to satisfy that demand. Apple seems to magically anticipate trends with all its product offerings.

Trading with the trends is the most important thing a retail trader can do. There are two big reasons for this.

One, trends are generally fast and directional, and follow along a fairly consistent path of higher highs and higher lows for an uptrend and lower lows and lower highs for a downtrend. If a trader catches a trend and is able to stay on it, profits can be a multiple of the risk taken at the outset of the trade.

The second reason that trading with the trend is so important is that doing so prevents oversized losses in the account from trading against the trend. It goes to reason that if the profit-to-loss ratio of trading with the trend is potentially high, then the reverse would be true if a trader positioned against the trend.

The fastest way to fail in trading is to be on the wrong side of a trend, not recognize the trend, fight the trend, overleverage against the trend, and ignore the trend. In addition, the longer a trader delays the process of getting on the trend, the greater the chance the market will reverse and really whip the trader's mind into mush as fear is increased.

So how do improve your chances of trading a trend?

The best way to catch a trend, trade a trend, and stay on a trend is to anticipate the trend. Just like Apple anticipates trends in consumer behavior, retail traders need to anticipate the trends in their market. Look at any chart. There are trends.

Most retail traders recognize a trend in hindsight. What most retail traders do *not* do is anticipate a trend. If you don't anticipate a trend, how do you know when one may be developing? You don't. In all likelihood you see a nontrending market that begs you to sell a high or buy a low. Why? Because that is what the market has been doing during the sideways market.

Do you look to anticipate a trend? Do you know of any market clues that would help you predict a trend-type move? If you had an idea a trend was on the horizon, the only thing you would need to do would be to get the direction right. Wouldn't knowing the market was poised for a trend allow you to attack the currency trend more successfully? Later in the book I will explain ways that traders can anticipate trends from the price action and the use of trading tools.

DON'T BE LIKE THE REST ... CHANGE!

Do you want to be the stereotypical trader who thinks trading is easy, who doesn't understand fear, who relies too much on fundamental trading yet does not pay attention to the important fundamental requirements that will keep risk down? Do you want to say you want to trade the trends but never can? Do you want to be in the fat part of the bell curve and continue to lose money doing it your way?

If you want to change from the norm—from the stereotypical retail trader—then take that look at yourself and make that change.

CHAPTER 2

The Six Attributes of a Successful Currency Trader

If you don't try what you can't do today, you will never know if you can do it tomorrow.

—Anonymous

What defines a successful currency trader? We have learned so far that it is not the trader who thinks it is easy, nor the trader who takes a hit-or-miss approach similar to flipping the proverbial coin. It is more than likely that the successful traders treat trading as a business and have the motivation to get better. Does that mean that you have to trade eight hours a day? Not necessarily, although the more time you spend the better. What does it take to be successful?

WHAT ARE YOU GOOD AT DOING?

Think of the thing or things outside of trading that you have shown a positive progression at doing. It may be parenting. It may be a job you currently have or had. It may be preparing for, taking, and passing the CPA exam like my wife did. It may be writing, performing, and recording a song like my son Matt does. It may be a card game or hobby like bridge or wood carving like my mother and mother-in-law do. It may be an athletic endeavor like golf, tennis, or biking. It may be enhancing your spiritual life, whether you are Catholic, Protestant, Jewish, Muslim, Buddhist, or Hindu. Maybe it's a skill like coaching youth baseball, public speaking, even authoring a blog or book—things that I started with a low knowledge level and have shown a progression toward success.

If you think back to when you first started a new venture, you may have said to yourself, "How am I ever going to do this?" You most likely thought of failure before thinking of success.

However, after overcoming your initial fear, if you truly liked what you were doing, that new passion most likely motivated you to work harder at it. Through that effort, you likely got better at doing it as well. Negative thoughts about failure were likely replaced with thoughts of success. Along that journey, you may have been rewarded with signs that your children did learn the lessons you taught them, or maybe a salary increase. Perhaps you saw your golf handicap come down or a new heavier weight lifted. Maybe you completed that 10K run for cancer or became a leader at your church.

If you are new to currency trading and it all seems daunting now, think of those things you are now good at and recall how imperfect you were when you first started. For those who are more experienced in trading, think of the steps you made that have contributed to your progression as a trader.

Just like the steps you may have taken to become better at cooking or running, there are steps you can take with your currency trading that will help you progress as a trader. You will learn how to execute a trade, the definition of a stop loss, how to set a stop loss, and what the currency acronym CHF means. I have heard it referred to as the Chinese franc, but CHF actually stands for Confederation Helvetica franc, which is the Latin name for the Swiss franc. Is the name something you need to know? No. Do you need to know you are trading the Swiss currency and not a Chinese currency (the Chinese currency is yuan, anyway)? Needless to say, yes.

For the more advanced trader who is several steps along, maybe your efforts have already led to monetary rewards—after all, making money is what we should all be striving to do as currency traders. However, you may not be achieving those rewards. In fact, it may be that a vast majority of you who are reading this book have nothing but losses from the steps you have taken to date. Something is amiss and needs to be fixed.

Just like professional baseball players, traders need to have a "spring training season" where the fundamentals of trading are reaffirmed and for some, learned properly for the very first time. The fundamentals form the foundation for your trading strategy. By building a stronger foundation, you will likely start to replace the "No, I can't" with "Yes, I can." Remember, if you don't try what you can't do today, you will never know if you can do it tomorrow.

THERE WILL ALWAYS BE PEAKS AND VALLEYS

Like everything in life that has a payoff, there is a level of effort that needs to be exerted, and there will always be peaks and valleys. Think of the peaks as the winning trades and the valleys as the losing trades. You will, of course, have your share of losing trades. You may also develop negative attributes that are not conducive to being successful.

Like the husband or wife who makes the mistake of focusing on a spouse's negative attributes, traders can be too focused on the negative attributes of trading. You will need to be able to focus on the positive. Focus and develop those attributes that will lead to your success as a trader and put all the bad off to the side.

Over the course of my career in the financial markets I have been able to uncover six attributes that most successful traders possess. These attributes help build the foundation needed to make money trading currencies. None can be ignored. To do so would seriously jeopardize the long-term success of the trader. In fact, lacking even one of these attributes, you are likely to fail. The attributes that I will define and illustrate have their roots in my experience as a trader and in my observations of thousands of currency traders and what makes them successful or not successful. Through time, I have also discovered that I can apply the same attributes to other jobs, life skills, or even hobbies.

For example, my middle son has the ambition to become a college football coach. Through our many conversations about the dynamics involved with his potential career choice, I found that applying my "Six Attributes of a Successful Currency Trader" could be massaged to the "Six Attributes of a Successful Football Coach."

Learning these attributes and striving to apply them in your trading will build a strong foundation for success. Don't take them lightly. Don't take any shortcuts. Focus on them. They are essential for developing your business as a successful currency trader.

1. SKILL OR APTITUDE

Let's face it, we are not all cut out to be anything or do everything. We each have certain God-given skills or aptitudes. Other skills or aptitudes we just don't have.

As mentioned, my wife is a CPA. I cannot be a CPA or work in the accounting field as a bookkeeper or other equivalent position. I do not have the necessary education, and although I could possibly go off to school to gain that education, I do not have the desire to spend the time to develop that skill or aptitude. It is one thing to say you want to be an accountant. It is another to actually go out and do it. Accounting is just not my thing.

The good news is that if you have the desire, you can develop the skills and aptitude needed to be a successful currency trader. There are numerous resources that can help you learn how to trade better.

There are books out there—including this one—that can and will improve your trading. However, there are also trading plans and ideas that I feel can be detrimental to most retail traders. I hope that with what you learn from this book, you will be able to pick out that which is beneficial to your trading and that which is not.

Other resources that can increase your skill and aptitude include things like traders' conventions where professionals give workshops. Local trader clubs are a good source for trading ideas and knowledge. The *Wall Street Journal* has a currency section. CNBC, Bloomberg Television, and Fox Business give economic and market news during market hours. Some currency brokers conduct free webinars. I personally conduct webinars on a regular basis that allow for the live analysis of current market conditions and also provide education on how to be a more successful trader.

As you develop your skill and aptitude, some of the information you will absorb will be good; some of it, although perhaps accepted by professional traders, can actually be bad for your trading. You will need to learn to filter the good from the bad.

At times, business television and sometimes print material can manifest the negative attributes of trading. I think this can in part be attributed to the natural instinct to be shocking. Shock sells, but it is often not good for retail traders to follow. For example, whenever I read an article or listen to an analyst that puts a target level for the currency pair at a level that is outside what is normal, I look to expunge the thought immediately from my mind.

In a *Wall Street Journal* article published on February 26, 2010, the headline read "Hedge Funds Try 'Career Trade' Against Euro," and the article talked about the EURUSD going to parity with the U.S. dollar (i.e., 1.0000) from the 1.3500 area. This type of article is the perfect example of something retail traders should simply ignore.

First, 3,500 pips is a pretty healthy move and would likely take a length of time that is outside a retail trader's normal tolerance for a trade period. A successful trader should focus on trade ideas that are more normal, not abnormal like 3,500 pips. Trading retail currency is not about taking the proverbial Black Swan position that is outside the norm and waiting for the desired result.

Second, these kinds of articles often don't mention the risk a trader might face. In my trading analysis, I always balance the current price with the risk that traders can expect to experience. If the risk is a 200-pip correction, what will that 200 pips do to your trading account? Will you be able to sustain a corrective move of this magnitude without closing out with the loss? Most retail traders will have a very difficult time with this type of trading in the currency market.

Third, a dramatic article like that can become the reason for a corrective move in and of itself. The trading gods tend to love doom and gloom articles. Many a top and bottom are made after a front-page article or cover story trumpets the end of some benchmark—including currencies. There is no explanation for this except to say that if sentiment is so bearish, it takes new added sellers to overpower the profit-taking/dip buyers. If the sellers are already short, sometimes the only way the market can go is up. Once the upside starts, shorts get scared and prices move even higher. Markets have and will always have periods of retracement.

In this instance, what specifically made me cautious was that the EURUSD had already come down from a high of 1.5100 to 1.3500, 10.6 percent in a relatively short period of time (three months). The pair was trading at the three-month low, and although the trend is indeed your friend, there were signs the pair might be bottoming or at a significant support level, because 1.3483 was the 61.8 percent Fibonacci retracement of the 2009 low-to-high trading range.

As shown in Figure 2.1, the day before the article was printed, the EURUSD closed at 1.3548. Over the next 14 trading days not a single day had a closing price below the 1.3548 level. Over that time the price rose to a high of 1.3817. The article picked a short-term bottom instead of leading to new lows.

Articles in the press and commentary on television or other media outlets, no matter how passionate, need to be put in a context that is congruent with your risk tolerance and trading style. Selling the EURUSD at 1.3548 and waiting for the collapse to 1.0000 becomes a different feeling in the gut of a shorter-term-oriented retail trader after a 260-pip corrective move higher. Are you prepared to take that longer-term look at the market? (I am not.) Is your trading more geared toward trading the trend in a shorter-term time horizon, while keeping your risk to a minimum? These are the questions you will need to answer before you put all your faith in something you may read that is designed to shock.

Ultimately, the EURUSD may indeed go to parity and those who wrote the article, and who were quoted in the article, can toast their good fortune. If you follow the rules of trading I will discuss in this book, you too will be toasting your good fortune. However, in your case you will do it the right way for the retail trader.

FIGURE 2.1 Evaluating the Risk First

Ultimately, I like to tell traders whom I mentor that it is my job to teach you how to fish for yourself. In other words, I want to develop your skills and aptitude for trading so you can do it, and do it successfully. I will look to guide you with specific clues to follow, but it is only through applying, doing, and believing in what you are learning that you will become a successful trader.

Although I like to think that everyone can learn how to be a better trader, not all will be able to develop the necessary skill or aptitude to be successful *enough*. You need to spawn the necessary love affair with trading by making money. Without a love (or at least a strong like), your skill or aptitude will likely slip. You will become lazy. Your skills will diminish.

At that point, your account balance will tell the story and you may have to look in the mirror and say, "I just don't have the skill or aptitude to do this or the desire to make it happen." That is okay. I cannot be an accountant. I cannot be a doctor. I cannot be a 10-handicap golfer. So, instead, find something you can be passionate about, and go do it instead. You will be happier, and more than likely you will be find success, too.

2. PRACTICE, PRACTICE, PRACTICE

A young man is walking down the street in New York City and stops an elderly man to ask, "Excuse me, sir, how do you get to Carnegie Hall?" The elderly man looks the young man in the eye and replies, "Practice! Practice! Practice!" Sometimes you don't like to do it, but some form of practice is needed in order to improve.

My mom loves playing bridge and has taken to online games. By playing online, she keeps her mind sharp. It also gets her ready for more serious tournament play where she really strives to excel. My son plays guitar and writes his own music. He compares his playing and his music writing to the professional musicians he admires. He gets better by playing his guitar every day and by comparing himself to the best.

Baseball players have batting practice each day so they can hope to hit a ball successfully three out of ten times. Basketball players practice free throws every day. Golfers putt hundreds of three-foot putts. Even stars in the big leagues need to practice.

Foundations for successful trading are also rooted in practice. I believe practice can have a few forms depending where you are in your currency trading career. One is through the use of a demo platform. Experienced and inexperienced traders can benefit from this method of practice. Most, if not all, retail brokers have a free demo platform. They tend to limit the demo period from one to three months, but often if you call up, you can have the demo period extended, keeping the continuity in place.

The purpose of the demo platform is to gain familiarity with the trading platform, including how to execute a trade, how to place stop and limit orders, how to cancel orders, how to utilize the chart packages including setting up the charts, and even training your eyes to watch the charts that you are most interested in. The more familiar you are with the tools of your trade, the better chance you have at success. Don't underestimate the importance of platform familiarity and the idea of training your senses to what you are doing.

Practice with your trading platform. Train your eyes; practice doing the keystrokes. If you use other senses such as sound, you need to practice without relying on that sense. The benefits of the practice far exceed the time commitment. Once that familiarity is achieved, trading practice needs to take place. In this book, I will teach a method for trading that will allow you to attack the currency trends in a logical way. You will need to practice what I preach and become comfortable with it. Doing it on the demo is one way of practicing.

A second way to practice is to trade on a live or real trading platform. By doing this, it puts some skin in the game. Demo traders often find that trading is more difficult when real money is in place. It shouldn't be, but it is for many.

Thankfully, in the retail market, a trader can vary the trade size fairly easily. A trader can trade a micro account (1000 units of the base currency) that has risk of around \$0.10 per pip. A mini account, which is 10,000 units of the base currency, has a pip value of around \$1.00 per pip. I would suggest using these amounts and building the trading size as your confidence grows.

A third way to practice is for more experienced traders who are fully familiar with the platform and other functionality of trading. It is a way that I practice and get better. The way is simply to observe and study the markets closely.

Most retail currency traders suffer from trading too much and not watching the market flow or rhythm enough. The currency market tends to have a rhythm to it. That rhythm can change just like the rhythm of music changes. At times, the rhythms in the market price are smooth and logical. I find this occurs during trending markets up or trending markets down. At other times the market can lack rhythm. During these times the market tends to be randomly choppy and irrational. This tends to occur during nontrending markets, when the market has no discernable trend.

For example, a key support level for your trading system may be breached and instead of continuing in the direction of the break, like the market *should* do, the price may reverse back above the old support level. Observing and studying what happens after a failure like this is telling and often leads to great trading opportunities—in the opposite direction.

Trading successfully is a lot about deciphering the clues the market is giving you and making an educated judgment about what *should* happen. If the clues you follow are consistent and reliable, make sense, are what the market should follow, and the market does not do what it should do, that tells you something.

Observing and studying what the market does, especially if you have a sound plan for your trading, will help to develop your confidence in what you are doing. It may seem like you are missing out on real trading— especially if the trade you would do is profitable. However, think of the time you spend observing and studying the markets as the price you pay to increase your understanding of the market and gain confidence in your trading methodology.

The more you practice by watching the markets, the easier it will be for you to see the low-risk/high-reward trading opportunities that present themselves over the course of a trading day. You cannot just go out and play and hope to be successful. Practice! Practice! Practice! You cannot get enough practice.

3. KNOW YOUR RISK

In life we are constantly evaluating risk. When we drive, we are processing the road ahead, behind, and to our sides through our mirrors. We pay attention to our speed partly in reaction to the risk of getting a speeding ticket and partly to consider the risk to injury of ourselves and others in the event of an accident. Analyzing risk is second nature when most of us drive. It becomes instinctive.

However, think back to the time when you were first learning to drive. If you can't remember that far back, perhaps I can jog your memory with mine. When I first got behind the wheel of a car, processing the risks was much more difficult than it is now. I was told to check the mirrors, watch the road, and monitor the speedometer. This was a process I had to think about carefully each time I got in the car.

Eventually, as I became more familiar and comfortable, the careful driving gave way to a more cavalier attitude. Now, friends were in the car. The cassette player was on full volume. Adjusting mirrors was a thing of the past. Speed was less of a concern. I realized that the risk of getting caught speeding was not that great. On the highways, if I led the pack, I did not have to worry about the guy stopping in front of me; he had to worry about me.

Then one day while pulling out of a parallel parking spot with a friend chatting in the front seat, and the radio blaring, I failed to check the blind spot. To my surprise, a car hit the side of my parents' Jeep. My heart started to race. The sweat started to bead on my brow. The police came and I made excuses. "I checked my mirrors, officer. I did not see the car. So obviously she must have been going too fast." Deservedly, I got the ticket, and I had to explain the damage to my parents. I had to pay the price both literally and figuratively.

Compare that to trading. When a trader first starts, the common reaction is fear. There tends to be an ultraconservative approach. This is mainly bred from the lack of experience. New traders are getting behind the wheel of the car for the first time. It happened to me. It happens to us all. So the evaluation of risk is congruent with that fear.

As time goes by, traders develop requirements one and two—that is, they advance their skills and aptitudes and they practice more. In the process, their feelings about risk start to change.

One reason is that they probably have some success. The success may extend from learning how to scalp the market—taking small profits quickly along the way and doing a lot of trades in the process. Traders become comfortable behind the wheel. Risk is less a concern. Trading out of the losses by doubling and tripling up (or even more), or waiting out the losses becomes the risk management employed by overconfident beginner traders. They may even get away with this strategy, which is the equivalent of the reckless driver. In this phase of the journey, the trader becomes giddy. With that attitude comes carelessness.

Then one day, the accident happens. The trader gets caught buying a dip in what ends up being the end of a bullish market, and the price moves lower. The trader buys against another support level and the price rallies a bit, but then sells through that support level. The trader looks for the next support level and buys against it. The market corrects a small amount, but not nearly close to the average breakeven price, and the market falls again. The accident is happening. The only difference between the car accident and this one is that in a car accident, *boom* and it's over. Trading accidents can be more drawn out.

When this happens, I often get an e-mail asking for my thoughts. I may note that the price has moved below the 100 day moving average, turning the bias to bearish, then below the 200 day moving average, which confirms the bearish bias. The price may have moved through the 38.2 percent retracement level, another key downside target and another bearish confirming level, and so on. The market is trending lower.

The client responds, "The Relative Strength Index [RSI] is oversold. We are due for a bounce." However, I need to warn him that RSIs can remain oversold in a trending market for an extended period of time, and I give him the proverbial trader's "ticket" for not following the rules of trading. The client was aware that he ignored looking in his trader's blind spot. He was overconfident in his trading abilities. He disregarded the market's rules for safe trading when his initial trade did not do what it was supposed to do, and consequently he got in an accident.

Over time, successful drivers learn the risks of the road. If they choose to ignore the risks, the consequences may need to be paid in the form of tickets or worse. Successful traders evaluate, know, and understand their risks, like conscientious mature drivers. Gauging risk becomes more instinctive the more successful you become, but it is never forgotten.

Rules for Risk

I have two rules when it comes to risk for traders. The rules are this:

1. If the specific risk of a trade is not known, then don't do the trade.
2. If the risk is too great, don't do the trade.

The first rule of risk requires traders to take responsibility for their trades. To not have a specific stop level is like driving with no regard for the rules of the road. The risk for an accident or ticket goes up exponentially. In life, and, yes, in trading, you need to take responsibility for all of your actions. In trading, it is called a stop loss. This defines your specific risk.

Successful traders get used to doing those trades that they see as being profitable. They also look to do trades at levels that limit their risk. That risk is often defined to a specific price. The reason the level is so specific is that successful traders will tend to look to trade at prices near turning points—near levels that I call *borderlines*. Borderlines are price levels where there is a sound reason (or reasons) for the market's bias to be bullish (or bearish) at one price, and bearish (or bullish) if the price moves through that price. By doing this, borderlines keep risk to a minimum.

I will discuss more about those low risk price areas—borderlines— later in the book. The important thing to learn now is successful traders know their exact risk; if it is not known, they don't do the trade.

The second rule, "If the risk is too great, don't do the trade," addresses taking on too much risk. It also addresses what I call a trader's worst enemy: fear. You may know your specific risk (the first rule) but if that risk is too great, then don't do the trade.

A guideline for most successful traders is to not risk more than 3 to 5 percent of the account value on any one trade. What does that translate into?

Assume you have a $10,000 retail trading account. The specific risk you feel comfortable trading is 4 percent of your equity. With that risk profile you should not risk more than $400 on any trading position ($10,000 × 0.04% = $400.00).

During most times, the market does not move fast enough for the $400 to be exhausted, assuming a position that is not overleveraged. However, an important economic report can come out that might send the price higher or lower quickly and in the process gobble up the $400 cushion rather quickly. U.S. Unemployment reports can move 75 to 100 pips in the first few minutes of trading. If the risk is expected to be too great, my suggestion is don't do the trade. You are just gambling. You are not trading. Instead, wait and look to do the trades near the borderlines where risk is not so great.

Jumping on the Bandwagon

Another time where the risk can be too great occurs after a fast-trend-type move. Many beginner traders will look to jump on the bullish or bearish bandwagon at trade locations that do not have a close enough stop level.

For example, assume the price of the EURUSD moves through key moving average support at 1.3428 and moves rapidly to the current price at 1.3370. You missed the initial break, but don't want to miss out on the rest of the move. You do what I call the "bandwagon trade" by selling without thinking at 1.3370. You simply jump on the bandwagon.

After doing the trade, you figure the closest stop level is if the price moves back above the moving average level at 1.3428. The risk on the trade is 58 pips. The dollar risk is $580 (58 pips × $10 a pip × 1 lot). You are not worried; after all, the market has broken support. However, your trading is not exactly close to the bearish or bullish borderline.

What often happens after a sharp directional move is that the market stabilizes, reverses, and corrects higher. We have all experienced this. It is as if the market was waiting for you to panic and enter. The correction is slow at first but then starts to ratchet higher. When the market moves above the 1.3400 level, you are now down 30 pips. You sold near the lows and your mind starts to think toward limiting the loss rather than making a profit. You hope for a 15-pip move down so you can book a modest $150 loss.

Since hope is for dopes, the price gods will push the price up to 1.3412. You are down $420, which would be your limit on a normal trade (4 percent). Your internal trading clock says, "I am at my limit." Instead, your stop is still 14 pips away, another $140. The market moves up to 1.3420, comes down to 1.3412. You close the trade out (out of fear) for a loss of $420. The price moves up to 1.3420 one last time, but then reverses and continues the trend to the downside. The market moves back below the 1.3400 level and trades between 1.3380 and 1.3400 for a while. You are now paralyzed, mad, fearful, and out of synch with the market.

The better approach would be to wait for an opportunity where you can define a risk that is more congruent with your risk tolerance. Wait. If you missed the bandwagon, don't try and jump on it. Wait to trade near the borderline. Your risk will be more comfortable. You are more likely to be able to live through the corrections if you are more comfortable with your risk.

Whenever I speak to traders, I tell them there is only one thing I can 100 percent guarantee them. That is, that there will always be another trade. Successful traders adhere to these rules and as a result, they avoid the accidents of trading. They also learn to quickly define and limit their risks.

4. CREATE AND EXECUTE A PLAN

The Division I college football team my son Brian works for as an undergraduate assistant had a keen understanding of the team's strengths and weaknesses as it entered the 2009 season. They needed a plan.

The offense was untested. The quarterback was a first-year senior starter. He lacked game experience. The receivers had more game experience and above-average speed. The running backs did not have a particular star. It would be a "running game by committee." The offensive line was intact from the year before, so they had experience. That was the good news. The bad news was that in the prior year the line gave up the most quarterback sacks in the conference.

The defense had a large number of returning players from a team that was solid. The defensive line had one of the nation's best pass rushers. The linebackers were fast, aggressive, smart, and they had good depth at the position. The secondary had experience but had some question marks with overall ability.

The special teams were anchored by a potential All-America place-kicker. The punter had a strong leg, but could be inconsistent. He also had difficulty with controlling distance on punts. This was important for pinning an opponent inside his own 20-yard line. The punt and kickoff return personnel had speed and were a threat to provide good field position. The other personnel on the kicking teams were unknown. Motivation is key in special teams play, and the players need to take pride in what they do and potentially can accomplish.

From this framework, the coaches devised the game plan for the season.

- The team would be dependent on the defense. The defense would be called on to hold the opposition deep in their own territory, force punts that would give the offense good field position, and look to create turnovers. Finally, they would use their swagger and intimidation to excite the crowd, motivate the offense, and intimidate the opposition.
- The next most important aspect would be the special teams. With an inexperienced offense, the punter and punt team would be used to pin the opponents deep in their territory. If our punter was better than their punter, the offense could benefit from better field position. Better field position would open the opportunity to take advantage of the All-American placekicker for needed points from field goals.
- The offense was the weak link. Inexperience at quarterback, lack of a proven star, and line uncertainty made the whole offense a big question mark. With the uncertainty, the offense could not afford to turn the ball over. As a result, the offense would be more conservative in nature. Risk would be minimized.
- The team needed to have fewer penalties than the opposition, and the team would need to force more fumbles and interceptions.

The plan was set. It was fairly simple. It defined what needed to be done. It was up to the coaches to implement the plan and the players (the tools) to execute the plan.

Traders need a plan, too. Know what you are going to do in various trading environments. You need to understand and define your risks. You need to understand what is going to make the most money; that's going to put the most dollars (i.e., points) in your account (i.e., on the scoreboard). You need to understand your limitations or weaknesses and how to avoid them so that hurtful trades are not made. You need to keep it simple. Being too complicated can cause confusion, and with it uncertainty. The trading plan should do all these things so you can maximize your profits.

Does having a plan and executing the plan guarantee that you will be successful most of the time? No. Trading plans that are designed properly are there to increase the odds for success. They don't guarantee winning trades all the time, but they should increase your trading results and your account value over time.

A trading plan should also set the stage for a key rule I have for becoming a successful trader. This is what I call the "If . . . Should" rule. The "If . . . Should" rule says this: "*If* the market does ABC, the price *should* do XYZ. If the market does not do what it is supposed to do, *get out.*" Putting it in terms of a market move, an example would sound something like this: "*If* the market price moves *below* the 100-day moving average, the market price *should* continue to move lower in the direction of the break. If the market price does not move lower, *get out.*"

This rule is a way to remain disciplined about your trading and it comes directly from a trading plan. There should be no doubt what you should be doing when you follow the rule. It also does something else important for successful traders. It puts the blame on the market. Blaming the market takes blame off you as the trader. This keeps your mind more positive, and being positive is important as you build trading success. If your plan is good—I will develop a plan for you to trade the trends—then if the market does not do what it is supposed to do, there is something happening that is not normal. Your trading plan needs to focus on what is normal, not what is abnormal. So whenever you expect the market to do one thing and it does another, get out and ask questions later. We will talk more about the "If . . . Should" rule in Chapter 4.

Of course, we all would like our trading plan to be successful a large percentage of the time. Most everyone would want his or her plan to win most of the time; let's assume 80 percent. But what good is the plan if the 80 winning trades make 5 pips each or 400 pips and the 20 losing trades lose 20 pips each or the same 400 pips? I would much rather be right 40 times out of 100 and make 30 pips for +1,200 pips and be wrong 60 times and lose 15 pips for −900 pips and a net gain of +300 pips.

What is important for success as a currency trader is the *quality* of the wins that your plan has the potential to produce. For a lot of retail traders, accepting this idea can be hard and can be a major contributor to being unsuccessful.

Medicine, law, engineering, and accounting are all professions that attract some of the smartest people. Does that demographic make for a successful trader? Not necessarily. The reason is that accepting failure on a trade is just not part of some people's makeup. Doctors can't afford to make errors. So they don't. Lawyers are hired to defend their clients. They cannot make errors that jeopardize their clients. Engineers need to have their calculations correct when they build a bridge or road, devise new chemicals, or provide the electrical schematic for a structure. There is no room for failure or error. Accountants are hired to be exact. It is not expected that the financial numbers will be changed.

When people in these types of professions look to trade, they are not used to losing. This is why having a plan, sticking to the plan, controlling your risk, practicing, and developing your skill and aptitude are all requirements to be successful in currency trading. The next two attributes are also key requirements.

So a warning to all those who got straight A's on their report cards: Get ready for some C's, but please avoid the F's in the process. The fastest way to an F is to not have a plan. I will develop a plan for your trading as the book progresses, using tools that will help you attack the trends while keeping risk to a minimum.

5. CONTROL YOUR FEAR

Fear is a trader's worst enemy! Fear tends to make traders do things they normally would not do. Most traders think that fear comes when money is being lost, and indeed it does. It also rears its ugly head at other times for traders. Successful traders are able to control their fear better than most. This gives them a major advantage in their trading results.

Most new traders experience fear literally at all times. The fear comes from many things, but not having the four attributes we have outlined so far is a major contributor to that fear. If you don't develop your skill or aptitude, you will have fear. If you don't practice and observe the markets enough during all conditions, you will have fear. If you don't quantify your risk or have too much risk, you will have fear. If you don't have a trading plan that helps define risk and plan for reward, you will have fear.

Looking at it from the other side, fear is reduced automatically if you develop your skills and aptitude. The more you know about the currency market, the better a trader you will become. So how specifically can fear be reduced?

Fear is automatically reduced when you:

- *Practice.* When market rhythms become familiar, when you understand the risk of big economic numbers, when you understand how markets should react when a key technical level is breached, then your fear becomes reduced. You need to practice to reduce fear.

- *Define the risk.* Defining your risk by having a stop loss will automatically reduce your fear. A stop loss level should always be at a price that says to you, the market was bullish, it is now bearish. If the market is now bearish, then why be long? A logical stop reduces your fear.
- *Create and execute a plan.* Part of a trading plan is to focus on the profit side of the trading equation. Part of it is to focus on where the plan goes awry. Trading plans have the stop loss as part of the plan. It also has targets along the way that give confidence to the trade. Both have the positive effect of lessening trader fear.

So the fifth attribute of a successful trader is the ability to control fear—an attribute rooted in taking care of attributes 1 to 4. If you take care of 1 to 4, you will have less fear. Most traders know about the fear of failure, but there is another fear retail traders tend to have: the fear of success. Let's take a quick look at both.

I certainly remember my early days as a trader when I would finally pony up the courage to do a trade, put the trade on, and immediately have a feeling that I would prefer to have my position in the exact opposite direction. So I would cover at a loss, go the opposite way, and have the trade move immediately against me. It is tough being a successful trader when you have fear as soon as you enter a trade. It also is a horrible way to set an example for future trades. Traders need to have conviction when they execute a trade. Not having that confidence is a sure way to not succeed as a trader. I call this type of fear the *fear of failure.*

Ironically, traders can also experience fear when they have a gain. I call this having the *fear of success,* and it is one of the chief reasons why traders do poorly trading trends. Even when a trade has been executed and a profit is secure, a fear can enter the mind of the trader that the gain will all be taken away by the invisible market thief. So instead of managing the position and benefiting from the good trade location, the trader cuts the position before it's time because of the fear of losing the gain. Later, after the trend is over, he or she looks at the missed opportunity and laments, "If only I'd kept my initial position."

Using a sports analogy, traders with this type of fear are like the coach who has a big lead and then suddenly abandons all the good the team has done and becomes ultraconservative. He sits on the lead.

When this happens, the lead is often whittled away instead of being enhanced. Sometimes the entire lead is lost, and the team loses. Coaches who do this have the fear of success. They also tend not to last long if the strategy becomes a habit.

Traders who have the fear of success also tend not to last long. Eventually, they will find their wins are not good enough to sustain the losses that inevitably arise. To be successful, you need some trading touchdowns. You need to score, not just get close.

The solution is to not fear the success, but anticipate, recognize, and attack the trend. By doing so, a trader is in a position to stay on the trend, instead of fearing the success early and covering too early in the trade. In Chapter 4, I will discuss the dynamics of the fear of success further and show specifically how this hidden fear can be so detrimental to many retail traders. Even at times more detrimental than the fear of failure.

If I were to blame one thing for traders being unsuccessful, it would be fear. Fear is a trader's worst enemy. You need ways to control your fear. Later in the book we will outline the ways traders can learn to control fear from the losing side and the equally painful winning side.

6. BE GREEDY ENOUGH

> *The point is, ladies and gentlemen, that greed, for lack of a better word, is good.*
>
> —Gordon Gekko, *Wall Street*

In the 1987 Oliver Stone film *Wall Street*, Michael Douglas, playing Gordon Gekko, said these oft-quoted words that have since become the reference for excess of greed—especially in the financial markets.

To say that greed is good after what has happened to the financial foundation of the global economy is hard to justify. Greed played a major role in the houses of cards in the financial markets being built and in those houses eventually falling down. Along the way, many benefitted financially. The ones who haven't necessarily suffered have been the ones who were the greediest, the gluttons, the ravenous, and the self-indulgent.

Think of the housing bubble in the United States. Who is to blame? Do you blame the mortgage brokers who wrote the no-money-down loans? They benefitted greatly from the writing of the mortgages, taking fees along the way with no regard for the creditworthiness of the customer. A lot of these people made a large amount of money, perhaps paid off their own mortgages in the process, and set themselves up for life financially. Could they have seen the risk instead of the greed for more and stopped the process? They could have refrained from making the riskier loans or the loans that leveraged the debt higher.

How about Wall Street, which bundled the mortgages up and sold them off to insurance companies, pension funds, and state and local governments? This group collected massive fees bundling and selling the securities with no consequence, and in the process encouraged the mortgage brokers to do more because more meant more fees for them.

Other greedy contributors on Wall Street were the massive internal mortgage-backed securities positions taken on by trading desks within the financial institutions. These positions put the firm and the depositor's money at tremendous risk. There was no trading plan. Most did not really know the extent of the risk. They clearly violated attributes 3 and 4 needed to be a successful trader. Moreover, they proved they did not have the skill or aptitude for doing their job, given the risk they were taking. Of course, during the run-up, the gains beget more and more greed and more and more profit. Massive bonuses were paid for the earnings. During the sell-off, those bonuses may have been reduced, but the damage was done that crippled the very foundation of the global financial industry. The repercussions will indeed be felt for years if not decades to come. Could they have stopped their greed?

The greed from the real estate debacle was devastating. The examples given were what I call "free option greed." The participants had unlimited upside potential with no downside risk. They also paid nothing for the options along the way. Some may argue that they ultimately paid in the form of losing their jobs or losing the value of the stock options they received along with their cash salary and bonuses. That is true. However, the job they lost and the stock options that became worthless were also at the expense of the lost jobs of many more people. There were very few beneficiaries from the greed that took place.

So how then can greed be good in currency trading? Does not Wall Street tell us that "bulls and bears get rich but pigs get slaughtered?" Doesn't this seemingly universally accepted trader axiom speak directly to greed? I think the saying is not so much a truism that all traders should live by, but instead a warning for inexperienced traders who don't define their risk or who take too much risk. It is for those who don't have a serious trading plan. If a trading plan is to take a large, overleveraged position looking for the big payday with no regard for risk, without a firm plan, without a stop loss in place, then this type of greed is not good. It may work in the short run, but in the long run, the odds of failure are great. The pig deserves to get slaughtered.

However, can a currency trader be successful with greed? The answer is successful currency traders are. What I like to remind traders is that pig farmers don't slaughter the pig when it is still running around the pigpen. To do so would not maximize the return on the pig. Instead, what the pig farmer will do is fatten up the pig until that point when the pig is on the verge of being too big to make it to the trough for its food. At that point, the pig has reached its maximum value and it is time for the slaughter.

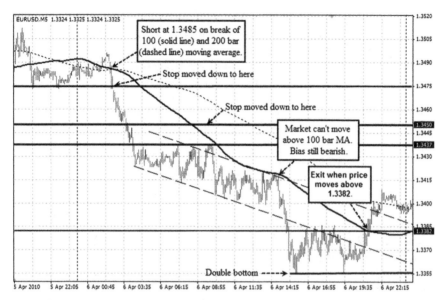

FIGURE 2.2 Greed Can Be Good

In the same way, currency traders need to let their account values get big and fat, and the way they do that is to attack the trends and stay firmly on the trend as long as they can; as long as the account equity cannot get any larger. When is the moment to exit? The moment comes when the market price decides it is going to change the bias from one direction to the other. At that point is when the successful traders "slaughter" their position and take their profit.

To illustrate, Figure 2.2 is the same EURUSD used earlier to demonstrate what goes through the mind of a trader who has the fear of success. In this case, I will explain the thought processes for a smart trend trader who has greed. Like the other trader, this trader gets short at 1.3485 too. He realizes, however, that the market is poised for a trend-type move. I will refrain from telling why at this point in the book, but I will explain why later.

The market does what it is supposed to do and moves lower. The trend trader enjoys the first leg down to the first targets at 1.3450 and 1.3437. The trader, because he is anticipating a trend, does not close his position. Instead he moves his stop down to 1.3475. This is just above the prior lows and just before the first sharp move lower. The market pauses at 1.3450, moves below 1.3437 and consolidates, allowing the moving average line (solid line) to catch up.

As the time goes by, the trend trader—still looking for trend move—can move the stop down to 1.3453, which is above the first support level, or alternatively use a move back above the moving average line to stop the position out. The stop levels do not get triggered as the price continues its moves lower. Instead, the trader is rewarded with another leg to the downside that takes the price down to the 1.3355 low, an impressive 129 pips from the entry level. The trend trader is playing with the house's money now as a gain is virtually locked in, and exits the trade either when the market moves back above the channel trend line or above the 100 bar moving average. He gets out at 1.3382 and books a profit of +103 pips.

The gain is made because he anticipated a trend move, because he managed his position and stops logically. He controlled his fear of success and had just enough greed to fatten his account. When the market could not go any farther and the bias turned bullish by going above the 100 bar moving average, he "slaughtered" the position and booked the profit. Bulls and bears make money, but pigs can and do get fat before getting slaughtered.

Greed can indeed be good as long as the prior five attributes of successful traders are firmly in place. Traders need to develop their skills and aptitude in order to create the desire to do better. They need the desire so they practice and begin to firmly understand markets and have a feel for risk. They need to evaluate and know their risk so they avoid the accidents of trading. They need a plan that will define their risk/reward, and they must accept failure as part of the plan. They need ways to control both the fear of failure and the fear of success, because fear is a trader's worst enemy. Finally, with all that in place, successful traders need the greed to attack the currency trends that allow the account to get big and fat.

A FOUNDATION FOR SUCCESS

Admittedly, I have begun to build the foundation by telling what needs to be done. However, I have not explained how it can be done. We do not have a plan. We do not know how to set our stops so we can control our fear. We do not know the tools we will use in our plan. We do not know specifically the profit targets we are aiming for or how to anticipate a trend. All these have yet to be developed.

Before we can do that, however, we must first continue to strengthen the foundation by introducing the mission statement for our trading and the game plan for attacking the currency trends. Let's move on with our journey and keep our step-by-step progression in motion.

CHAPTER 3

The Mission Statement

Before *Mission Impossible* was a series of movies starring Tom Cruise, it was a television show. The program started with a tape recording that detailed a mission for Mr. Phelps, played by actor Peter Graves. The distinctive recorded voice would say "Your mission, should you decide to accept it . . ." with a brief explanation of the goal of the mission. The final words would warn "this tape will self-destruct in five seconds," at which time the tape recorder would smoke and the tape was destroyed.

Mr. Phelps was always focused on the mission. He knew what he had to do. However, to do it, he needed to develop a game plan. Of course, by the end of the program (consistent with the Hollywood tradition) he was able to perform the impossible by following the game plan.

In life we all have missions that seem impossible, but we are somehow able to solve a lot of them. Many of you may be parents. I know when I think back to the day my first son was born, my wife and I had no clue what to do or how to do it. We felt anxiety not just for the near term, but the long term as well. We were only 25 years old, and it just seemed like a lot for a young couple. It was a mission impossible for us.

Apart from the little hurdles like changing diapers, feeding, getting by on little sleep (now it seems I get even less sleep), my wife Debbie and I knew that our mission as parents was to mold Matt into a responsible adult.

Our game plan was to protect him and keep him safe from harm. We wanted him to understand right from wrong. We wanted to give him the opportunity to succeed as best we could. We did not want to be his best friends, but we wanted to be his best parents, whom he could depend on as a baby, toddler, child, teen, and young adult. That became what I now call the *game plan* that would satisfy our mission—to have Matt become a responsible adult.

How about something less pressure packed then parenting? I have always loved the game of golf. In my youth, when I had more free time, my mission on the golf course was to lower my handicap. If I did not lower it over the course of a season, the season was a failure. My game plan for accomplishing the mission was to hit more fairways with my drives, reduce my putts, and improve my bunker play. I had it all mapped out. Maybe you have something similar in your life.

Over the next two chapters, I will outline a mission statement and game plan for retail currency traders. These two pieces help to lay and strengthen the foundation for success as a currency trader and, like the six attributes of successful traders outlined in the previous chapter, can often determine success or failure.

Whether it is something serious like raising a child or something not so serious like golf, success is built from having and committing to a mission and a game plan. Your mission, should you decide to accept it, will take you closer to profitability in your currency trading.

A TEAM OF ONE

When I have a speaking engagement, I often ask the traders to honestly answer a question. Do they have a mission statement for their trading? What I find is that very few hands go up.

Now I know that the mission statement is part of many a corporate motivational exercise, and it sounds great during an off-site team-building weekend. However, it is often forgotten on Monday morning when the "rah-rah" of the weekend is over.

I have been there and felt rejuvenated by off-sites, but I think it is hard to get everyone to drink the corporate Kool-Aid and make permanent changes for the good of the firm. Management knows it works, but unless the team members rally together, it is difficult to keep the momentum going forward. As a result, success of mission statements may not be as great as most would think. In the corporate world, it takes persistence, a strong leader, and, most importantly perhaps, the team behind the idea.

What I do know, however, is each year there is a champion crowned in baseball, in football, in soccer, in rugby, in basketball, in many sports, and the common thread in most championship teams is the individuals' willingness to put team ahead of self.

True teams become families. Family members will often do anything for other family members. In fact, the 1979 Pittsburgh Pirates used the Sister Sledge disco hit "We Are Family" as their theme song for their baseball championship run. Post-game interviews of champions tend to always reference how "we couldn't have done it without the dedication of everyone on the team." That is often the mission statement for groups of people and especially in sports.

In currency trading there is usually no team. By and large, trading is a lonely business. Most retail traders don't have physical face-to-face human contact with other traders. In recent years there has been more contact through message boards, but most participants are anonymous, just another pictured face behind a pseudonym.

I am not all that surprised by the loneliness of trading. Let's face it, trading can be humbling. Losing is unavoidable, and most people shy away from being put in a situation whereby their faults are so exposed—even if they are overall profitable.

The fact is that successful traders can be wrong more than half the time and still be profitable. That can be tough for some people who grew up getting all A's on their report cards, went to a top university, went to business, medical, or law school, and are now retired and looking to trade currencies. It is tough being wrong 50 percent of the time when in your prior profession you had to be right 99.9 percent of the time or you were out of a job (or sued because of your "incompetence"). I certainly am glad I have a cushion as a foreign currency trading analyst when compared to my CPA wife, who had better get the tax return right, or the IRS will be on her client's tail.

Once, early in my career, I traded with someone as a team member and, quite frankly, it did not work out. We both ended up abandoning the idea. Upon reflection afterwards, we both came to the realization that we compromised to the detriment of our trading beliefs. It wasn't so much on our decisions about getting into a trade but more on how and when to get out of a trade.

For example, when we had a losing trade, we both felt like we had to keep it open longer than normal, for fear of being considered a chicken, or not committed to the trade in each other's eyes. When we had a winning trade, we were often more quick to take profit because of the fear that if the position turned around, we would be questioned by the other as to why profit was not realized. In both our eyes, it was safer to take the small profit even if it was premature and well before its time to do so.

Could we have fixed the team and traded more profitably? In theory, we could have, but we thought we would do better on our own, using our own styles, making our own decisions. We thought being a team put more stress on our trading and created more fear. We both knew that was not what either of us wanted. We realized that trading was not really a team sport for us.

So if currency trading is not all that suited to being a team sport, do we still need a mission statement? Of course we do. In fact, because most retail traders trade as a team of one, it makes the dynamics of following through on the mission statement easier. The only person who needs to buy into the idea—into the mission statement—is you. You and you alone are the family.

A TWO-PART MISSION STATEMENT

When I went about creating my mission statement for trading, I looked at it as not some far-off dream that is something to achieve in the future (i.e., "My mission is to make a million dollars") but instead a path to follow today, a broad guiding light toward success, however that may be defined and accomplished. The mission statement is the rock that all else is built upon.

So when I went about deciding on what my mission statement for trading should be, I wanted to make sure it was something that I could focus on each and every day. Of course I wanted to make it simple and succinct—small enough to fit on a note card. I wanted each word to be important.

Contrary to what some may think, a mission statement alone cannot make a trader more profitable. After all, my mission statement for golf does not automatically lower my handicap. Becoming a profitable trader is accomplished through things like my game plan, the rules I follow, the trading tools I use (and perfect), and the clues I look for in the market that allow me to trade successfully. Knowing that I wanted a guiding light as well as a rock to build my trading foundation on, my mission statement for trading currencies became: "To make the most money with the least amount of risk."

Let's take a look at each of the two parts of the guiding light and rock for trading currencies.

"To Make the Most Money . . ."

If you are reading this book (and you are not my mom or a family member), you either are currently a currency trader, have the desire to be a currency trader, or perhaps just want to increase your knowledge about trading trends. You heard that this book lays the progression down in a logical, easy-to-understand format. Whatever your reason for getting to this point, what all traders are trying to do is take some pool of money or capital and make more money through trading. Clearly, if traders do not have this as their mission, then they are cheating themselves and should not trade at all.

Making money is what it is all about. Traders should think about making money. They should focus on the positive and keep the thought of losses off to the side. Will there be losses? Of course there will, but before we talk about them, let's focus not only on making money, but making the most money.

I could have easily said the first part of the mission statement was "to make money," but instead I added the qualifying word "most." Needless to say, I think the word is very important. Let me explain.

With my experience, I could trade the EURUSD and make a pip or two pretty easily. The bid-to-ask spread is fairly narrow. The price has good high-to-low trading ranges, and the market has enough up and down volatility. In fact, there are plenty of auto trading programs for sale that take advantage of these characteristics and try to entice beginning traders to their high win/loss scalping programs.

Is it the way to make the most money trading? I don't think so. In fact, it can and often does the opposite. In Chapter 1, I outlined the case where including and paying away the bid-to-ask spread of 2 pips, a move of 3 pips is needed to scalp a 1-pip profit in the EURUSD. That same 3-pip move in the opposite direction of the trade creates a 5-pip loss with the normal 2-pip bid-to-ask spread.

Including the spread, being right 84 percent of the time using a scalping strategy of making a 1-pip profit would bring in 84 pips of profit. The 16 losing trades of 5 pips would subtract 80 pips. The 4-pip overall gain for such a success rate is a lot of pressure to be right.

What if you were only right 75 percent of the time? In this case 75 pips of gains (75×1 pip gain = +75 pips) would be made and −125 pips of losses (25×-5 pip loss = −125 pips) would accrue for a net loss of 50 pips. Being right 75 percent of the time is a great success ratio. Losing 50 pips is not a great result for being right so many times.

This way of trading is not the way toward making the most money. Successful traders—the ones who make the most money—have to work harder. How is it done? Our game plan in the next chapter will start to explain the hows and whys of making the most money, and the rest of the book will take us further along the trend-trading journey.

Will We All Make Money?   To make the most money, you need a combination of market and trading knowledge, and quite frankly, a little luck. The luck part of the equation may sound random, but as I will explain later in the chapter, successful traders tend to make their own luck. First, let's look at the market and trading knowledge needed for making the most amount of money.

Market and Trading Knowledge   In this book I have already told you the six attributes of successful traders. Follow them. Failure to follow them will likely lead to trading losses. I have now told you the mission statement for currency traders. Use it as your guiding light and foundation. There are other things I will tell you that will increase your market and trading intelligence and provide a logical progression for increasing success as a currency trader. In other words, for making the most money, I will start broad and will get more specific as the book progresses.

For example, in subsequent chapters I will tell you what the game plan is for the mission statement. You will need to know and follow the game plan. I will tell you the rules for the game plan. You will need to know and follow the rules. I will tell you what technical tools to use and why. You will need to know and use the technical tools and have faith in them. I will tell you the clues the market gives for anticipating trends and why. You will need to know and follow the clues the market gives you. I will tell you to stay on the trend until it tells to you exit the trade—especially if you are anticipating a trend. You will need to be disciplined enough to stay on the trend.

I will tell you all these things in a progressive step-by-step process, but ultimately, you need to do it all. If you do, you'll be a smarter trader who naturally makes the most money, just like the mission statement says.

Retail currency traders need to focus on making the most money they can each and every day given their abilities. The amount they make is largely dependent on market and trading knowledge that they will learn over time. It is unrealistic to think that someone will automatically be a five-star trader from day one, even after reading this book. That is a lot to ask for. Trading is just not that easy.

However, having a mission statement to make the most money does help focus attention on a guiding light, on the rock of foundation for your trading each and every day, and the lessons from this book will be built upon that rock. Traders should think and perhaps even say out loud, "My mission today is to make the most money."

The Right Kind of Luck   There are two types of luck. One type of luck is the bet-red-or-black blind luck. This is the bad luck that ultimately leads to failure. The other type of luck is a risk-defined luck. Successful traders tend to benefit from this type of calculated luck. It is a piece of making the most amount of money.

Traders who trade *without* a reason—who buy because the market price is rising and sell because the market price is falling—tend to rely on blind luck for making the most amount of money. This is the bet black or red on the roulette wheel type of luck, but worse. The reason it is worse is that since these traders do not have a reason to do a trade, they probably don't have a reason or price level to get out of the trade either. Failure to know specific risk means the risk of loss is unlimited. The trader does not know when he is wrong. He does not know when the market bias is no longer bullish and is now bearish.

These types of traders tend to have losses that are larger than those who trade because of a reason. They need to rely on luck being on their side, and a lot of it. I have seen these types of traders come and go rather quickly. If you are this type of trader, my advice is to change. It is unlikely you will have any long-term success.

Other blind-luck-reliant traders are the ones who put on a new position right before the monthly U.S. Unemployment report (or another key economic release or event) because they have a hunch it will be stronger or weaker than expected. The fact is that there are 300 million people in the United States; if Nonfarm Payroll is plus or minus 150,000 people away from consensus, it can cause a violent reaction one way or the other. If a trader guesses right, it is pure, blind L-U-C-K. The trader who does this type of trade does not know why the scheduled report would be off consensus. Professional economists with PhDs at companies such as Goldman Sachs, Morgan Stanley, Citibank, or Deutsche Bank get paid a lot of money to model and estimate how many jobs are created any given month. I would think that they would know more than the average trader who has a hunch.

A retail trader who comes up to me at a trade show and tells me how he put a new position on through Unemployment (or another key release) and made a killing in 30 seconds is telling me that he drank the devil's Kool-Aid. If someone who does this wants to be your buddy, distance yourself from him or her. Down the road, that trader will do the same thing, and when it does not work out as hunched, the loss will be larger, because getting out of a losing position is harder than taking a profit in a fast market. That trader will disappear in time. If you are this type of trader, change. This is not the way to make the most money.

I like to tell traders that successful traders make their own luck, and with that luck they are in a better position to make money. How do successful traders make their own luck? Isn't a lucky trade something that should not have happened, but did? Therefore, how can successful traders predict a lucky turn of events that leads to a successful trade?

It isn't so much that they predict what may happen; it is more that they protect themselves from the trade going against them, and therefore limit the loss. If a lucky event is in their favor, then a successful trader is prepared to profit. Let me explain.

Successful traders will do trades for a reason—for example, the price fell below the 100 hour moving average or it broke a key trend line. By doing a trade for a reason, the trader automatically has a reason to get out of the trade. What is the reason to get out of the trade? It is the opposite of the reason to get into the trade, *plus* a reasonable cushion. This is the stop loss. We will go through pinpointing the specific risks and reasons in Part II of the book.

If some unexpected event occurs (by the way, unemployment is *not* an unexpected event), at least the trader knows his stop, and hopefully that stop is in the market with his broker. The loss can be limited by virtue of the fact he was a smart trader and was prepared for a random event beyond his control. Sure, it is tough luck. It may take a gain and make it a loss. However, it happens to the best of traders. It is not his fault, but his loss is likely limited. He is more likely to survive to trade another day and the mission is still intact.

The random event can also go the trader's way, and the market can be pushed in the direction of the original position. The trader who did the trade for a reason and understood his risk gets lucky, but successful traders tend to make their own luck by quantifying their risk and benefitting from an unknown outcome of an event. Moreover, successful traders—traders who are knowledgeable about the market and trading—are also better suited to manage that lucky gain and are often able to parlay the initial profit into even larger profit in their account.

Remember all the while they understood their risk and had limited risk even before the luck kicked in. Do you see the difference between the two types of traders? One had no reason for the trade and traded with blind luck and unlimited risk. The other had a reason and because of it, understood and knew his risk and benefited from the luck. The traders who make the most amount of money benefit from increased market knowledge and, yes, a little calculated luck as well.

The next section will take a look at the next part of the mission statement—"with the least amount of risk."

". . . with the Least Amount of Risk"

When I think of trader's risk, I can't help but think of a champion boxer. A champion boxer is able to balance the offensive with a firm understanding of the risk from what the opponent can do on any given punch—no matter how overmatched the opponent may be. Even when a champion boxer is ahead in a fight, he is always looking out for the punch that can knock him out. All it takes is one uppercut to the jaw.

He understands his risk and is disciplined enough to maintain his boxing position, keep his arms up, keep moving, keep bobbing and weaving—making sure he is taking the least amount of risk in the process. He knows when to lock up and have the referee pry them apart. He studies his opponent and measures his weaknesses. He starts to think like his opponent. He *anticipates* the opponent's punches and avoids them. Then when the time comes, when the opponent lets his guard down, the champion makes his offensive move, but even then, it is not without protection against a counterpunch at any time, for any reason.

The successful trader needs to think like a boxer. He needs to understand the risk of the market and realize that no matter how sure he is that the market price is going down or up, an unsuspecting reversal can knock him out. A successful retail trader has risk in his mind during the whole trade and uses the least amount of risk at each step to reap the reward of a trading profit, and in the process, avoid being knocked out by that one swift uppercut.

The second part of the mission statement is "with the least amount of risk." Understanding risk and knowing your risk is paramount for success as a trader.

Without some sort of evaluation of risk before every trade, you are doomed to fail. It does not matter what you know, what fundamental news is out, what the circumstances are that make you sure of the direction of the market. Without a specific knowledge of risk, you never know where you are wrong in the trade. Not knowing where you are wrong in your trade leaves the door open for an oversized loss. There is no stop loss except the pain from the equity in the account getting smaller and smaller. In fact, as the loss gets larger, the retail trader often gets more stubborn with the position and may in fact double and triple the size of the losing trade. Excuses such as, "the market is oversold (or overbought) and is due for a correction" permeate the vocabulary. Sound familiar? This strategy ultimately ends in tears. If you have traded long enough, you have most likely experienced this sensation, and it is not a good feeling.

Contrast that with the trader who knows where his risk tolerance ends. If the market does not go in the intended direction, the position is closed with a limited loss. The trader survives to trade another day with a clearer head as well. He does not get knocked out by an unsuspecting market punch.

As with the first part of the mission statement, the second part includes a qualifier that is an extreme condition. The use of the word "least" (in contrast to "most") accentuates the importance of controlling risk. Some traders I speak with are surprised with the use of the word "least." They reason is that they are trading, and trading is supposed to involve risk, so why should they avoid risk and use the least amount of risk? Others will interpret the saying "No risk, no reward" as "The greater the risk, the greater the reward." I like to counter that traders should and need to assume some risk. Clearly, on every trade there is risk. However, the risk needs to be known, and it should be as small as it can be. What is also true is the larger the risk, the greater the chance for a large loss, and it is large losses that successful traders look to avoid.

The "least amount of risk" phrase is also used in context with the first part of the mission statement. That is, the currency traders should strive to make the most money, with the least amount of risk. If there is always risk, the amount used should be the least needed to make the most.

How do I define the risk in a trade? I like to define the risk in the following way: "The risk of any trade is the difference between the current price and that level where the bias switches from bullish to bearish if the trade is a bullish trade or where the bias turns from bearish to bullish if the trade is a bearish trade."

Of course, the big question now becomes, "Where does the trading bias turn from bullish to bearish and bearish to bullish?" Where is the borderline that switches the bias? That is, the level that becomes the risk area, the stop loss level for the trader. As long as that area is known, the trader is protected and risk is limited. To visualize the trading borderlines, let's talk about our real borders, from the eyes of my youth.

FINDING TRADES THAT SATISFY YOUR MISSION STATEMENT

When I was a child, my parents would treat us periodically to a trip to New York City from our home in the New Jersey suburbs to see a Broadway show, to visit a museum, or to go to the circus.

As I was one of seven children, it was no small feat, but we would all pile in the station wagon—two in the way back, four in the middle bench, and one in between my parents in the front seat.

The trek would take us across the Hudson River, and we were in awe at the wonder of crossing under the water through the Lincoln Tunnel. Halfway through the tunnel there was a line in the tiled walled that had New Jersey on one side and New York on the other. We would all look for it and sometimes if we were in traffic (or if there was no traffic), my parents would stop on the line so we could be in both states at the same time. For a child, it was a thrill.

Borderlines are now my new thrill as a trader.

The point on a chart where the bias is bullish on one side and bearish on the other side is what I call the borderlines in trading. These areas are where successful traders focus their attention. They look for that border-line for two important reasons.

First, it becomes a level to initiate trades with a reason. As we have learned, successful traders often have a clear reason to do a trade. The borderline on a chart gives traders a clear reason to do a trade. For example, the simple act of buying because key trend-line resistance is broken is a logical reason to do a trade. Do traders need a logical reason to do a trade? YES! Traders who buy because the market is going up and they have to be on that momentum move do not have a sound reason to do a trade. We called them blind-luck traders. They are just buying on the back of the current momentum move and oftentimes that reactionary trade is at an extreme when the market stalls and corrects. If it doesn't stall, it is just blind luck.

Smart traders in currencies trade for reasons. They don't trade because of short-term momentum. They often look to take advantage of the momentum—don't get me wrong—but they will have a sound reason for the trade. Buying a break of a trend line is one example of a reason to do a trade. It is also a clear borderline trade. When a trend line is broken on the top side, it is a clue the market should go higher. The line from New Jersey (bearish bias) to New York (bullish bias) was broken. A lot of currency traders likely see that same trend line, and it should attract buying interest. It should be a self-fulfilling prophecy.

The second reason for trading at the borderline is that it gives a reason to get out of a trade. If the market breaks a key trend line to the upside, the price should continue to go up. If it does not break (with a reasonable stop), then the trader should get out of the trade. Why? Because the market price failed in the attempt to change from bearish to bullish. It was as if the family car crossed into New York but quickly turned around and went back to New Jersey.

Contrast this type of trader to one who buys because the market is going up. Does that trader have a reason to get out of a trade? No. The reason to get in the trade was that the market was going up. The reason to get out of the trade therefore should be because the market is going down. How far down? I don't know. Neither does this type of trader often. Risk is undefined.

Finding those borderline prices, where the bias is bullish on one side and bearish on the other, makes defining risk easy. The closer you can get to the borderline with your trades, the least risk you will endure. It also opens up the possibility of satisfying our mission statement of making the most money with the least amount of risk.

Where are the borderline trades? A trend line is obviously one. On one side, the bias is bullish. On the other side, the bias is bearish. There are, of course, others that will be explained as I outline the tools for trading. Right now, however, as we develop our foundation for trading success, what we need to focus on is our mission and game plan. From there, we can begin to take the subsequent steps forward with the details that color in our picture for success.

Does "The Greater the Risk, the Greater the Reward" Make Sense?

For anyone who has ever taken an introductory economics class in college, there probably was a point where the professor drew the risk/reward profile. The graph of the risk/reward has reward/return on the x-axis and risk on the y-axis. The profile is an upward-sloping line that says as the risk increases, the potential reward/return also increases. Figure 3.1 shows the standard risk/reward graph.

Most people are familiar with the saying, "the greater the risk, the greater the potential reward." This is often the case when speaking in terms of the risk from investing in bonds or notes versus investing in stocks. A government bond has a yield and will pay that yield to maturity, whereas a stock has a dividend yield but that may or may not stay the same, and the price of stock can fluctuate up and down. Therefore, the risk is higher for stocks, but the potential reward is also higher over the same life of the bond.

How does currency trading fit in this idea? Of course, trading currencies is risky. Currency can fluctuate up and down like the price of a stock,

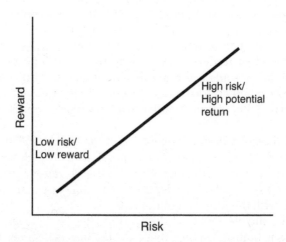

FIGURE 3.1   Risk/Reward Profile

and when compared to the yield on a bond, there is nothing guaranteed with the currency trading return. So from an investment standpoint for a fixed period of time, bonds are safest; stocks and currencies have more risk. Note this is over a fixed period of time. If you get the direction right, however, you could earn a greater return on both stocks and currencies.

What about the risk/reward profile for trading? That is not over a fixed time horizon. In other words, instead of a fixed investment period, what happens if a trader is trading bonds, stocks, or currencies over a shorter time horizon with no set end date? One can argue that risk in stocks, bonds, and currencies is very similar. All are exposed to market risk. Government bond prices fluctuate up and down according to the changes of interest rates. Stocks fluctuate in price due to company-specific risk and market risk, which includes a host of fundamental variables. Currencies like the EURUSD have market risk that is tied to country-specific risk and a host of other fundamentals.

What determine the winners in any trading market are the traders who manage their risk and are able to catch and stay on the trends. If this is done correctly, the successful traders actually have a trading profile whereby the risk taken can be small, while the potential reward is great.

For example, I try to look at and anticipate trends. I also look to trade at the borderlines. In doing this, the risk can be quite small—maybe 10 to 20 pips for the more liquid currency pair—but the potential reward can be a multiple greater than three to four times the risk (and sometimes more). Risk is small. Reward is great.

This idea runs counter to the normal risk/reward profile some retail traders may think are the keys to success. Many retail currency traders think that in order to make a greater reward in trading they need to take on more risk. They need to have a position on during the more volatile/risky economic releases like U.S. Unemployment. They need to use maximum leverage. They need to have stop/losses 100 pips away to let the position develop. All are not true. Successful traders focus on the least amount of risk to make the most amount of money. They look for trends. They look to anticipate trends.

How Much Is Enough Risk?

Traders will often ask me, "How much risk should I take on a trade?" Although there are books written on the subject of money management, and this is not necessarily one of them, there are some general guidelines for the maximum risk a trader should take on a position.

The general rule of thumb per trade is 3 to 5 percent of the account equity. Personally, I cringe at losing 5 percent. I think it is too much to downside to assume. Mathematically, a string of five consecutive losses of

TABLE 3.1 Profit/Loss Profile from Successive 5 Percent Trade Losses

Trade	Starting Account Balance	5% Loss Effect
1	$10,000.00	($500.00)
2	$9,500.00	($475.00)
3	$9,025.00	($451.25)
4	$8,573.75	($428.69)
5	$8,145.06	($407.25)

5 percent would take a $10,000 account down to $8,145 or -18.55 percent $(($10,000 - $8,145.06)/$10,000 = 18.55$ percent). Table 3.1 outlines the progression.

In contrast, a 3 percent loss limit per trade would lead to a loss of $1,147.07 to $8,852.93, or 11.47 percent for the same five consecutive 3 percent losses. This is something I could live with as a trader. This is outlined in Table 3.2.

That is the negative effect of a string of losses. What about a string of gains? After all, we want to be positive with our results. If we were to target a 6 percent gain, twice the 3 percent loss limit, and we had five consecutive gains of 6 percent, the account would compound to $12,155.06, or a gain of 21.55 percent after five consecutive trading gains of 5 percent. Table 3.3 shows that progression.

THE IMPORTANCE OF STAYING ON TREND

Traders should strive to risk less than what they make on trades. Although I am not one to say that you need to make a set ratio when you put a trade on, traders should look to make a multiple of the amount of risk. If you are to trade the trends, that definitely would be the goal for your trading. So believe it.

TABLE 3.2 Profit/Loss Profile from Successive 3 Percent Trade Losses

Trade	Starting Account Balance	3% Loss Effect
1	$10,000.00	($300.00)
2	$9,700.00	($291.00)
3	$9,409.00	($282.27)
4	$9,126.73	($273.80)
5	$8,852.93	($265.59)

TABLE 3.3 Profit/Loss Profile from Successive 6 Percent Trade Gains

Trade	Starting Account Balance	6% Gain Effect
1	$10,000.00	$600.00
2	$10,600.00	$636.00
3	$11,237.50	$674.16
4	$11,910.16	$714.61
5	$12,624.77	$757.49

To demonstrate the power of trends, let's look at three traders who are very similar except for a few subtle differences. They all are patient traders who look to make a profit that is a modest multiple of the losing trades. Each has only a 33 percent win/loss percentage, though. That is, they win one and lose two, in that order. Each trader does only 50 trades a year. I said they were patient.

Let's take a look at each more closely and see how each does with his or her respective trading for the year.

Trader 1 starts with $10,000 and will risk 3 percent, but wants a 7 percent return for a 7:3 risk/reward ratio. With his starting account, he will risk $300 or 30 pips with one lot (to start), to make $700 or 70 pips with the same one lot. If his account is greater or less than $10,000, he will adjust his position size so he only risks 30 pips and 3 percent but requires that 7 percent or 70-pip gain.

For example, assume his account grows to $15,000. His maximum loss on the next trade is 3 percent of $15,000. So 3 percent $\times$ $15,000 = $450 of risk. Since the trader will risk a set 30 pips per trade (he trades near borderlines), he would do $450/$300 = 1.5 lots. A loss of 30 pips $\times$ 1.5 lots $\times$ $10/pip = $450 maximum 3 percent loss. On the win side, 7 percent required gain of $15,000 = $1,050 gain needed. If 70 pips are needed, then 70 pips $\times$ 1.5 lots $\times$ $10 = $1,050 gain.

How would Trader 1 do?

On a $10,000 starting account balance, the profit/loss profile would show a maximum gain of $845 ($10,845 − $10,000) and a minimum gain of $67.63 after 10 trades, a maximum gain of $1,369 and a minimum gain of $483 after 30 trades, and a maximum gain of $1,918 and a minimum gain of $989 after 50 trades. Over the 50 trades there would be just 17 winning trades and 33 losing trades. The maximum percentage gain over the 50 trades would equal 19.18 percent. Although the win/loss percentage is low, staying on the trend even modestly reaps a more than respectable gain for the year (see Table 3.4a).

Trader 2 is another trend trader but occasionally falls off the discipline wagon and lets a loss get away from her. She has the same 7:3 risk/reward

TABLE 3.4a Starting Equity of $10,000, Win/Loss Percentage of 33 Percent, Risk/Reward Ratio of 7:3

After # Trades	Maximum Account Value	Minimum Account Value	Max%/Min% Return
1–10 trades	$10,845	$10,067	8.5/0.7
11–20 trades	$11,141	$10,273	11.4/2.7
21–30 trades	$11,369	$10,483	13.7/4.8
31–40 trades	$11,679	$10,697	16.8/7.0
41–50 trades	$11,918	$10,989	19.2/9.9

ratio and is right once for every two losing trades (a 33.3 percent win/loss percentage). She does have that discipline problem that results in a 10 percent loss on the 12th, 24th, 36th, and 48th trades of the year (once a quarter she has a bad undisciplined trade). What would the 4 misguided trades out of 50 do for this trader's account? Table 3.4b shows us.

After the year of trading, this trader would have a loss of between 5.4 percent and 17.4 percent of her account during the last quarter of the year. It was not a good year. Those 10 percent losing trades really cost her.

Finally, there is Trader 3, who is also disciplined. He does 50 trades a year, and just like the others, for every winning trade, he loses two. This trader picks key borderline trades that require him to risk only 20 pips, or 2 percent of his $10,000 account per trade. However, because he risks less, he looks to make only 60 pips or 6 percent on his wins with a $10,000 account. This is a 3:1 risk/reward ratio.

The other thing he does is to look to trade a longer trend if the opportunity presents itself. During those instances, he will look to make 10 percent four times a year (once a quarter). On a $10,000 account, that is 100 pips.

Like the other traders, he will adjust his position size to account for any increase or decrease in his account value, but he will only risk 20 pips and look to make 60 pips per trade (except those four 10 percent trend

TABLE 3.4b Starting Equity of $10,000, Win/Loss Percentage of 33 Percent, Risk/Reward Ratio of 7:3 with Four 10 Percent Losing Trades

After # Trades	Maximum Account Value	Minimum Account Value	Max%/Min% Return
1–10	$10,918	$10,067	9.2/0.7
11–20	$10,591	$9,531	5.9/−4.7
21–30	$10,407	$9,085	4.1/−9.1
31–40	$9,920.30	$8,660	−0.8/−13.4
41–50	$9,456.94	$8,255	−5.4/−17.4

TABLE 3.4c Starting Equity of $10,000, Win/Loss Percentage of 33 Percent, Risk/Reward Ratio of 6:2 with Four 10 Percent Winning Trend Trades

After # Trades	Maximum Account Value	Minimum Account Value	Max%/Min% Return
1–10	$11,605	$10,180	16.1/1.8
11–20	$12,244	$11,032	22.4/10.3
21–30	$13,406	$11,759	34.1/17.6
31–40	$14,942	$12,875	49.4/28.8
41–50	$16,359	$14,350	63.6/43.5

trades). He succeeds in catching four trends on the 10th, 22nd, 34th, and 46th weeks. His impressive results are shown in Table 3.4c.

What the exercise in the numbers demonstrates is that the mission statement of making the most money is found by looking for, and staying on, trends. Trader 3 who risked only 2 percent of his account per trade (20 pips) was able to stretch out his wins just a touch to have a 3:1 risk/reward ratio. Even though he had to do this, he only had to make 60 pips, which was 10 pips less than the other traders. The other traders were not as good with their borderline levels, so they had to risk more on their entry trades. Trader 3 was able to make 6 percent thirteen times a year and 10 percent four other times. He had 33 losing trades, but each only lost 2 percent per trade (20 pips). He used key borderlines that made him either wrong or right, and he lived with the results.

Trader 1 did fine for himself, too. He made a nice return. He did not stretch his wins any further than he had to, and he had to risk 3 percent (30 pips) on his entry trades, as he was not as good with his borderlines. He felt he could do better with his win/loss percentage and entry levels, but he was happy.

Finally, Trader 2 lost money. She had some good winners, but she blew up four times during the year, and like Trader 1 was not all that happy with her entry trades.

Knowing the numbers behind what trends and entry levels can do for you can be eye opening. They highlight how trading near borderlines and staying on the trends are the key to success.

The next chapter will take our next step forward by looking at the game plan for successfully trading and attacking the currency market.

CHAPTER 4

What's Your Game Plan?

B y now, you have probably deduced that I find parallels between sports and trading. For me, success on the athletic field is a nice comparison to success in trading. In football, if you complete 60 percent of your passes, you are a starting NFL quarterback. In trading, if you are successful 60 percent of the time, you should be a success. In golf, controlling risk, or employing proper "course management," will keep high scores off the scorecard. In trading, controlling and knowing your risk will keep the big losses out of your account. Tennis is a game of risk and reward, baseball has a large degree of failure that has to be managed and controlled, and soccer is also a game that requires working through little failures but takes a big trend-type move to lead to a goal.

I would be willing to wager that if athletes and traders got together in a room and talked generally about the mind-set and hurdles each has to go through to be successful and how they solve the mental challenges, the similarities would be startling.

The last chapter introduced a mission statement for all currency traders: "To make the most money with the least amount of risk." Using another sports metaphor, now the ball has to be moved farther down the field to refine how the mission will be accomplished. It's time to develop a game plan to go with our mission statement.

EVERY MISSION STATEMENT NEEDS A GAME PLAN

A football coach might have as a mission statement, "To win the most games possible, with the fewest injuries." The first part is similar to making the most money as a trader. If a football team does not want to win as many games as possible (i.e., make the most money), it should not play the games. Does it mean the team will win all its games? No. But given what they have, all members should strive to win the highest number.

The second part, "with the fewest injuries," addresses the importance of keeping the best players playing. With fewer injuries, the team stands to win more games.

Contrast this to the "least amount of risk" part of a trader's mission statement. If you take too much risk, you will likely fail. Fear will be increased. So use the least amount of risk.

Our fictitious football team now needs a game plan. That game plan would likely focus on the strengths of the team and getting the most out of the weaker parts. So if the team is strong on defense, the game plan might be to limit yards gained rushing and force a certain number of turnovers. On offense the game plan might be to keep penalties to a minimum, keep turnovers down, establish a running game to keep the clock moving and the team's defense off the field (so it remains strong and rested). Another part of the game plan would address the injury side of the mission statement. So the game plan for that may be to commit the team members to strength and conditioning, limit contact at practice, and look to perfect technique in an attempt to steer clear of avoidable injuries.

The game plan must be focused on the team's mission statement, but it must also speak more specifically to *how* the mission can be accomplished. Now, what should be our game plan for trading? Specifically, how do traders make the most money, and how do they do it with the least amount of risk? The game plan comes in two parts: Trade the trends and keep fear to a minimum.

TRADE THE TRENDS

Focusing on the first part of our mission statement, it is common knowledge that traders should trade with the trends, and that if they do, they will stand to make the most money. As a result, this is the first part of our game plan: Trade the trends.

There are a few reasons why trading the trends offers the best opportunity to make the most money:

- Trends move in one direction with higher highs and higher lows when in an uptrend, and lower lows and lower highs when in a downtrend. If trading with the trend, the account equity should not go negative and should continue to go higher with each successive directional trend leg up or down.
- Trends tend to move faster with corrective waves that are shallow and sometimes quick. This should keep profits accruing at an accelerated rate. The faster a trend moves, the better chance a successful trader has to manage the trend without getting scared and covering. Plus, the trader has more money to play with in the account, which also works to his or her mental advantage.
- Often a trend trading range can be multiple of the range of a nontrend. A larger range increases the potential for a larger profit.

Trends are a powerful profit dynamic for traders and one that should therefore be a focus if the trader is geared toward making the most money. What retail traders do not realize is that for the same reasons that trading with the trend is so profitable, trading against the trend can be devastating to the account equity.

When a trader trades against the trend:

- Instead of account equity not having a chance to go negative, the account equity has no or little chance of going positive.
- Instead of profits accruing quickly, losses accrue quickly.
- Instead of leading to profit, the larger trading range leads to larger losses.

If you want to see equity disappear from your account quickly, then simply trade against the trend.

Why Don't Retail Traders Trade the Trend?

Do retail traders trade trends well? The answer is *no*. Over the last 10 years in the currency business, I have found that most retail traders do poorly trading the trends. What I see is also supported by generally accepted estimates for active traders. Although there is no proven statistic as to the percentage of active traders who will ultimately lose money trading, the estimates do range in the vicinity of greater than 70 percent.

The reasons are varied, but one can safely assume that it is trading against the trend that tips the scales against most retail traders. Losses simply accrue too quickly when traders go against the trend. They tend to wipe out any chance for success while they wipe out account balances and confidence in the process. Moreover, if retail traders were good at trading with the trend, profits from that should lead to oversized account balances. That is, there would be more profitable traders. The fact is, there are not.

So who makes all the money trading with the trends? It seems the institutional traders make the most money, or that is what their earnings show. Why do they make the most money? Because they tend to trade and stay on the trends. They may have an informational advantage at some point—there is no denying that—but the information is reflected in the price in the chart, and institutional traders see the same charts retail traders see. If the information says be long, the price is going to go higher. Everyone sees the price. So how can a retail trader do as well as an institutional trader? Trade like an institutional trader. In other words, trade the trend and stay on it as long as possible.

To solve a problem, it is often beneficial to understand why the problem exists. Although there are a number of reasons why retail traders don't trade trends well, the following are some of the main reasons.

They Don't Think It's Worth It   One reason retail traders can't seem to trade the trends is that they simply don't pay enough attention to trends or the potential for a trend. If you were to look at a daily chart of a currency pair, most of the activity is either nontrending or correcting a trend move. Therefore, traders tend to think the trends are not so important.

Although trends occur less than nontrends and corrections on a daily basis, with the currency markets trading 24 hours a day, there usually are periods where the market trends intraday. When looking at 5-minute, 15-minute, or even hourly charts, there are many more trend trading opportunities. These are trends that traders can either profit from or get hurt trading. Traders have to be aware of intraday trends. They can be a great benefit to your trading account's profitability.

What is also important to realize as a trader is that longer-term trends—the kind that happen less often—start from shorter-term trends. You can bet that if there is a longer-term trend, there are a bunch of shorter-term trends in the same direction that, combined, made up that sustained directional move. So, although we don't know what the future may bring, the trends from the shorter periods start the progression that leads to a longer-term trend. As the book progresses, we will look at the progression of a longer-term trend that has its roots firmly established in the shorter-term market.

Traders Don't Anticipate Trends   Another reason for the failure to trade the trends successfully is that most traders do not consciously think about anticipating a trend.

Think about your favorite major league baseball player. He hits a home run to win the game. He is being interviewed by the television announcer, and more times than not, the player will say something like "The pitcher fell behind two balls and no strikes. So I was looking for a fastball for a strike and I got it." The batter anticipated the pitch and he hit it out. Home run. Game over.

Think about Apple and the iPad (or any of Apple's other products). One of the selling points in its television ad says simply, "You already know how to use it." That is what Apple does well. It minimizes the learning curve. It anticipates what the consumer will do with the iPad from a usability standpoint and as a daily informational tool, and this is one of its main attractions. I am willing to bet that on one of Apple's designer's white boards for the iPad, someone wrote the word "ANTICIPATE."

Traders need to anticipate the trends, too. If you can anticipate a trend, you are more ready to trade a trend. Not only that—if you anticipate a trend and it starts to trend, you are now more willing and able to *stay* on the trend. If I told you the market had a good chance of trending and you believed me, would you be more willing to ignore the little corrections? I would. The good news is, you don't have to believe me. What you have to believe is what the market is telling you through the price and tools applied to the price. If you believe those tools, and you are anticipating a trend, you will be more likely to stay firmly on the trend until the market tells you to get out. This is what the institutional guys are doing.

How can you anticipate when a trend is going to happen? Much the same way that a baseball player anticipates a fastball or Apple anticipates how a user would use an iPad. The baseball player knew the pitcher needed to throw a strike and that came via a fastball. For Apple, applying human logic to technology and understanding what the consumer wants and needs via the apps allowed designers to anticipate what users would do with the product in their hands.

In trading, the clues the market gives from technical trading tools allow successful traders to anticipate a trend-type move. Does anticipating a trend always lead to a trend move? Not always. Just like a pitcher may not always groove a fastball down the middle of the plate, the currency markets may not always be ready to trend when you think they might. Nevertheless, the best traders always look to anticipate the trend moves.

Later in the book I will outline the ways that traders can better anticipate trends by using key technical tools. This will allow the traders to take advantage of the predictability of the market. Pretty soon you will be taking the grooved fastball out of the park, too.

Traders Are Too Complicated Pete Tomasino, a colleague of mine at FXDD, is a character. He has much more personality than most. He also is not shy when it comes to expressing an opinion. It certainly helps add to his personality. I always surmised that although Pete may not have been on his high school debate team, he most likely would have beaten the pants off of them if he wasn't too busy excelling on the athletic fields. The reason is that Pete has a bunch of plain old common sense.

One of the more logical proclamations that Pete abides by is "Life is simple. People choose to make it complicated." Retail traders may or may not make their lives complicated, but they most certainly make trading, and trading the trends, complicated. This helps explain why they are not successful trading trends.

Most retail traders' charts will have a Relative Strength Index (RSI), Stochastic, Commodity Channel Index (CCI), or Moving Average Convergence-Divergence (MACD) on them. They will have three to four different moving averages and a Bollinger Band. They might analyze candlestick patterns and include an Ichimoku cloud. They will have trend lines coming up and down from all sorts of obscure angles. They will follow oil, the S&P, and gold for the intermarket relationships. They might have Bloomberg and CNBC on two separate television monitors. They might subscribe to some premium news services and have 10 different books on trading on their desks. I realize my book is adding to that pile, but I hope it simplifies your trading thoughts and becomes the bible for your trading.

These traders will often be one of two types. The first type will rarely have a position because they have successfully confused themselves with all the input running through their brains. When they do get the courage to trade, something on their charts that will tell them to go the other way and the position will be squared up.

The second type will go to the other extreme. They will have positions in the EURUSD, GBPUSD, USDCHF, AUDUSD, GBPJPY, and AUDCAD or some similar combination at the same time. They too will go back and forth as the different tools kick in from bullish to bearish and bearish to bullish and back again.

Most likely both stay up well past their bedtime. The trader from the first group will stay up without executing a trade, lamenting how his eight-point signal was not triggered. The trader from the second group will eventually tire as the lethal cocktail of caffeine, adrenaline, and trading losses leads to a trading coma. Neither will be focused on trading trends.

Baseball players have a choice between a fastball, curve, or changeup. Golfers agonize over a 9-iron or pitching wedge to the green. Ice skaters choose to do either the triple toe loop or the quad toe loop during their long routines.

Traders feel a need to clog their heads with all sorts of technical indicators, with the thought that more equals better. What they fail to realize is that the more tools they use, the greater the chance a trend will never be found or traded. In the revised words of Pete Tomasino, "Trading is simple. People choose to make it complicated."

KEEP FEAR TO A MINIMUM

The second part of our traders' game plan is to "keep fear to a minimum." Fear is an emotion that I never, ever liked. In fact, I don't know anyone who thrives on fear. Fear causes you to do things you normally would not do. Yet controlling fear is also very difficult thing to do. It almost is impossible to control some forms of fear.

When I was a young boy, I will always remember how two friends set me up by having me go get a board game in my friend's dark basement. Little did I know that one of my friends, who I thought was going to get a drink, actually snuck down to the basement and hid in the dark. When I went down and tried to turn on the light, the light failed to go on. I entered the room anyway, and from a dark corner in the room a flashlight went on, focused on a masked monster face. Immediately, my heart raced, I bolted out of the room, and I screamed my way up the stairs. Needless to say, my friends thought it was hilarious. For me, however, the fear was real. It was lingering. I could not get the sight of that mask out of my mind's eye. I had trouble sleeping. I kept lights on. I opened closet doors when I entered rooms. I certainly did not like going in any basement. Fear overcame me. It became my enemy. I could not do anything about my fear for a good long while.

A Different Type of Fear

Traders have a different type of fear. It is not the horror fear that I experienced as a child, but it is fear nevertheless. Most people know about the fear of failure. That rears its head when a trader fears losing money. If you put a position on and immediately feel that you would rather have the complete opposite position, that is an example of the fear of failure.

Traders also have what I call the fear of success. This is a fear most traders don't know about, but which I think contributes to retail traders' inability to trade trends. I introduced this fear in Chapter 2.

Before discussing and explaining in greater detail the two types of fear, it is important to realize that for a trader, fear is directly proportional to risk—the second part of our mission statement. That is, if a trader's fear is increased, trader's risk is likely to be increased as well, and vice versa. So to control risk—that is, to keep the least amount of risk—traders should search for ways to control their fear. If they can control fear, it is likely that they will be using the least amount of risk—the second part of our mission statement.

What is also important to realize is the seesaw balance of our game plan, which is "Trading the trends and keeping fear to a minimum." Most traders know that the "trend is your friend." What most traders don't realize is that fear is a trader's worst enemy. Fear makes you do the wrong things. It will make you scream and yell (inside, of course); it will increase your heart rate; it will make you avoid trading; it will muddy your mind. If a trader can stay with the angelic trend and steer clear of devilish fear, there will be a greater chance for success.

As already mentioned, there are two types of fear that retail traders face. One is obvious. The other is not so obvious. The next sections will go through each in more detail. It is important to know your fears and find ways to overcome them.

Fear of Failure   The most common fear that traders have is the fear of failure. As mentioned, this fear is specifically tied to the notion that the trade initiated will lose money. I think some fear is better than no fear. The trader with no fear is one who takes the stance that he is right, the market is wrong, and no matter what, the position will remain—even when it is clearly wrong. That is one extreme that I do not recommend, as there usually is no limit to the loss side of the trading equation.

The other extreme is the trader who does a trade and almost immediately wishes to have the opposite position. Invariably, this trader will switch the position, close the position quickly, tell himself the position is right as a way to quell the fear (even though the fear is still there and high), and keep a losing trade longer than he should. What he will *not* likely do is keep the position on for an extended trend-type move. He is too scared. Missing trends is not what traders should aspire to do.

Traders who fear failure have fear similar to the fear of monsters I experienced as a child when my friends scared me in the basement. To overcome my fear, I had to condition myself to listen to what my parents were telling me: "There are no monsters in the basement." I had to change my negative thought (monsters were everywhere) to a positive thought (they are not everywhere). I took it slowly from there until I could say there were no monsters anywhere.

If you have the fear of failure in your trading, you need to do the same thing. You need to *understand* that you have this fear (i.e., listen to your emotions. Perhaps listen to me.). You need to *condition* your mind that you have this fear and a solution is needed. You need to solve the problem by conditioning your mind to think more positively about your trading and find ways to control your fear, and in the process, rid your mind of the negative thoughts/fear.

When this is all done, the fear will be dispersed. It may not be all gone, but it will be lessened, and as a result, you will be back in control of your trading position—instead of leaving fear in control. Needless to say, I will look to show you how to do this—but as the book continues; it's a step-by-step process.

Fear of Success   In Chapter 2 I introduced the fear of success. This is a fear that a vast majority of traders are probably not aware of. It is the silent fear and causes more retail traders to actually trade against the trend rather than with it.

The fear of success is the condition whereby a trader fears the success he has on his trade will be taken away. As a result, the trader will take his profit well before it's time—often for no apparent reason.

In this situation, there should be little fear of failure. After all, there is a profit on the trade. However, if the mission is to make the most money, and the game plan is to trade the trends, then getting out of a trend move early is not a good thing. In the words of the old proverb, a successful trader should "make hay while the sun is shining." Traders who get out of a potential trend trade are not harvesting the hay.

Fear in Action

I know what most are thinking. The old Wall Street truism that "No one went broke taking a profit" makes my fear of success theory fail to stand up. Admittedly, you are right if the trade is taken as a single event. If a profit on a single trade is booked, it is a net addition to the account value. However I like to add an addendum to that old Wall Street saying, and it goes like this: "No one went broke taking a profit, but you can go broke after the next three trades."

How can that be? Let me explain. Trading successfully is a lot about staying in synch with the market. It is about staying in rhythm. Staying on the beat and pulse of the market. A lot of traders have the sell high, buy low idea down pat—especially when a market trades in a nontrending, defined range for an extended period. During these markets, traders get used to selling the high. They get used to buying the low. They are in synch with the market. In their minds, the ranges are well defined and predictable. As a result, when the price is at an extreme, they tend to take profit as they fear that the success—the profit they have in the trade—will be taken from them.

What we know is that at some point, the market will transition from a nontrending, range-defined market to a trending market. A trending market is where the most money is made. However, it is during this transition from nontrending to trending that the unsuccessful traders fall out of rhythm with the market. They fail to adjust from the nontrending market to the trending market that may be breaking to the upside or downside.

For example, assume a market is in a defined nontrending range and the most recent move is to the downside. The trader has sold at a higher level and is profiting from the move from the high. When the price reaches the low end of the range, the trader does what is now familiar—buy at the low and book the profit. He reasons that no one goes broke taking a profit. Besides, the trader fears that the price will rebound higher and his profit will be taken away. This time, however, the price does not rebound but continues to fall. The market transitions into a downward trend.

The price falls to the next support level. With the price now cheaper, the trader's instincts say buy. After all, he is supposed to buy low and sell high and that is what he will be doing. He buys even though it is now against the downward trend. The price rebounds a little—but not to the last floor level—and then the trend continues down. At the next support level, the trader does not prepare to exit with a loss, but buys again, doubling his position. Why? Because the price is lower. He is buying a dip. He envisions the rebound back to the old floor. He ignores the clues of the bearish trend that the market is clearly giving.

The market rebounds a little, but reverses back down again. Finally, it reaches a new low, and the market is oversold on the RSI. The trader is blind to the obvious downward trend. If he were a dancer, he would be so out of rhythm he would be stepping all over his partner's feet. Nevertheless, the trader is sure the market will snap back, so he buys one last time. The market rebounds a little and then heads down yet again.

The next trade is the liquidation trade. The large loss is booked and the trader is wondering how he failed to see and trade the trend.

The fact is the trader was short and on the trend—but he had the fear of success. He worried that the market would continue nontrending in the range and his profit would be taken from him. As a result, he closed out the profitable short position well before its time. From there, the brain was doing what it does: Think logically given the last event. If the last event was a success, it often gives an even more positive signal. Success is good. Pavlov's dog salivates, and the trader buys again, at a cheaper price. The brain ignores the bearish trend clues because it has not been programmed to look for them.

Ironically, after a fear of success event like the one described, I find the fear of failure dissipates in unsuccessful traders. The trader becomes more cavalier and suddenly forgets about fear. Without fear, risk is forgotten and the mission statement of "Making the most money with the least amount of risk" is ignored.

If you are trading now, I challenge you to go back and find the trade where you lost the most money. Look at the trade(s) just prior. Look at the chart from that period. See if you did something similar—that is, took a quick profit. Did the next trade in the same direction of the profitable trade. Doubled up. Tripled up. Liquidated. All against the trend. Although you did not realize it, the fear of success was your enemy at the very beginning.

No one went broke taking a profit, but you can go broke after the next three trades. Don't be one of those traders. Don't always fear the success you may have. Instead, when the time is right, look to anticipate a trend, and above all, don't ignore the market's directional clues.

Overcoming Your Fears

Understanding the potential problem is one thing. Solving the problem is another. So how do you do it? How is fear dispersed? Let's tackle the fear of failure first.

In order to conquer fear of failure, you need to be able to tackle the cause of your fear—the monster. One monster is the fear of losing money trading. Losing money in trading is the equivalent of failing. The score in trading is cut and dried—you either make money or lose money. So how do you make money? By trading and staying on the trends. Can you stay on the trend with the fear of failure? Not likely. Something will spook you.

From this vicious circle we are actually getting closer to a solution. What I know is if a trader can stay on a trend, he will make the most money. Also, fear can *potentially* be reduced. Why? If the trading is making money, it is easier to convince him to try and not fear the success.

Alternatively, I can also say that if we keep fear to a minimum, we are likely to be able to trade and remain on the trend. So fear and trading trends go hand in hand. That is why it is our game plan.

So how is it done? In the last chapter we discussed the borderline levels as a way to take the least amount of risk. Borderlines, once again, are those areas, or price levels, where the market is bullish on one side and bearish on the other. By knowing this and being confident about these levels, a trader can initiate trades at or around these levels, and in the process clearly define risk.

For example, if a downward-sloping trend line is being approached from below on a corrective rally, a trader can sell against the line in anticipation of the trend line holding and the market price moving back down.

What is the risk to the trader? The risk is simply that of the price moving above the trend line. If the price moves above the trend line, the bias turns from bearish to bullish. If this happens, the market did not do what the trader thought it was supposed to do. In other words, the market's bullish conviction is stronger than the trader thought it would be. I have never seen an individual trader tell the market what to do and have the market listen. As a result, when the price moves above the trend line and the bias turns from bearish to bullish, the trader should *get out* or close out the trade.

Of course, because the trader initially has a borderline reason to do the trade, and because the trader defines his risk, the trader is more confident. What does more confidence do? It lessens the fear. Does trading against borderlines get rid of all the fear of failure? Not all. There is still the fear that the stop will be triggered. However, traders who define their risk have done Step One in controlling fear. They know what the maximum loss will be. Step Two is deciding if the risk of the trade is acceptable. In other words, can you accept the loss? If the answer is "yes," fear should automatically be lessened. Is it likely to be all gone? No. There will always be some fear, but it should be at a minimum and that is the game plan—the least amount of risk.

What happens if the trade does what it is supposed to do? What happens to fear? Your fear on profitable trades should become less and less and less. Why? The worst you are most likely to do is lose profit. You should not lose money in your account. That's good! That's great! As a result, take your level of fear down. Don't fear your success. Think that the worst you can now do is break even. That is a comfort. Disperse your fear.

So what about the fear of success? Earlier in the chapter we talked about taking profit before its time. I have to be honest with you. Sometimes it is good to take profit. If you are not anticipating a trend move, then it might make perfect sense. However, what a trader needs to realize is that he or she should have a really good reason to take profit.

For example, in Figure 4.1, if you sell the GBPUSD on a break of the trend line, the market price should continue lower. If the price now

FIGURE 4.1 GBPUSD Price Moves Below Trend Line but Finds Support against 200 Day MA

approaches the key 200 day moving average (dashed line), it is likely that the market is going to pause at the key moving average.

I could not fault a trader from taking partial profit or even all profit against the key support level. However, if the price moves through the key level, the trader should realize that the short should be reestablished. Why? The reason is that the 200 day moving average is another borderline. Being below the moving average increases the bearishness. The price is below both the trend line and the moving average. Make sense?

Now, is selling on the break of the moving average easy to do? Is it easy to reestablish a short after taking a profit by buying? The answer is *no*. It is hard to do that trade especially after buying and taking profit against a key support level. Human nature says you should be buying the lower level—buying the dip.

However, what is important to realize is if you cannot reestablish the short, in this example, by reselling on the break of the 200 day moving average, don't do the opposite trade—that is, buy the new low because it is cheap. This is a mistake made by most retail traders and is the continuation of the fear of success progression, buying because that is what was done last. Instead, wait until you are more comfortable with your fears and you can get in rhythm with the market bias and the trend.

NEVER UNDERESTIMATE A STRONG FOUNDATION

The one thing I have not explained is how to anticipate a trend. What I *have* done is continue to build the foundation for trading success. A strong foundation of knowledge allows traders to better anticipate the trends, stay on the trends, and manage the profits of a trend trade.

When we get to the point of the book where I outline how trends can be anticipated, there will be charts. There will be technical tools we will introduce to help attack the trends. I will show the specific clues the market gives traders as well.

Quite frankly, I purposely kept charts and technical tools out of these earlier chapters because a mission statement and game plan are not meant to be the playbook. (Plays—I mean charts—come later on.) They are meant to broadly define the objectives for becoming a successful trader. I want you to be aware of what you are trying to accomplish and why, from a broad perspective. From a foundation that includes a mission statement and game plan, you can outline the details of how specifically it can be done.

Surprisingly, most retail currency traders have no concept of a mission statement or game plan to steer them toward success. In my mind, it is the development of this foundation that will give you a chance to succeed. Ignoring it is at your own peril. Think about your mission. Think about your game plan. They will serve you well.

In the lingo of *Mission Impossible*, your mission, should you decide to accept it, is to believe in the mission statement and follow the game plan. If we have a game plan, we need some rules for the game. The next chapter will outline the rules for our trading as we progress toward attacking the currency trends.

CHAPTER 5

Rules for Attacking the Trend

You have to learn the rules of the game. And then you have to play better than anyone else.

—Albert Einstein

Having a game plan implies that a game or sport is being played. Well, trading is not a sport per se, but it does have characteristics of one. Sports have winners and losers. Trading has winners and losers. Sports have a game plan. Trading has a game plan. The participants in sports have differing abilities. Traders have differing abilities. In the same way that athletes can improve their skill through things like practice, traders can improve their trading results through practice. And just like in sports, there are rules that need to be followed in trading.

I have five rules that traders should follow. They are common sense rules, but then again, rules are meant to instill some common sense to games they govern. The difference with the rules in trading currencies and rules in a game is most rules in a game are meant to prevent an unfair advantage to the rule-breaking player or team. In trading, the rules are meant to protect the trader from an unfair disadvantage. Traders who break rules only hurt themselves.

Together with the game plan and mission statements presented earlier, these five rules will increase the retail currency trader's success at attacking the trends.

RULE 1: KEEP IT SIMPLE (BUT STAY POSITIVE)

Most people know, or think they know, the K.I.S.S. principle. In fact, I will often poll the audiences at seminars and ask who knows the K.I.S.S. principle and invariably nearly all the hands go up. When I then pick a random audience participant to share what it is, he will confidently say "Keep It Simple, Stupid."

Well, in this case, nothing is that simple. The correct answer in my eyes was actually given to me by a friend named Joseph I met at a trade show a few years ago. He and I were talking and he asked me the K.I.S.S. principle question, and I gave the customary "Keep It Simple, Stupid" response.

Joseph looked at me, and with a grin, replied "No. It stands for 'Keep It Simple to be Successful.' " I was taken aback by the logical simplicity of changing "Stupid" to "Successful." Joseph knew that the slight alteration to the translation was right up my alley. He understood that I liked to keep things simple, and he also knew that I look to keep things positive with my trading approach. The one-word alteration really changes the meaning of the K.I.S.S. principle, and I will never think of it any other way. So what does it mean to "Keep It Simple to be Successful" for a retail currency trader? Let's take a look.

Start by Keeping It Simple

In the last chapter, I spoke of how retail traders like to make things more complicated than they should. Retail traders tend to use a number of technical tools. They will incorporate oscillators on top of moving averages, use candlesticks and trend lines, and look for pattern recognition. They will listen to as many people as possible and take their word as gospel. Some will create their own proprietary indicator. How do I know? I know it because I have been there and done all that, and in the process complicated my life as a trader. Although I thought I was doing the right thing, I was actually making trading more difficult and I could see it in my profit and loss. If your charts look like Figure 5.1, you are probably overcomplicating your trading.

It is my feeling that traders who make trading more complicated increase uncertainty, and with increased uncertainty comes more fear. We know that fear is a trader's worst enemy. Fear makes traders do things they normally would not do. Traders who cannot control fear cannot trade trends or stay on trends, and trends are where traders make the most money. Traders need to focus on steering clear of fear. If a trader wants to keep fear to a minimum, he or she should keep trading simple. Don't

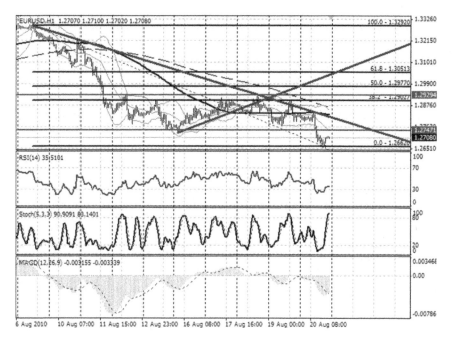

FIGURE 5.1 Are You Overcomplicating Your Trading?

make trading complicated. Don't look to add uncertainty or do things that elevate fear. It is that simple.

There is another reason why retail traders should keep it simple. That is, I have found that the currency market likes to keep things simple as well. So, how do I know the market is simple? To address that, I first need to define the market.

Who Makes Up the Currency Market?   The currency market is the collection of traders from around the world who determine the current price for a currency pair. The price is made up of the collective buy-and-sell influences at a point in time. The buy-and-sell flows in the market may include demand from an exporter who wants to remit earnings from overseas back to his home country. It may include demand as a result of an international merger. It may include an overabundance of buyers of one currency versus another after a stronger than expected economic statistic that may make a central bank raise rates sooner rather than later. It may include the demand from a hedge fund or perhaps even a central bank. These and many other influences go into determining the price of a currency pair.

If there are more buyers than sellers for a currency pair, the price will go higher. If there are more sellers than buyers, the price will go lower. Again, it is that simple.

Will a retail trader know all the influences that cause a price to go up or down? No, never. They might know the main influence, which could be the effects of interest rate policy, economic statistics, or something even more fundamental like the sovereign debt crisis that sent the EURUSD down in 2010. However, as time goes by, all those influences will be priced into the market.

Now, will institutional traders (i.e., traders other than retail) know all the influences that cause a price to go up or down? No, never. They do not know it all either.

What they may have at times is an advantage because of their size. As a result, they do have the ability to move the market price in one direction or the other. The fact is they have more zeroes in their account value than retail traders, and therefore have more influence when they do enter the market. They will tend to be the ones who give the market the push needed to move it out of a nontrend into a trend and also can keep it on the trend at key levels—like when a correction runs into trend line resistance. They can help influence the market to remain below that key trend line level.

However, the institutional traders can also fight each other at times. That is, one institutional trader can take on another with one buying and one selling, and keep the market at bay—in a nontrending range. So any single institutional trader cannot influence the market for long. There has to be a consensus of traders to move the market in a trend. That consensus can and often does include the smart retail trader.

The net effect is that there are a vast number of traders, retail and institutional, from around the globe who collectively make up what I call the market. They collectively have an auction each minute of every day, where a price is determined. That price is at one level one second and can move to another level in the next second. If there are more buyers than sellers, the price in the auction goes up. If there are more sellers than buyers, the price in the auction goes down. Because the larger institutional traders have more power, they do have more influence on direction, but it typically takes a consensus of money into the market to make the market trend.

The good news for retail traders is the price they see is the same for them as it is for the institutional traders. There is what is called *transparency*. Retail traders see the same price; that is, their charts are the same as those of the largest, most influential traders in the world. That is a comfort to me and should be a comfort to you.

The other thing that is important to realize is all institutional traders need to make money trading. They are driven to excel and are paid well to succeed. They too need to make the most money with the least amount of risk. In order to succeed, they too need to trade the trends and keep fear to a minimum. If they trade against the trend, will they make money? No. They will lose money just as fast as the retail trader. If they take on too much risk, will they have fear? Yes. Like retail traders, institutional traders put their pants on one leg at a time. Once again, they are more like retail traders than most think.

Can you as a retail trader benefit from what institutional traders do? Absolutely. Remember, most money is made trading the trends. Institutional traders have the influence to start the trend and keep the trends moving. That is what you, as a retail trader, need to have happen in order to make the most money with the least amount of risk. As a result, institutional traders are more your friend than your enemy. They give you the chance to succeed as a trader by trading with the trends and pushing the trend up or down. All you have to do is follow what they do and trade with the trend. That is how they make money and that is how you will make money.

In my mind, the retail trader is playing on a more level field with the institutional traders than one may think. If you come to that realization and start to think like them, you will begin to trade trends more effectively. You will also stop thinking of them as your enemies and instead think of them as your allies.

What Does the Market See?   If the field is more level, the retail currency trader needs ways to uncover the bias from the price that the market is creating at any one time. That is, the trader needs to uncover if the market has a bullish bias or a bearish bias. This objective should be the same for all currency traders. In general, if the bias is bullish, the trader should be long. If bearish, he or she should be short. It is that simple.

To do this, if a trader watches the market price and uses technical tools that the market uses to determine a trend direction, then the trader will have the market's bullish or bearish bias. From there it is all up to the trader to be long if bullish or short if bearish.

Is it worthwhile to try and predict the market bias by creating a proprietary technical tool or oscillator that works faster, that is, predicts the bullish or bearish bias early? Many traders, including myself, have tried to be smarter than the market, to preempt a market bias by trying to be creative—to be trailblazers.

Early in my career, I had a self-developed tool that looked at a number of different technical indicators. If I got a score that was bullish, I would execute a buy. If the score from the technical indicators was bearish, I would execute a sell.

The tool worked sometimes. It didn't work other times. So I refined the tool and found the same thing occurred—sometimes it worked, sometimes it did not. It was the equivalent of halving a number and continuing the process until you get to zero. You never get to zero. I was constantly trying to find that perfect indicator.

I soon realized that I was trying to tell the market when it was time to go up or down. I learned that the market does not care what I think. I cannot tell the market what to do. In fact, the market did not follow my trading system. The market had no idea what my tool was saying. Individually, I am insignificant, as are the vast majority of currency traders who make up the market. I like to say, "As individuals, we all don't matter."

As a result, I realized I had to think like the market. I also found to be true that the market is simple. It looks for clues that others can see easily.

For example, if a trend line is broken, the market can see that the trend line is broken, and I can too. This visual is available to everyone and is contrary to my misguided attempts to find the perfect proprietary indicator that no one but myself could see. Instead I learned to buy when the market is buying and sell when the market is selling. I learned to follow the trends.

All the influences in the market are reflected in the price. With that price, it becomes as simple as listening to what the price is telling you as a trader. If you use the right tools—the tools that the majority of the market use—they will tell you what the bias is and which way the market price should move. Moreover, they will also give you clues for anticipating trends.

The first rule to follow is to keep it simple. Making trading complicated is not the path to success. Trying to not think like the market is not the path to success. Instead, understand that the market is simpler than you think, and the trick is to follow it, not try to lead it.

Success Is Important

Traders not only should strive to keep it simple, but they should also strive to be positive in their trading. So although the main focus of Rule 1 is to keep it simple, traders should not lose sight of the importance of the SUCCESS we all strive for in our trading. Being positive is important because it helps to keep fear down. So focus on success. Don't focus on failing or being stupid or other negative thoughts when trading.

If you keep positive, you will be more successful not only in trading but in everything you do. Like Joseph told me, think "success," not "stupid."

RULE 2: HAVE A REASON TO PLACE A TRADE

In Chapter 3, I touched on this rule as it relates to the game plan. Having a reason to trade instills confidence in a trader and makes it possible to quantify risk.

The reason to place a trade often acts as a reason to get out of a trade as well. For example, traders will buy because the price moved above a trend line. However, if the price goes above the line by 20 pips and then reverses back below the trend line, the reason to trade is no longer valid.

By having the reason to trade, the specific risk for the trade is known. As long as the trader is comfortable with that maximum loss, a trade should be executed with little fear. With limited risk and little fear, the trader is more likely to stay confident about the trade and keep the door open for a potential trend-type profit that can be a multiple of the initial risk.

A simple example outlines the importance of having a reason to trade. The simple moving average (throughout this book I will use the abbreviation MA to designate the simple moving average) takes the closing level of a time period (say five minutes or one hour or one day) and accumulates a series of the closes—say for 100 periods—then finds an average closing level over those 100 periods. This has the effect of smoothing out the price fluctuations. I find that the market tends to watch the 100 bar MA. The price either finds support or resistance against this MA level. Alternatively, it can move through the level and in doing so, switch the trading bias from bullish to bearish or bearish to bullish.

For example, if the price of a currency pair moves below the 100 bar MA, it should lead to further selling pressure as the bias switches from bullish to bearish. A price move below the moving average becomes the reason to execute a trade.

In Figure 5.2 the price of the EURUSD falls and closes below the 100 bar MA at the 1.2298 area. This is the first sell option for a risk-conscious trader who looks for a reason to trade. What is the risk? The risk is of the price moving back above the moving average plus a volatility cushion.

After falling to a low price near 1.2250, the market price rebounds to the 1.2292 area. This gives a second selling level for the opportunistic bearish trader. Why? The price remains below the 100 bar MA. As long as the price is below the moving average line, the bias is negative or bearish.

What is the risk? The risk to the trader is if the price moves above the moving average line plus a small cushion. If this happened, it would shift the bias back to bullish. In the example, a stop loss level of say 1.2308 could be set for each of the trade options. If set at that level, the total risk is 16 pips (from 1.2292 to 1.2308).

FIGURE 5.2   Finding Reasons to Trade

By defining risk and knowing the risk, the trader has a reason to trade. As long as the 16-pip risk is acceptable, fear should be dispersed and the trader need only let the market price dictate success or failure.

If the trader is correct and the market price stays below the 100 bar MA, he should remain short until that time when the bias turns from bearish to bullish. In our simple example, the trader remains short until the price moves back above the 100 bar MA at 1.2190 (see Figure 5.2). At that point, the trade bias turns from bearish to bullish and the position should be closed. The risk on the trade was 16 pips, while the gain totaled just over 100 pips.

Did the trader have a reason to do the trade? You bet. Did the trader know the market was going to continue lower? He had a reason to believe it would, but he also understood the reason to enter the trade and that became his risk if the market did not trend lower. As long as the risk at the inception of the trade is within the trader's comfort zone, the trade makes sense, fear is dispersed, and the market is in charge.

Traders who don't have a reason to trade—the ones who just buy or sell because they feel the price is going up or going down—do not have a clear picture or understanding of the risk on the trade. As a result, any corrective moves against the position tend to increase uncertainty and cause additional fear. It is not likely that the trader will be able to sit through the corrective phases without booking a loss or taking profit too soon. Also, the

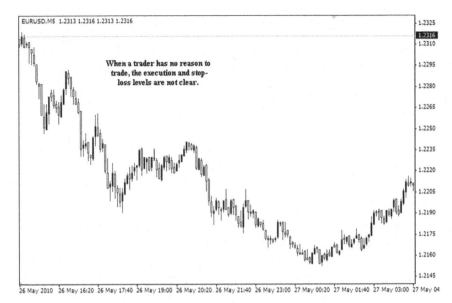

EURUSD,M5 1.2313 1.2316 1.2313 1.2316

When a trader has no reason to
trade, the execution and stop-
loss levels are not clear.

FIGURE 5.3 A Blank Canvas Gives No Reason to Trade

trader is more likely to think that the trend will reverse and go the other direction without tools that say otherwise.

Comparing Figure 5.2 with the simple downward sloping trend line and moving average to Figure 5.3, a simple price chart, illustrates the importance of tools to aid in formulating a reason to execute a trade. In Figure 5.2 the price is trending below the trend line and moving average. In Figure 5.3, there are no clues from the price other than that the price direction is to the downside. The road map is clearer with the tools that define the trend and provide the direction for following the trend to its conclusion.

Successful traders always have a reason to do a trade. Being able to identify that reason will increase profit potential, limit risk, and decrease fear. The next rule will outline the requirements of the tools I use. Later, in the second half of the book, I will further develop the use of the tools and outline how they can be used to anticipate a trend, stay on the trend, and attack the trend.

RULE 3: BE PICKY ABOUT YOUR TOOLS

We touched on the use of the 100 bar MA as a technical tool in what I call the trader's toolbox. The tools in a trader's toolbox need to be specific for the mission statement and game plan. The game plan—trading trends and keeping fear to a minimum—sets the requirements for the tools that I will use. If a tool does not conform to my requirements, it will not be used. As a result, I will not use some of the more popular trading tools that others may use every day. I am not being stubborn. I am also not suffering by not using them (in fact, I benefit). I simply have standards that my tools must conform to. I will go through some of those nonconforming tools later in this chapter.

I have three requirements for the technical tools I use. They must be trend defining, risk defining, and unambiguous.

Trend Defining

The first part of game plan is to trade trends. So it makes sense to use tools that will help define trends. Most trend-defining tools use slope of a line to define the direction of the trend. We already spoke of the 100 bar MA. If the slope of the moving average line is positive and the current price is above the moving average, the trend is bullish. Conversely, if the slope of the moving average line is negative and the current price is below the moving average, the trend is bearish. Another possibility is that the slope is sideways. When this happens, there is no trend. Can a nontrending market help a trader define a bullish or bearish trend? Not immediately, but later I will discuss how a nontrending slope can be a key clue for traders looking to trade trends. Needless to say, the simple moving average is one of the trading tools I use that helps define trends.

The other tools I will use, and explain later in the book, will also need to define trends. If they do not, they are not worthy of use. They will do more harm than good. They will break Rule 3.

Risk Defining

The second part of the mission statement is to use the least amount of risk. The only way to use the least amount of risk is to know or define the risk.

As a result, the technical tools I use need to help define risk. By knowing the risk, the trader is able to decide if the potential loss on the trade is acceptable or not. If the risk is too great, the trader should not do the trade. If, on the other hand, the risk is acceptable, then the trade can be done with little or no fear. If fear can be dispersed, the trader can focus on trading and attacking the trend.

Retail traders tend not to focus enough on defining risk. Not doing so often leads to unlimited risk and oversized loss potential. This ultimately destroys a trader's account equity. Successful traders cannot tolerate a trade or trades that destroy account equity. The tools used need to define risk so that large losses can be avoided and the focus can be on attacking the currency trends. You need the combination to succeed as a currency trader.

Unambiguous

The first two requirements are pretty straightforward. If we are looking to trade trends, our tool should help define trends. Also, if we want to use the least amount of risk and keep fear to a minimum, then using technical tools that define risk makes perfect sense.

The third requirement—that the tool needs to be an *unambiguous* tool—needs a further explanation.

What I define as an unambiguous tool is one that gives a clear bullish or bearish bias. The tool should not give an oversold or overbought condition. It should not give an 80-percent correlation clue. It should not be a tool that is not fully committed to being either bullish or bearish.

I like to say that the ideal tool gives a green or red trade signal, not a yellow one. It is yes or no, not maybe. It is white or black, not gray. The tool used gives a cut-and-dried bullish or bearish bias.

An unambiguous tool defines risk and lowers fear in the process. The reason is that successful traders tend to use the price levels from the unambiguous tool to trade against. As a result, the risk is defined, and as long as the trader is accepting of the risk, fear should also be dispersed and lessened.

Using our simple moving average example from earlier in the chapter, the trader sells on a break of the 100 bar MA, an unambiguous trading tool. It is unambiguous because below the line means bearish, above the line means bullish. Therefore, using an unambiguous trading tool like a simple moving average helps define risk, and with it fear can be minimized. The requirements of the game plan and mission statement are achieved.

If unambiguous tools are what we want, what does an ambiguous tool look like? The best way to describe an ambiguous trading tool is to say it is one that does not give a bullish or bearish bias. In trading, the main ambiguous trading tools are the technical tools that give overbought and oversold conditions. Saying something is overbought or oversold means that the market *should* go down, if overbought, or *should* go up, if oversold. It does not say it is unequivocally bearish or bullish.

More importantly, it does not define risk. If a market is said to be overbought, there is nothing to say that the price cannot get even more overbought. If this can happen, where is the stop loss? Where is the position closed out? There is no price for the stop. It is more of a guess. Guesses tend to increase fear over time. Successful traders look to steer clear of fear, not increase it.

In addition, if a market is overbought and the price continues to rise, what does that say about the higher price? It should be overbought as well. As a result, traders will add to their position by selling as the market trends higher.

If the market is trending higher, the trader is now trading against the trend. In other words, the game plan to trade trends and keep fear to a minimum is being ignored. It is ignored because the ambiguous trading tool said the price was overbought. Needless to say, it was not fully overbought.

More account equity is destroyed by using ambiguous tools that predict overbought and oversold conditions and lead to traders' positioning against a strong and directional trend. As the trend continues, fear eventually increases and the trade is eventually closed with a large loss.

The RSI and Stochastic Have No Place in My Game Plan   The most widely used overbought and oversold indicators used are the Relative Strength Index (RSI) and the Stochastic Oscillator. These two are oscillating indicators—that is, the index that is derived for each oscillates up and down with the market movements. As they oscillate, they give oversold and overbought conditions. The problem is that these indicators do not work well in trending markets, and that is where the most money can be made with the least amount of risk. If they do not work well in a trending market and they add to risk, they do not conform to the game plan.

An example will clearly outline the problems with using an ambiguous tool like the RSI.

The RSI is thought to be oversold when the oscillator goes below the 30 level. The EURUSD in Figure 5.4 first had the RSI dip below the 30 level when the price moved below 1.3127. This signaled the price was oversold and due for a correction. A trader who follows the RSI might be inclined to buy or close out a position at this level.

The market continued to sell off and moved toward 1.2930, where a modest rebound occurred. The RSI moved back higher and peaked when the price reached the 1.3005 level. This is well below the 1.3127 level where the market was first oversold. There is no reason from the RSI to get out at that level. The RSI barely got above the 30 level on the correction.

The market moved lower and became oversold (below 30 RSI) again at 1.2919. The market price did not rebound, but continued to sell off. The highest close came in at 1.2795 when again the RSI peaked not far above the 30 level. The market then sold off again and moved all the way down to 1.2521—all the while with the RSI moving above and below the oversold 30 levels.

A trader who focused on the ambiguous RSI would have bought the market looking for the oversold bounce as high as 1.3127. The market never

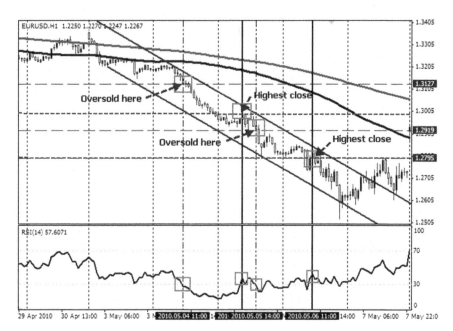

FIGURE 5.4 Using RSI Can Cause a Trader to Trade Against the Trend

closed above that level. The bounce never came. What is the stop level for the trader who is looking for the oversold market to bounce? There is none. What is the profit level for the trader who focuses on the RSI? There is none. Traders who use the RSI are likely looking for dips to buy during the entire trend down. If they are able to avoid the first oversold area, they are not likely to miss the subsequent oversold levels along the way. Instead of riding the trend, the trader is fighting the trend and trading against the trend.

When it is over, if the trader has not lost a large portion of the account (the EURUSD did move from 1.3300 to 1.2500), he or she would have likely missed the trend opportunity of the year. Eight hundred pips in four trading days do not come along very often. As mentioned earlier, you have to make hay when the sun is shining. Traders who focus on the RSI likely do not make hay. Like the RSI, the stochastic oscillator will often give the same oversold/overbought signals that could cause the trader to trade against the trend. That is simply not the game plan.

Does it make sense to use these ambiguous trading tools? For me, it flies in the face of what successful traders try to accomplish—trade trends and control risk and fear.

FIGURE 5.5 Using Unambiguous Tools to Uncover Oversold Markets

Can Other Tools Give Oversold or Overbought Hints? The tools I will introduce allow for the trader to look for plenty of clues that indicate the market is likely to be overbought or oversold. Those levels can also be fairly close to the tops and bottoms, but the difference is risk is defined.

For example, in Figure 5.5, the EURUSD bottom in June 2010 had a number of clues the market was oversold and ready for a move back higher. First, the price was a good distance away from the 100 hour MA line. The 100 hour MA was at 1.2180, the price was at 1.1880. When the price is too far away, there tends to be a period of consolidation and/or a correction. Does it give a buy or sell decision? No. However, the trader has a basis to think the bottom is in place and can use the low as a stop-loss level.

Second, once the bottom was established, the market price kept making higher lows and a trend line support level was developed. The trend line defined another risk level. If the price is above the trend line, the bias is bullish. If the price moves below, the bias is bearish. Since risk is defined, traders can buy against the trend line with little fear. If the price moves below the trend line, the trend down continues and the long position is sold. It did not. Instead, the market used the line as support on a number of different occasions.

Three, the market price eventually moved above the 100 hour MA on June 9. This is also a bullish trigger. Although on June 10, the price did dip back below the 100 hour MA, that dip was temporary. In fact, the price dip lower tested and held the bullish trend line, keeping a bullish bias versus that tool. When the price reversed back above the 100 hour MA, the bullish bias was reestablished, and the price surged higher.

The final clue was the test of the support at the 1.2006 level. When this floor level held, it paved the way for the trend move higher. At the trend line, at the MA line, at the floor, risk was defined. If the price remained above each line, the bias was bullish. If the price dipped below the lines, the bias was bearish. The longer-term trend was down, but there were clues the market was oversold and ready for a corrective move higher. The unambiguous tools used defined the risk and paved the way for the subsequent trend move higher, without risking a lot of equity in the process.

Using an RSI or Stochastic does not define risk so well. It simply says the market is oversold and it may rally. There is no certainty. There is no stop loss. There is no defined risk. With the increased uncertainty, trader fear is increased.

I know what I suggest may be shocking. I know plenty of traders who use tools like the RSI and Stochastic to detect oversold and overbought conditions. However, there are unambiguous tools that are better and that will keep from trading against the trend and keep traders on the trend. So heed my advice or warning.

More Rules for Tools

If you need more help choosing the best technical indicators for your trading, there are two more rules to consider:

1. *Stick to using three tools.* I have already spoken about how retail traders like to overwhelm their charts with a whole myriad of technical tools and indicators. Perhaps it makes them feel smarter. Perhaps it is part of the 10-step plan that will guarantee perfection, just like it did in other jobs or disciplines. In trading, "the more the merrier" does not work. Just because a chart has a bunch of lines and colors does not mean it is infallible.

    So what is the perfect number of tools to use? I like three. Two is too little. Four is too much. Three for me is just right. Most traders can focus on using three tools without too much stress, confusion, or uncertainty. There also is just enough for you as a trader to be able to handle when one may be bullish while another is bearish.

Traders who use more than three are likely using too many, and too many increases uncertainty. Uncertainty leads to more fear, and it is our goal to steer clear of fear.

2. *Tools must be universally used and simple.* In Rule 1 I talked about the K.I.S.S. principle for success and spoke about proprietary tools. Traders who create their own proprietary technical tools don't get the fact that the market is simple, and as such it focuses on the most obvious, most of the time. If you use a tool that has a cult following, don't use it. The market is bigger than the cult. The market does not care what the small percentage of traders think. The market that controls the price cares about what the most traders are thinking and doing.

In the hit movie *Caddyshack*, Ty (played by Chevy Chase) tells Danny to "be the ball" when describing being in the "golf zone." But how could he possibly "be the ball"?

Athletes on many levels put themselves in a zone where they feed off the game and go into a mental trance. The ball appears bigger, the speed slows down, the sounds disappear, and all outside influences are dulled or silenced. When this happens, they are, in effect, "being the ball."

As traders, try to think about being the market. As an individual, you can't beat the market. So instead be the market. To do that, I use the tools that the market uses, and if there is a choice between simple and complex, choose simple. For example, simple moving average or exponential moving average? Simple. I can teach nearly everyone who wants to trade how to calculate and understand a simple moving average in five minutes. I could not teach nearly everyone how to calculate and understand an exponential moving average.

The tools I use will be universally used by many and simple. If I do this, I stand the best chance to be the market.

Tools of the trade are important in any profession. In that common expression, the word *tool* typically refers to something that performs a helpful function. It could be a hammer for a carpenter. It could be casebook for a lawyer. The word *trade* in the expression is synonymous with a job. In other words, what things are needed to do your job better?

A currency trader needs tools too. My tools need to define a trend, define risk, and be unambiguous. If they do that, I can do my job better. Tools have another meaning to traders in particular. That is, they will be used to determine buy or sell decisions. The tools I choose will dictate my trades. So they not only allow me to do my job better, but will also tell me what to do in my job.

Are the tools used in trading important? You bet. They help me and they tell me what to do. That is why I am so picky about the tools I use.

RULE 4: THE "IF . . . SHOULD" RULE

Unambiguous trading tools may have been a mystery when I first introduced them, but hopefully, that mystery is now gone. The next rule, which I call the "If . . . Should" rule, is likely another mystery for most. However, I promised to keep it simple, so do not fear.

The "If . . . Should" rule says this: "*If* the market price does ABC, the price *should* do XYZ. If it does not, *get out*." Filling in the ABC and XYZ with a trading example, the "If . . . Should" rule would sound something like this: "*If* the market price moves below the 100 hour moving average, the price *should* continue to go lower. IF it does not, *get out*."

The rule seems simple, doesn't it? However, by looking at each part you can better understand the impact it is designed to have on a trader. Let's go through the pieces.

If the Market Price Does ABC . . .

"If the market price does ABC" implies that the trader is looking for a condition for the market price to be met. *If* a condition is met, it also is another way to say *if* there is a reason to do a trade. Of course, the rule does not say to do the trade, which leaves the door open to accept the condition or not. However, the "If . . . Should" rule is meant to be a guide for traders who have a position, so don't get too caught up in the omission.

What the first part does not say is the conditions or reasons for doing the trade. Those conditions will be set when we go through the tools we will use to satisfy our game plan and mission statement. The important thing to note is that the trader is looking for the price to do something specific.

. . . the Price Should Do XYZ

The second part of the rule says, "the price *should* do XYZ." This part outlines what the effect *should* be from the condition of a trade being met. Needless to say, *should* is the key word in this part of the sentence. Using *should* implies that there is a chance that the price action after the trade does what the trader thinks it will do. However, the door remains open for the price to *not* do what the trader thinks it will do as well. Of course, the

XYZ is what the trader is expecting the price to do, and that is either go up or go down.

The combined statement makes the trader set a condition or reason for a trade and then requires the trader to understand that the price may or may not go in the intended direction. Implied in the reason for executing the trade is that the bias just turned bullish or conversely the bias just turned bearish.

If it Doesn't, Get Out

The final part of the "If . . . Should" rule outlines what to do if the price does not do what it *should* do. The rule is to get out or exit the trade.

I have found that retail traders need to remind themselves constantly to be disciplined in their trading. If conditions change contrary to the intended trade direction, the trader needs to exercise discipline and accept the loss. This is not easy to do. There is often a lot of time, and mental conviction, spent to enter a trade. Having a positive conviction about a trade is a good thing, but being married to the trade until "death do you part" is *not* a good thing.

A lot of unsuccessful traders become married to their trades and have a difficult time exiting at a loss—even if it is small. As discussed earlier, not being used to failure or accepting defeat can be difficult. Traders have a tendency to be stubborn, until that time when fear overcomes stubbornness. Then things really go bad.

The fact is, if a trade is done for a reason, then the price should move away from the price that triggered that trade idea. In our rule, *if* ABC happens and it triggers a buy, the price *should* go higher. If it does not, guess what? The price is not doing what it *should* do. That is not your fault. Your analyses all pointed toward the price going higher.

When the price does not do what it *should* do, I personally like to blame the market. Something I don't know about—it may be a large corporate seller, it might be some comment from a central bank figure, it may be a merger and acquisition money flow that caused the market to move the price in a different direction from where it *should* go.

Think of a baseball player. Imagine the batter works his way to a count at the plate of two balls and no strikes. In this situation, he might expect that the pitcher is likely to throw the pitch right down the middle. In addition, he might expect the pitcher to be less careful with the location of the pitch. The batter reasons that the pitcher would not want to walk him but would prefer to take his chances that even if hit, an out will be made. So in this situation, the batter might be looking for a fastball, just above knee high and down the middle of the plate.

The "If . . . Should" rule for the batter is, "*If* the count goes to two balls and zero strikes, the pitcher *should* throw a fastball that is down the middle, just above knee high."

If the pitcher throws a curveball instead, and that pitch is thrown for a strike, the batter is likely to not hit the pitch. He *should* resign himself to having the count go to two balls and one strike. The pitcher wins. It is not the batter's fault. He did all he could given the information he had. He accepts the fate and prepares for the next pitch.

Successful hitters accept that the pitcher is in control. The pitcher throws the pitch. The batter has to hit it. If the batter is not prepared, the pitcher will win.

Trading is just like that. A successful trader is able to process what he knows, like the market price, and uses tools to help give a bullish or bearish bias. The trader's count goes to two balls and no strikes when he does the trade. If the market does what it *should* do, the trade is a profitable one. If the market throws a curveball and goes the opposite direction, then the trader should get out or exit the trade. Strike one. Get another pitch. It is not your fault. The market is doing something you did not expect. There are forces beyond your control. Don't blame yourself. Blame the market.

The market throws the pitches. The market is in control. You as a trader must be prepared, must develop the skill and the plan to beat the market. If you don't, you will fail. If you do, you will get one strike, but you have another shot. It is because you accept the strike and get out that you survive as a trader. You follow the "If . . . Should" rule.

Successful traders, like the successful baseball player, process the "If . . . Should" rule instinctively. They train their brains to think ahead, to anticipate by using tools they believe in. They practice and hone their skills. Then when they do a trade, they are confident but are prepared to blame the market if it doesn't do what it *should* do. They accept defeat without falling apart. They accept limiting their risk. They have conviction but don't become married to that conviction.

I like to tell all traders to think about the "If . . . Should" rule whenever they do a trade, until that time when it becomes instinctive. If it requires making a note card with the words on it, do it. Tape it to your desk or on your computer screen. Whatever you do, follow the "If . . . Should" rule.

RULE 5: LOOK AHEAD, BUT NOT TOO FAR AHEAD

If you want to move ahead, you need to have a destination in mind. This is true with trading, but most traders don't have a destination for their trades—especially the trend trades. The EURUSD is going down or the EURUSD is going up, but there is no idea to where or how that journey may unravel—if it does at all.

Equally hurtful is if a trader has a destination but that destination does not make realistic sense. For example, when in 2010 the EURUSD was trading near the 1.2000 level, I often heard comments about how the pair was going to 1.1209—the 61.8 percent retracement of the EURUSD move up from the all-time low to its all-time high.

OK. That is fine, but what roadblocks will the trader run into along that journey? What about the 200 month moving average at 1.1963? What about the area between 1.1826 and 1.1873, which contained five monthly lows between July 2005 and March 2006? Won't that provide some good support? What about the 1.1640 low from November 2005? What about the 200- to 300-pip corrections along the journey caused by some change in fundamentals or perhaps a shift in focus from the hardships in the Eurozone to hardships in the United States? Do those traders who see the EURUSD going to 1.1209 just sit and wait for the target level to be reached during the 300-pip corrections?

Traders in currencies need to be more flexible because it is a market that will trend for a duration, but can then correct, and the corrections can be significant.

So if not having a destination is not good and having a destination too far ahead is also not good, what is just right? Successful traders execute a trade and although they may have an ultimate destination in mind, the route traveled will take a step-by-step progression.

My friend Scott Barclay gave me the visual by comparing a trade to traveling along a highway. If you are long and anticipating a trend-type move, you are on the Bullish Highway. If short and expecting a bearish move, you would be on the Bearish Highway. Along a highway there are exits. The exits correspond to the next target levels. The target levels are key levels of resistance if on a Bullish Highway or support if on the Bearish Highway.

For example, in order to continue in the direction of the Bullish Highway, the price has to reach the next exit and go past. If the market cannot get past that exit, guess what? Either the driver is stopped on the highway—the bias is pausing—or the driver has turned around and is now on the Bearish Highway, going the other way.

How do you determine the exits on the highway? You do this by using trading tools that reinforce the trend or reverse the trend. If an exit is reached, the trader should have added confidence in the trend, and with added confidence fear should be eased. Focus is now on the next exit down the highway. As for the risk, the trader should now be able to move the stop up and manage the profit rather than the loss.

At each successive hurdle or exit reached, the trend rumbles on—the miles start to rack up on the odometer—the profit starts to accumulate. Traders should stay on the highway until that point when the bias turns around and the trader notices that the bias is no longer fully bullish but showing a bearish bias instead. The car is turned around.

To follow this trading strategy, traders must stay focused on the trend and where it is going in a step-by-step process and not on some unrealistic far-off target that can change and turn around, leaving the trader going the wrong way on a one-way highway.

Following this approach also reminds the trader of the risk. By using unambiguous trading tools and things like the "If . . . Should" rule, traders begin to see and understand the rhythm of the market.

For example, assume a trader buys because the price moves above the 100 bar MA. He knows that the "If . . . Should" rule says "*If* the market price goes above the 100 bar MA, the price *should* go higher. If it does not, get out." He expects the market to rally.

The trader buys and is now on the Bullish Highway with a stop 10 to 20 pips below the 100 bar MA (the "get out" point plus a buffer).

The next step is to start to map out the next exit. That might be the 200 bar MA. If the price goes above the 200 bar MA, the next target will be spotted, which may be the upper end of a channel trend line.

The "If . . . Should" rule is also revised to say, "*If* the price moves above the 200 bar MA, it confirms the bullish move and the price *should* go higher. If it does not, get out." As a result, the stop might be moved up to the 200 bar MA less a 10-pip buffer. The trader remains on the trend and in the trade. The stop now guarantees a profit. This step-by-step process continues until that time when the bias turns around from one of the trading tools monitored.

In Figure 5.6, the AUDUSD is in a trending market to the upside. A channel is drawn connecting lows and the highs. The top trend line becomes a target on the Bullish Highway. When the price reaches that target or exit, the market momentum stalls and the price reverses. This is a bearish development. The price is not able to get through the exit, so the car on the highway has stalled, and it can only turn around and go the other way. Traders can sell against the level with a defined risk. If the price moves above the trend line, the long can be reestablished. If the price moves lower, the bias is bearish and the target for the bearish move becomes the bottom trend line.

This is exactly what happened. When the market corrected to the lower trend line target, the bulls returned and bought. Risk for buyers was a break of the trend line. If the trend line broke, the bias would be confirmed to the downside and another exit on the Bearish Highway would be targeted.

AUDUSD.Daily 0.88670 0.89080 0.88570 0.89010

Trend is up, but the price runs into the target channel trend line resistance. This becomes a reason to change the bullish bias. Market corrects down.

When the price comes down, the bearish bias turns to bullish when support target at the trend line holds here.

FIGURE 5.6 Defining Targets or Exits on the AUDUSD Bullish Highway

Trading a trend requires that you constantly look ahead and target levels to overcome. The purpose of this rule is to increase confidence in the trend by providing realistic goals, managing risk by providing definable risk levels, and taking advantage of profit-taking levels. The rule also allows the trader to stay in synch with the trend's step-by-step progression. Failure to follow this rule will lead to increased uncertainty and increased fear, and will likely lead to traders' exiting trends before their time.

Follow the road ahead. Reach the exits along the way and attack the currency trends one realistic and meaningful step at a time.

RULES RULE

The game of trading that we all play is really a free-for-all. You can do what you want when you want with little restrictions. However, just because there is freedom does not mean you should shy away from self-imposed discipline. Successful traders look for discipline in order to keep risk to a minimum and keep fear down.

In the next chapter, I will formally introduce the tools in the trader's toolbox; this will finish the foundation needed for success as a currency trader looking to trade the trends.

CHAPTER 6

The Trader's Toolbox

Tools are designed to make jobs easier and workers more productive. The ultimate goal is to make the job more profitable. Some tools are better than others, and then there are those tools that can actually be counterproductive.

Recently, my youngest son Bobby and I participated in a Boy Scout service project. The troop was building a three-sided, covered structure called an Adirondack at a campsite in memory of a father of a scout who had recently passed away. The only requirement was to bring a hammer and a desire to help. I found my tools—a hammer for me and a hammer for Bobby—and headed to the camp.

Upon arriving at the site, the project foreman, who also happened to be a professional builder, took one look at the hammers in my hand, smirked and said "You can put your hammers back in your car. I would prefer not to have to take you or Bobby to the hospital for treatment."

Apparently, a hammer is not a hammer anymore. My hammers were wooden handled, which made them susceptible to breaking, especially if they were old and dried out like the ones I was carrying. The newer models are lighter, have handles made of composite material, and have bigger heads so that fewer fingers get smashed.

The tools I had were not only inferior, they were potentially dangerous. It could have been counterproductive if a finger was smashed or a flying hammer head hit an unsuspecting worker (or me).

Traders need a well-stocked toolbox as well. Like the hammers of today, the trader's tools should get the job done, make the trader more productive and profitable, and not be *counterproductive*. This chapter will introduce the tools I use to attack the currency trends. I will also outline a tool that may be counterproductive to your trading. You may be surprised.

RULES FOR THE TOOLS

In Chapter 5, I outlined the rules for the tools that traders should use. Specifically, one requirement is that the tools should help the trader define trends. If our mission is to make the most money and the game plan is to trade trends, then tools that do not help define trends are counterproductive toward our mission.

The second requirement was that the tools used should define risk. Once again, our mission statement is to not only make the most money but to do it with the least amount of risk. If a trader cannot define risk, then knowing what the least amount of risk is cannot be done. Using a trading tool that does not define risk would be counterproductive. Those types of tools should not be used.

Finally, I outlined that the third requirement for our trading tools is that they be unambiguous. Unambiguous trading tools give a definitive bullish or bearish bias. By doing this, they define risk, which keeps fear to a minimum. By being unambiguous, they also do not carry the negative implications of an ambiguous trading tool.

For example, and as outlined in Chapter 5, unambiguous trading tools do not give oversold or overbought signals like the Relative Strength Index or Stochastic Indicator. Both of these widely used technical trading indicators I consider to be ambiguous trading tools. Both can contribute to not staying on trends or even trading against the trend. They also both fail to define risk or give a stop loss level that traders need to exit losing trades. This adds uncertainty and fear to trading. Remember, traders need to steer clear of fear. Trading against the trend without being able to define risk is totally against our mission statement and game plan.

HOW TO USE FUNDAMENTAL ANALYSIS

What I did not really address when talking about the ambiguity of some tools in the last chapter was how fundamental news—that is, all the other influences other than technical tools—affects the price of a currency pair over a time period and whether it fits in a trader's toolbox. A lot of traders—and especially those who are just starting to trade—use fundamental analysis almost exclusively. But is it a useful tool? Is fundamental analysis an ambiguous or unambiguous tool?

If you recall in Chapter 1, I commented on how fundamental news may not move the market in the direction that is always expected. The reason is the inputs that make up fundamental news and events are vast and can offset each other.

For example, in recent economic times, the cycles for many countries have been in synch. The United States entered a recession. So did Europe and Great Britain. When the global economy rebounded, the health of the major economies also rebounded together. As a result, the market's price reaction to individual economic releases was not so cut-and-dried compared to another time when one country's economy was weak and another's was strong. This dynamic would tend to lead the strong economy to have the strong currency and the weak economy to have a weak currency.

There may also be other fundamental factors that cause the price to move in directions not necessarily expected by the perceived fundamentals. Multinational businesses may have currency flows that affect the supply and demand balance of a currency pair. If McDonald's, Coca-Cola, or IBM wants to remit foreign profits back to the United States, they may look to sell foreign currency and buy dollars at times when fundamentally the dollar is perceived to be weak. Merger and acquisition flows can also be a fundamental influence that can cause a currency pair to move in directions against what the fundamentals may suggest. Options on currencies may also have an effect on trading flows. Traders with large option exposure at a specific strike price will often look to defend that price level and look to halt a directional bias. Central banks, which are controlling their own reserve balances, can have a huge influence on the movement of currency rates that may be counter to the perceived fundamental direction.

I like to tell retail traders to think of the fundamental inputs all going into a brew in a big black cauldron. The ingredients make up a price for a currency pair. That brew is constantly changing, with new ingredients being added all the time. As a retail trader, you can see and interpret some ingredients. You see and know that retail sales came out stronger. You see that the central banker said that it "would keep rates low for an extended period of time." You see the change in Nonfarm Payroll and know that it was weaker than expected. Any one of these influences can make you bullish or bearish a specific currency pair—from a fundamental standpoint.

What you do not see is the hedge fund or central bank that executed a large order through a bank or perhaps on the institutional electronic platform. You do not see the multinational repatriating funds back to the home country through a global bank. You do not see the option flows. You do not see the large hedge fund traders who are buying against a key technical level. You may not see the comments from the central banker until the price has already moved. You do not see the flows into the risk currency pairs instead of the major currency pair, even though the economy of the major currency pair is strong. These are influences on the market that leave a fundamental retail trader wondering, "What just happened? Why isn't the market going the way the fundamentals say it should go?"

What I often hear from inexperienced traders, and that includes prominent analysts on television, is a list of fundamental reasons why the market price of a currency or currency pair might go up or down. These are some from recent memory:

- The sovereign debt crisis in Greece, Spain, and Ireland will only get worse and this will lead to the EURUSD going to parity.
- There is a war brewing in the Middle East with reports that the military is building up for an attack, which will lead to the U.S. dollar moving sharply higher.
- We are just a terrorist attack away from investors fleeing or moving into the U.S. dollar.
- All the fiscal spending will lead to a sharply lower U.S. dollar. (There is no escaping this fact.)
- The BRIC nations (Brazil, Russia, India, and China) do not want the U.S. dollar as the reserve currency. They want to diversify into the euro.
- The BRIC nations are fleeing the euro and are looking into diversifying into the Canadian and Australian dollar.
- Inflation is just around the corner, and when it comes, investors will flee the U.S. bond and stock markets and the U.S. dollar.
- Gold will go to $2,000/$3,000/$4,000 and the U.S. dollar will plunge.
- Gold will go to $2,000/$3,000/$4,000 and the euro will plunge.
- Nonfarm Payroll will be stronger than expectations on Friday and this will lead to the USDJPY and the other risk pairs soaring higher.
- Gisele Bundchen, the super model, is demanding to be paid in euros as her earnings in the dollar are being eroded day by day. More and more people will be doing the same thing given the weak dollar policy the U.S. government is following.

These types of traders will have a fundamental view based on one or more stories or analyses. In addition, they will often add an addendum to their view that, "If the euro goes higher, it will just be an opportunity to sell more." In other words, "If the price is trending higher, I will sell even more against the trend."

That type of thinking is one sure way to *not* attack the trend. It also is a recipe for your account to lose value. Remember our game plan is to trade the trends; it is also to keep fear (and risk) to a minimum. It does not sound like either is being addressed by the purely fundamental trader.

What I also often hear from inexperienced traders is the comment that "Ultimately, the fundamentals will take over and win out." What I like to reply with is "When is 'ultimately?'" Is it after 50 more pips, 100 more pips, 200 more pips, or 300 more pips? How far does "ultimately" have to go before fear is too high and a large loss is booked, or before the account blows up? How far is "ultimately" until you realize that the fundamental reason for taking the position is now reversed and that some other fundamental story in the cauldron is driving the market? In other words, how do you define risk and control fear when there is no basis for knowing when you are wrong? The answer is "You can't."

Fundamental news is important, but it is not a tool retail traders should use to base trades on. Although, in the long run, the fundamentals may do what was expected, there are technical tools that will also be right in the long run. I guarantee those technical tools will catch and ride the trend if and when the EURUSD goes to parity. They will catch the trend in the euro (or the U.S. dollar) as a result of gold going to $2,000 an ounce. Those technical tools will catch the trend if overspending fiscally in the United States leads to a sharply lower dollar.

Those same technical tools will also be able to prevent the trader from losing when the market does not do what it is "fundamentally" supposed to do in the mind of the trader. It will not necessarily prevent losses, but if used properly technical tools will limit losses more effectively than fundamentals. The good news is they will also confirm your fundamental view when both are in synch.

Fundamentals can be ambiguous and because of that, traders should not base trading decisions solely or even principally on them. They should be a secondary tool in your trading decision-making process. Fundamentals can then be used to explain yourself and your market conviction to your dinner guests so you sound smart. Apart from that, follow the one thing we all can agree on—the price—then, to provide the reasons to trade, apply the right technical tools to that price. The combination, given the right tools, should lead the way toward attacking the currency trends.

THE ONE THING WE CAN AGREE ON: PRICE

I work for a retail currency broker, and at my firm we have tens of thousands of live accounts. We are just one firm in the world. There are many others like us in the retail space around the world with a similar account base.

Take all those retail traders and add the institutional money managers, hedge fund managers, international corporate treasurers, bank traders, insurance company portfolio managers, and so on and you can now imagine why the currency market is the largest market in the world ($3 trillion to $4 trillion a day is transacted).

Now understand that all those traders and investors are looking at a relatively small number of currency pairs. As a retail broker we have around 20 different pairs we quote our clients. The major pairs are against the world's reserve currency, the U.S. dollar. Those major pairs include the euro versus U.S. dollar (EURUSD), the British pound versus the U.S. dollar (GBPUSD), the U.S. dollar versus the Japanese yen (USDJPY), the U.S. dollar versus the Swiss franc (USDCHF), the U.S. dollar versus the Canadian dollar (USDCAD), the Australian dollar versus the U.S. dollar (AUDUSD), and the New Zealand dollar versus the U.S. dollar (NZDUSD). From these you get the cross-currency pairs including the EURJPY, EURCHF, EURGBP, GBPJPY, and so on.

Of those currency pairs, roughly 40 percent of all trades are executed in the EURUSD. Thirty to thirty-five percent are executed in the other major pairs against the U.S. dollar, and the rest is in the cross currency pairs including the EURJPY, EURCHF, and so on.

So there is a whole lot of volume, and that volume is traded in a relatively few currency pairs. Compare and contrast to the global equity market with thousands of stocks and volume (and often thin volume) spread over all those thousands of choices. I don't know about you, but having so many traders trading a relatively small amount of currency pairs is a comfort to me. I like the idea that there is a huge amount volume with a whole lot of traders big and small contributing to those currency pairs' price movement.

All the thousands of currency traders, focusing on a few currency pairs, determine a price 24 hours a day from Sunday at 5 PM EST to Friday at 4 PM EST. That price has all the influences in our cauldron mixed up. All the fundamentals are in the pot, the mergers and acquisition flows are in there, the comments from central bankers, the economic expectations and economic releases get mixed in, as do the option-related flows and the flows from central banks. All these influences, and more, are in this huge cauldron.

The net result is the price. The price is what *all* currency traders see. It is what the global currency traders can all agree on. It is the score of the game. It does not lie. Because of the global nature of the currency market and the fact that it is an electronic market, the price is the same whether you are in New York, Sydney, Tokyo, Dubai, Frankfurt, Paris, or London. It is also largely the same for retail and institutional traders. As such, the price is said to be transparent.

The net supply and demand from the traders causes the price to move either up or down. That price movement is moved by all the influences that traders—including you—can see and not see. As a result, I think of the price as the most important piece of information at any one moment for traders. However, on his or her own, can a currency trader make money trading the price movements and momentum? Let's take a look at this idea.

Price Momentum Has Its Limits

The current price and price momentum, whether it be up or down, is important, but as far as its usefulness for trading, it has its limits. Traders who watch the price can see or follow the price direction. Many beginning traders will look at the price action or momentum and base trading decisions simply on that movement. If the price is going up, they will buy. If the price is going down, they will sell. Moreover, the more momentum there is in a specific direction, the more excited the trader will be about getting in on that move.

As a result, the inexperienced trader will buy when the price has already gone up and sell when the price has already gone down. Sometimes it works, and the price continues to go higher or lower and the trader feels happy. Sometimes it doesn't, and the price reverses and the trader is sad and often confused. "Why didn't it do what it did last time I traded like that?" the trader will often say.

In reality, because the trader does not have a reason to trade, trading is random. Trading is done because of the thrill of the trade, the thrill of the momentum. It is similar to a gambler betting red or black on the roulette wheel over and over again. The gambler continues to bet because the thrill of the wins and the vision of the potential wins. There is no real rationale to think the next spin's odds will be any different than the previous spin.

In trading, the trader remembers the winning trades too. However, unlike the gambler who most likely thinks he is lucky when he bets red or black and wins, the high from the random wins in trading is often *believed* to be because of a trading aptitude and prowess. The trader thinks he is fully responsible for making the trade and having a gain. They were good trades. "Nice trade," he says to himself, and often he cannot wait to tell someone about it.

In reality, the trader is likely more lucky than skilled. After all, there was no reason other than price momentum in a direction to do the trade. To me, that is not enough. Price momentum just tells me a direction now. It does not tell me at what price level I am wrong. It does not tell me where my stop level should be, except when the price momentum fades or goes the other way. It does not define risk. It runs counter to my mission statement of keeping risk to a minimum, because I cannot define risk. If I cannot define risk, I don't know if my risk is minimized. (Remember: I want to make the most money with the least amount of risk.) It also does not tell me at what price I should be bullish or bearish. As a result, price momentum is an ambiguous trading tool.

When there is no price level that determines a trade decision of either bullish or bearish, the trader is left with hoping that momentum continues in the direction.

We have all gotten caught up in the emotion of buying a fast-rising market only to have the market reverse or even slow down. Suddenly, visions of buying the high price flood our mind, and rightly so. There was no reason to do the trade. The trade was simply a reactionary bet that the price would do what it already has done.

The traders who have purchased near the high simply on price momentum all have this same reversal fear. As a result, if buying slows, a flood of selling by the overzealous, out-of-synch buyers often causes a sharp price correction in the opposite direction. Typically, if the momentum buyer does not sell on the correction back down, the corrective move has likely scared the trader to the point of simply getting out as close to breakeven as possible. Thoughts like "If the market gets back to my entry point, I will get out and reevaluate the market" or, for the religious, "Please God, just get me back to breakeven and I promise I won't be an impulsive buyer again." Is this type of trading the way to keep fear to a minimum? Not in my mind. The game plan is in shambles.

Of course, there will be times when the price momentum trader will see the momentum continue in the direction of the trade, and the trader may even make some good money. In my mind, even if the trader does find "success" in this approach from time to time, it often simply encourages the continuation of bad trading habits—trading habits that rely on the luck of the momentum continuing before fear is increased. Trading habits that do not have any concept of risk.

This is the equivalent of giving a misbehaving child a piece of candy in order to distract her from what she is doing wrong. The child does not learn. When the candy is gone, the misbehaving will continue and your child's dentist bills will also rise.

There is an old saying, "I would rather be lucky than smart." A lot of less-experienced traders rely on that luck by trading the price momentum. As with so many sayings, however, there is always what I call the "dot, dot, dot" that gets forgotten over time. In this case it may be that "I would rather be lucky than smart . . . but luck always runs out, while learning lasts forever."

Trading Price Ranges

Inexperienced traders who get burned trading price momentum—if they don't lose all their money—tend to regroup and realize that buying or selling market price momentum is not a way to make money consistently. What typically happens is that fear and uncertainty are just too high, luck runs out, and losses mount.

So instead of buying new highs and selling new lows with the price momentum, the trader switches tactics and starts buying low and selling high. The old Wall Street axiom to "buy cheap and sell dear" becomes the new trading strategy.

Unfortunately, like trading price momentum, the strategy fails to address what exactly is cheap and what is expensive. Moreover, there is no reason to trade other than the price is lower or higher. In other words, what is the stop level if a dip is bought and the price continues to make new lows? The trader is supposed to buy dips, and most will, doubling up on the position. The market moves lower, and they will buy another dip. Pretty soon, the trending market to the downside leads to a large loss or liquidation.

Of course, this strategy can work just fine in a nontrending market. In Figure 6.1 the price is trading in a confined range for the USDJPY between 91.07 and 91.79. Buying at the dips and selling at the peak would have yielded seven profitable trades of 72 pips for a total of +504 pips over an eight-day trading period. Not a bad gain.

At the point marked "1," the market starts what is a trend move. For the dip-buying trader, it represents a dip to buy. The first buy occurs at 91.07. The next buy occurs at the cheaper price of 90.87, the third at 90.35, and so on. A total of five buys are executed. In addition, since the trader is good at buying dips (I will give him the benefit of the doubt), all the price lows are bought. Note that the corrective waves higher are all shallow, which is typical of a trending market, and the trader is never in a position to break even or make a profit. Finally, when the price falls sharply at point 6, the trader's fear is just too high, his account value is largely depleted, and the entire position is liquidated. The total loss on the five dip-buying trades totals minus 1,364 pips, which far outpaces the gains from trading the low-to-high trading range. The time period it took to lose over twice the amount was around eight trading days—the same length of time to make the 504 pips in gains. Trends move quickly and losses accrue quickly too.

What range traders typically find out is that buying low prices and selling high prices only goes so far, especially during trending periods. The price only tells you that the current price is cheaper or more expensive than in the most recent past. It does not tell you how cheap or expensive

USDJPY,H1 88.66 88.67 88.61 88.67

Sell at 91.79

7 trades x 72 pips = +504 pips

Buy at 91.07

Buys on Dips

① =91.07 (−382 pips)

② =90.87 (−362 pips)

③ =90.35 (−310 pips)

④ =89.25 (−200 pips)

⑤ =88.35 (−110 pips)

Sell stop at 87.25

⑥ =87.25 (−1,364 total pips)

7 Jun 2010   9 Jun 20:00   14 Jun 13:00   17 Jun 05:00   21 Jun 22:00   24 Jun 14:00   29 Jun 07:00   1 Jul 23:00   6 Jul 16:00   9 Jul 08:00

FIGURE 6.1   Buying Cheap and Selling Dear

the market price will get, nor does it define the risk of the trade. In addition, it also leads to trading against the trend. Trends are where the most money is made. It is also where the most money can be lost. As seen in the example, the price in a trending market can get cheaper and cheaper and cheaper, and with it so can your account value.

Although the current price and price direction are no doubt some of the most important things a trader needs to follow, they are not the answer to success as a trader.

Instead, traders, like carpenters, like lawyers, like software programmers, need to apply tools to that price. The tools are filters that take the price and transform it into a meaningful bias for the trader—a bias to be bullish or a bias to be bearish. In the transformation, the tools should make the trader's job easier. They should make the trader more efficient. They should make the trader more profitable. They should *not* make the trader counterproductive. They should not cause uncertainty or fear but encourage certainty and confidence. Using the analogy from the beginning of the chapter, the hammer head should not fly off the handle and hit the trader in the head.

THE TOOLS

The next sections will outline the three tools I use to attack the currency trends: moving averages, trend lines and remembered lines, and Fibonacci retracements. In the subsequent chapters I will outline how you can use each tool to become a successful currency trader.

Moving Averages

As introduced earlier, the moving average, or simple moving average, is one of the tools that I use to attack the currency trends. In the book I will use the abbreviation MA to designate both. A simple moving average takes the closing price level over a variable number of periods and calculates the average over that period.

For example, if a trader wants to calculate the simple moving average for a 10-day period, the calculations shown in Table 6.1 would be made given the following closing values over the last 10 days.

The cumulative sum of the closing values over the last 10 days totals 12.323. Taking that total and dividing by the days used for the cumulative sum or moving average period, equals the MA. In our example, taking the cumulative total of 12.323 and dividing by 10 periods or days equals the 10-day MA. So:

$$12.323/10 \text{ days} = 1.2323$$

$$\text{The 10-day MA} = 1.2323$$

The simple moving average is designed to smooth out a series of prices and take the volatility out of the series. The shorter the MA, the faster the

TABLE 6.1 Calculating the 10-Day Simple Moving Average

Day	Closing Daily Price	Cumulative Total
1	1.2220	1.2220
2	1.2331	2.4551
3	1.2309	3.686
4	1.2388	4.9248
5	1.2373	6.1621
6	1.2312	7.3933
7	1.2270	8.6203
8	1.2310	9.8513
9	1.2333	11.0846
10	1.2384	12.323

average will react to current price trends. The longer the MA, the slower the average will react to current price trends.

From a technical perspective, the MA levels are placed over a chart of price bars, candlesticks, or even a line graph. In this book I will use candlesticks and bar charts in most of the graphs. I will use the generic word "bar" to describe a candlestick and "bars" to describe a series of candlesticks. The MA on a chart is in the form of a line. That is because for each bar, there is only one MA.

A moving average can be calculated using bars on a chart that can show any time period. That is, you can have a moving average on a minute chart, a 5-minute chart, a 15-minute chart, a 30-minute chart, an hourly chart, a daily chart, a weekly chart, or even a monthly chart. In each, the calculation is the same—take the closing value of a series of bars, sum them up, and figure out the average over x periods.

You can also vary the x-periods used to calculate the MA on the chart. For example, you can have an 18 bar MA, a 34 bar MA, a 50 bar MA, a 100 bar MA, or a 200 bar MA, and anything in between. Although there can be a moving average for any x-period, the periods listed are some the market tends to favor over others. In the next chapter I will outline the moving averages I feel the market is most focused on.

When looking at the 100 bar MA, the convention for a daily chart is to say the "100 day MA." For an hourly chart, the same convention is used. That is, I would say the "100 hour MA." For less than an hour chart, such as a 5-minute, 15-minute, or 30-minute chart, it is not correct to say the "100 5-minute MA." Instead, I like to say the "100 bar MA on the 5-minute chart" or the "100 bar MA on the 30-minute chart." For a minute chart, the convention would go back to the "100 minute MA."

From what we have learned, there can be many chart time periods. There can also be many MA time periods including the 18 bar, 34 bar, 50 bar, 100 bar, 200 bar, and any MA time period in between.

The question becomes which moving average to use and on what time period charts. In Chapter 7, I will outline the time periods that I focus on and use to evaluate the market for entry and trading the trends. In the next sections, I will introduce the basic use of the MA lines, and why it is a tool I need in our trader's toolbox.

What They Do   When analyzing a chart, the current price will be either above or below the moving average. Dependent on if the price is above or below the moving average will determine if the bias is bullish or bearish. The following rules apply:

- If the current price > x-period moving average = Bullish bias
- If the current price < x-period moving average = Bearish bias

FIGURE 6.2   100 Bar MA on the 5-Minute Chart

In Figure 6.2 the 100 bar MA on the 5-minute chart is represented by the solid line in the chart. When the price is greater than the MA line the bias is said to be bullish. When the price moves below the MA line, the bias turns bearish.

Of course, the price can also be at the MA level. At these levels, I like to say the price is at the borderline, where the market is neither bullish nor bearish. In Figure 6.2, note how the price comes up to test the 100 bar MA level on the chart and trades on the borderline level, but then moves back down and continues the bearish trend down. We will discuss how traders use the moving average lines in more detail in the next chapter.

How They Fit in the Toolbox   If we are to use the moving average as a tool, we know it must conform to our trading rule. That is, moving averages need to define a trend (or nontrend), define risk, and be unambiguous. Do the moving averages conform?

An MA line helps traders define trends, but it can also be used to help define nontrends. We know that if the price is above or below the moving average line, it gives either a bullish or bearish bias. Does that indicate that there is a trend? Not necessarily.

In Figure 6.2, the price moves below the 100 bar MA at around the 1.2265 level. This turns the bias bearish. However, the slope of the line at that time is positive or moving higher in the chart. This is because the move from the top was pretty steep. The moving average line needs some time to react or adjust to the sudden change of direction. Should the trader be bearish? Yes. The price is below the MA line. If the price is below the MA line, the bias is bearish. As a result, the trader should be short if he has a position. Is the market trending? Not necessarily, or at least not yet.

Eventually, in the chart the moving average line flattens and then turns down from around the 1.2270 level. Since the price remains below the 100 bar MA line and the slope of the MA line is starting to move down, the bearishness is confirmed and the trend is confirmed.

Another benefit of a moving average line is it can also define nontrends. If the moving average is going sideways, it often can be a prelude to a trend-type move.

In Figure 6.3 the 100 bar MA on the 5-minute chart is moving sideways between 1.3487 and 1.3492 in the gray shaded area. The market is nontrending in a narrow range. Markets that are nontrending can only continue to nontrend or eventually trend. In this case, the nontrend transitioned into a bearish trend. The price started a move down to a low of 1.3355.

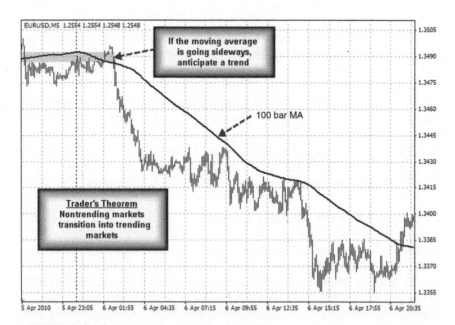

FIGURE 6.3 Nontrending to Trending Using MA

In the next chapter I will talk more about using the moving averages to anticipate and attack currency trends like this example demonstrates.

The second requirement for the tools we use is that they define risk for the trader. The moving average gives traders a clear bullish or bearish bias. The line that makes up the moving average is the equivalent of a borderline. If the price is above the line, the bias is bullish. If the price is below the MA line, the bias is bearish. In Figure 6.3, the price was consolidating below the MA line in the chart as the market consolidated around the sideways 100 bar MA.

Toward the end of the shaded area, the price moved back above the MA line. Although this gives a bullish bias for traders, the price could only move 8 pips above the MA line at 1.3488 to 1.3496 high before moving back down and below the line. Remember the "If . . . Should" rule from the previous Chapter 5. The "If . . . Should" rule says "*If* the price moves above the 100 bar MA line, the price *should* move higher." If a price can't move higher, there is only one way it can go—down. The trend started to the downside.

What is the risk to the trader who shorted the market on the move back below the MA line? The risk is if the price were to move back above the MA line, plus a buffer for volatility of 5 to 15 pips. Risk is clearly defined. Risk is limited.

With risk defined, the trader is fully able to evaluate if the exposure is acceptable. If it is, the only thing left to do is execute the trade. Once done, fear should be dispersed. It is now a question of what happens. Does the trend begin and the market move lower, or is the trade stopped out?

No one knows for sure what will happen. There are clues, however, that give traders more confidence in the trades. What we do know is that using moving averages satisfies the requirement of defining trading risk, and by defining risk, fear is kept to a minimum.

The final requirement for the tools for trading is if it is an unambiguous trading tool. Since a moving average gives a bullish signal if the price is above the moving average line and a bearish signal if the price is below the moving average line, it is indeed an unambiguous trading tool.

Being unambiguous allows the trader to define risk and to keep fear to a minimum. It also allows the trader to be patient and wait for opportunities to trade when the price moves closer to the moving average line. Doing so keeps risk to a minimum. This is a major advantage of using unambiguous trading tools like the moving average.

In Figure 6.4 the EURUSD is trending higher with the moving average line sloping to the upside. The corrective moves off the higher highs approached and tested the 100 bar MA line and found trend following buyers. When the market price finally broke, the bias turned bearish and the price turned lower. When unambiguous tools are used there is no guessing as

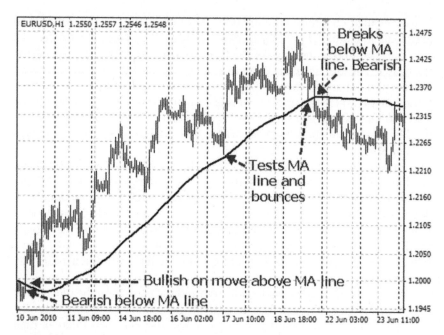

FIGURE 6.4   Moving Averages Are Unambiguous Tools

to the directional bias—price above the MA line is bullish, price below the line is bearish.

In Chapter 7, I will explore using the moving average in more detail, including what moving averages I use, how to use moving averages to anticipate trends, and how to use moving averages to stay on the trend.

Trend Lines and Remembered Lines

In Chapter 5, Rule 1 was to follow the K.I.S.S. principle. That is, "Keep It Simple to be Successful." We also are fully aware by now of the requirements for our trading tools of defining trends and risk and being unambiguous.

The second tool that I use to attack the currency trends is about as simple as you can get, and it also satisfies the requirements of our trading tools. The second set of tools is trend lines and what I call *remembered lines*. Most traders are familiar with trend lines. "Remembered lines" is a term I coined to represent a type of trend line. It is explained in more detail shortly.

In the Introduction, I spoke of how my father used hand-drawn charts to follow and trade the trends in the market. He used graph paper and each day drew the bar charts and point-and-figure charts for the respective instruments he followed. When the lapse of time or a market move outside the range required a new graph page, he simple taped the new page to the last and spread the extended pages across his desk to analyze.

Calculating a moving average was something he could do, but it had to be a shorter-period moving average such as an 18 day MA. Longer-period moving averages were not an option. They were simply too time consuming without a personal computer for help.

Besides point and figure analysis, he would take out a pencil and ruler and draw trend lines. They told the story of the trends. They told the story of nontrend periods. If he had two higher lows, he would connect the points and see the uptrend. If he had two lower highs, he could connect those points and see the downtrend. The more connected points along a line, the better the support or resistance. They provided clues for trading trends back then, and they still provide clues for trading trends today.

What They Do   When I look at a chart, I immediately look to see if there are any trend lines I can draw that I can rely on for trading clues. The typical trend line I will draw will connect higher lows, signaling a bullish trend, or lower highs, signaling a bearish trend.

The general trend line trading rules are the following:

- If the price is above an upward-sloping trend line that connects higher lows, the trend is bullish. Traders should use that trend line as a buying opportunity when the price is tested on dips.
- Conversely, if the price is below a downward sloping trend line that connects lower highs, then the trend is bearish and traders should use that trend line as a selling opportunity when tested.

In Figure 6.5 the EURUSD has higher lows signaling a bullish trend line formation. Connecting points 1 to 2 originally sets the upward-sloping trend line. In the chart, buyers entered the market on dips that approached or tested the trend line at points 3 through 7. Each time the market bounced off the line. Each test provided a low risk trading opportunity for traders.

In Figure 6.6 the USDJPY is in a downward trend as lower highs create the trend line. This is a bearish trend line formation. The main trend line was tested no fewer than 12 times in this move lower. Each test of the line provided a low-risk opportunity for a trader to sell and stay on the trend.

The trend is thought to end when the price moves below a trend line if it is a bullish trend. On a downward-sloping bearish trend line, the trend is over when the price moves above the trend line.

The basic bullish or bearish trend line is just one way to draw and interpret trend lines. There are other trend line formations that I will use

FIGURE 6.5 Bullish Trend Line

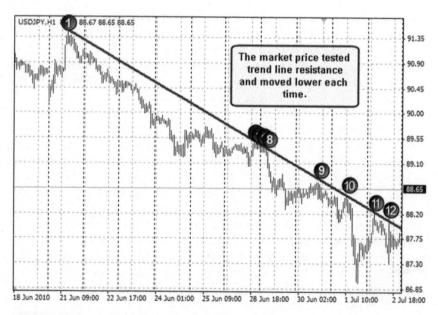

FIGURE 6.6 Bearish Trend Line

to look for clues for trends and nontrends. Chapter 8 will go through the ones that I find useful in following and staying on the trend and others that will help anticipate a trend (and attack currency trends!). If a trader can anticipate a trend, he or she is more apt to stay on a trend and reap the rewards of a directional, fast-moving market move.

Remembered Lines: Lines without a Slope   Earlier I explained how to draw a trend line by connecting higher lows for an uptrend and connecting lower lows to create a downtrend. This creates a sloping line. For a bullish trend, the slope is positive or moving higher. For a bearish trend, the slope of the line is negative and moving down. There is another type of line that I draw on charts that does not have a slope like a normal trend line. I call these "remembered lines." A remembered line is a horizontal line (or narrow area) that connects highs to highs, lows to lows, or highs to lows.

I find that the market will "remember" certain prices and use those levels as a point of deflection when approached again. They can form during consolidation periods when the market is not sure of the directional move it wants to make. They can also be old lows or highs from years gone past that are remembered, especially by those traders who search for low-risk trading clues from the past chart history.

When the market consolidates in a nontrending range, it will often consolidate around a remembered price or area. The price usually is started after a high or low is made and a correction ensues. Subsequently, when the market returns to the area, traders will look to initiate a new trade or take profits against the level. If the level holds, a remembered line can be drawn connecting the two points.

Typically, although the market may return to the price or area a number of times, the market tends to not trade in the area for long. Instead, it moves either higher or lower away from the remembered line (or contained area). Since the market is often consolidating (nontrending) during this time, and not sure of the trend direction it wants to go, the market price tends to move away from the remembered line, find support or resistance, and return back to the remembered line. Eventually, the market will break away from the area and trend either up or down.

In Figure 6.7, a high for the EURUSD was initially made at points 1 and 2. When the market rebounded at point 3, it found low-risk sellers against the borderline level. We know that successful traders will look to sell against borderline levels as risk is defined and limited. A remembered line can be drawn connecting the tops.

Then during the period between 4 and 12, the market goes through a number of instances where the price moves up to the remembered line and comes off. It tries the upside but also runs out of momentum. Finally, after

FIGURE 6.7 Remembered Price Area between 1.2660 and 1.2666

a move back down where the market decline stalls at the remembered line at points 13 and 14, the price pushes through and a momentum move to the downside ensues.

The breaks away from remembered lines (at 3, 12, and 14) are quick bursts that act like a springboard (a sharp quick move). At 3, the market was coming off a pretty quick but volatile leg up from the lows. When the "remembered price" area was reached, sellers emerged. At 12, the price was at the end of an up-and-down range where the market tested the downside, then the upside. When support held at 12, the buyers emerged and the price bounced sharply higher.

Finally, at 13 and 14, the market tried going higher off the remembered line, but failed to gather upside momentum after similar 20-pip moves. When the market failed on the second move up, the conditions were ready for a smart and quick move lower. Smart traders watch these ebbs and flows closely while the market is consolidating and will use the remembered price or area as the bullish or bearish bias borderline. When it breaks through, they expect a sharp move and react.

Figure 6.8 shows the price action after the fall below the 1.2660 level. The trend move led to a 110-pip move lower from 1.2660 to 1.2550. Remembered lines give valuable trading clues.

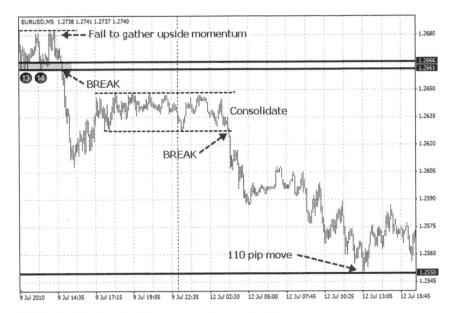

FIGURE 6.8 Break of Remembered Line at 1.2660

How They Fit in the Toolbox   Do trend lines define trends? Yes. An upward sloping trend line defines a bullish uptrend, while a downward sloping trend line defines a bearish trend. Do trend lines define risk? Yes. If the price moves below a trend line, the bias turns from positive or bullish to negative or bearish. Traders should look to exit positions when the bias is reversed. Therefore, trend lines define risk. Are trend lines an unambiguous trading tool? Yes. Price above trend line = bullish. Price below trend line = bearish. There is nothing ambiguous about the trader's bias using trend lines.

Remembered lines are an important tool because they do not necessarily define an uptrend or a downtrend. In fact, they tend to define a nontrend. However, knowing a market is nontrending is often more important than knowing a market is in a trending phase. I will explain this more in Chapter 8 when I look more closely at the use of trend lines and remembered lines.

Fibonacci Retracements

In recent decades, we have had one-word-named celebrities including Prince, Madonna, Sting, and even Pele. In the end of the twelfth and beginning of the thirteenth centuries there was an Italian mathematician who is known to all traders as simply Fibonacci. Fibonacci (also known as Leonardo Pisano Bogolio, Leonardo of Pisa, Leonardo Pisano, Leonardo Bonacci, and Leonardo Fibonaci) devised a sequence of numbers used to estimate how a population of rabbits multiplied. The sequence, which has also been applied in other scientific disciplines, has been adopted for use by the financial markets.

In Chapter 9, I will discuss in more detail the sequence of numbers and the importance, but for now I will simply say that by following the Fibonacci sequence of numbers, financial market technicians calculate retracement percentages. The use and acceptance of these percentages by traders helped make Fibonacci retracements an important tool for measuring market corrections.

The percentages used most by the market are 38.2, 50, and 61.8. These percentages are applied to any significant trend that extends from a low to high or high to low. For example, if a low-to-high range extends 100 pips and then tops out, the 38.2 percent retracement would round to 38 pips from the high. The 50 percent Fibonacci retracement would be 50 pips from the high and the 61.8 pips would be rounded to 62 pips from the high. Traders measure those levels from the extreme and anticipate corrections that should pause or stop at those levels.

If you trade, even for a short period of time, or take a look at any chart, what you will immediately notice is the market's movements are a series of ups and downs. Sometimes the ups and downs are more or less equal to each other. That is, the market makes its way from one level to a higher level via a series of smaller intermediate steps higher, and then makes its way back down to the low level, through a series of smaller intermediate steps lower. This is a sideways nontrending market. A range-bound market.

A trending market will also have a series of steps, but the steps will be directional with larger steps followed by smaller corrective steps. Within the larger steps will tend to be the same pattern for what is an intermediate trend.

What They Do   Fibonacci retracements are ways for traders to anticipate and measure a correction in a trending market. Since they are also static lines on a graph, they also are very helpful in giving traders borderline levels where they can execute low-risk trades. Traders can get on a trend by trading against a Fibonacci correction level. They can also do it with a defined risk.

Fibonacci retracements can also be used to trade the corrections or counter trends. To do this, another tool, like a moving average or trend line in conjunction with the Fibonacci, is often used. I will outline this idea in more detail later in the book. I like to think of Fibonacci retracements as a tool that allows traders to stay in rhythm with the market, and in

FIGURE 6.9 Fibonacci Retracements Give Corrective Targets for Traders

particular, with a trending market. They help traders to attack trends with added confidence. However, they also give a definable bullish or bearish bias and define risk, and as a result are also an unambiguous trading tool.

Chapter 9 will take a closer look at the use of the Fibonacci retracements. For now, I will provide an example of the use of this important trading tool and discuss why it qualifies as one of my three trading tools.

An Example   In Figure 6.9, the market starts a trend move higher. The trend is characterized by a number of up candles or bars, interspersed with a smaller number of down candles or bars. The direction is clearly higher and the price move takes the price from 1.2045 to 1.2298, or 253 pips.

After the high is reached, a correction begins. There are three down bars that start the correction, giving the trader a clue that a top is in place. At this point, a trader can use the tools available in most charting software to draw the Fibonacci retracement levels. Since the trend is bullish, applying a Fibonacci retracement off the move from the low at 1.2045 to the high at 1.2298 is in order. The three horizontal lines that cross through the middle of the chart represent the 38.2, 50, and 61.8 percent Fibonacci retracement levels. They are the shaded areas in the chart and come in at 1.2201, 1.2172, and 1.2142 respectively.

On the corrective move to the downside in the chart, the price stalls at the 38.2 percent retracement level at 1.2201. This level, like a moving average or trend line, is a borderline. Traders who sold near the top will take profits on shorts against the level. New longs are also likely to be established at the price. Remember the major trend is bullish; buying should be a priority. The risk for buyers is if the price were to move below the Fibonacci level. On a breach, traders will exit long positions and will anticipate the next down move to target the 50 percent retracement level.

In the example, the price consolidated at the 38.2 percent Fibonacci level at 1.2201, but then broke through the level. This led to a quick fall to the 50 percent Fibonacci area at the 1.2172 area (1.2166 was the actual low). When downward momentum slowed at the 50 percent borderline level, it gave traders the signal to reenter the market from the long or bullish side with a defined risk (a fall below the 1.2166 level). Support holds and the trend higher resumes with five successive up candles in the chart.

Figure 6.10 is a continuation of the example's trend move higher. The bullish price momentum led to a trend move to 1.2353. This move is represented by the shaded area in the chart during which the price surged 181 pips from 1.2172 to 1.2353.

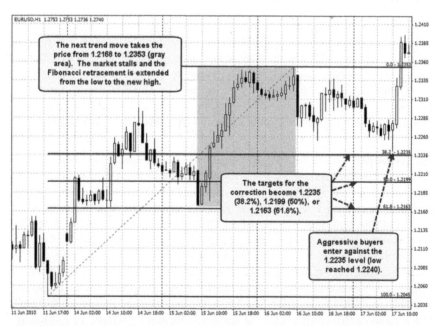

FIGURE 6.10 EURUSD Corrects to 38.2 Percent Fibonacci Retracement Level

At the high, the market consolidates, and a double top is formed. This is often a clue a top is in place. Traders can close long positions against the tops, or even sell against the level, anticipating a corrective move lower. Risk is a new high above 1.2353. The Fibonacci retracement lines can be extended up to the new high as shown in the chart (from the low at 1.2045 to the high at 1.2353). The three new Fibonacci lines that dissect the chart now come in at 1.2235, 1.2199, and 1.2163 respectively. These levels become targets for the corrective move lower. The market corrects down and finds buyers against the 38.2 percent retracement level at 1.2235. The borderline level holds and allows the trend following bulls to reenter the market once again. The trend higher is reestablished.

How They Fit in the Toolbox   What the example illustrates is the use of Fibonacci Retracement levels as another borderline that can be used to target or to trade against. On a trend-type move, if a top or bottom is formed, I will immediately apply a Fibonacci to the bullish or bearish move and will target corrective moves. If I am confident in the extreme (i.e., a double top), I can even trade against the trend, with defined risk being the extreme. When the Fibonacci level is reached like the 38.2 percent retracement line, I use the level as a borderline to trade against much in the same way I would use a moving average or a trend line. On one side of a Fibonacci line the bias is bullish; on the other it is bearish.

This borderline characteristic of Fibonacci lines also defines risk for traders—another requirement for our trading tools. For example, if a trader buys against the 38.2 percent Fibonacci retracement level, the stop would be if the price fell below the calculated level. If the trader sells against the Fibonacci level, the stop would be if the price moved above the level. Risk is defined. With risk defined, fear is lessened.

Do Fibonacci levels help define trends? Better question: How can retracements help define trends if they typically run counter to a trend?

What I like to tell traders is that retracements are actually an integral part of a trend. The reason is that markets do not trend in a straight line. Successful traders are aware of the corrections and can use Fibonacci retracements for clues as to the strength of a trend. They also use them to enter a trend or add to a position on a trend. Some even use them to trade countertrends for even more profit potential. Countertrends can run hundreds of pips and there are ways to anticipate them just like trends. Chapter 9 will show what to look for and when.

For example, if a market reaches an extreme and reverses the trend, traders assume the correction will at the least reach the 38.2 percent Fibonacci retracement level. If the correction stops or falls short of the 38.2 percent Fibonacci retracement level, it represents a shallow correction and is a clue that the major trend is likely to resume. Traders can be aggressive on a move through the old extreme and anticipate a new trend move.

Moreover, traders who may have missed the start of the trend will look at the Fibonacci retracements as an opportunity to get on the trend during these corrective phases. Using the retracement levels allows them to define their risk and as a result, be more comfortable and less fearful of their trade location. Successful traders will be patient and wait for the corrections to enter a trend rather than force the position without a clearly defined risk.

What is important for a retail trader to realize is that retracements are often where inexperienced traders start to trade against the trend and where losses start to mount. Remember, most money is lost by retail traders trading against the trend. Retracements often kick-start that process.

As a result, be aware that retracements are indeed an integral part of a trend. They need to be recognized, defined, and measured, and if this is done they provide additional insight needed to attack currency trends.

In Chapter 9, I will take a closer look at the Fibonacci retracements and outline in greater detail the ways traders can use this most important trading tool.

IF I HAD A HAMMER

Price alone is like an old hammer with a dry wooden handle. It is not an ideal trading tool, but perhaps a way to get your account injured. Successful traders need to take that price and use a trading tool—and an effective tool—that will define trends, define risk, and give an unambiguous trading decision that keeps fear to a minimum. I have narrowed the list down to three: moving averages, trend lines (or remembered lines), and Fibonacci retracements. There is no need for more or any other. In fact, more are likely to add a layer of uncertainty, and with it fear, to your trading. Master these three simple tools and understand the clues they give each and every day, and you will have a hammer that can be used to build whatever structure is in your dreams.

Tools and Strategies

T he foundation for trading trends needs to be developed and understood in order to trade a trend. In Part I, I laid the foundation for success for a trader who is focused on attacking trends. This all needs to happen before a trader can properly analyze or execute a trade. Develop the foundation and you will be a better trader.

Part II of the book will show how to attack currency trends that allow traders to make the most money with the least amount of risk. It will introduce in detail the tools needed to trade trends effectively. The tools will be used to help anticipate trends, define risk, get on trends, stay on trends, control fear, and exit trends. You will continue to connect the dots that allow for trading success. All strategies outlined in Part II will focus on the foundation developed in Part I. There will be no stray concepts or ideas. It is all about trends, risk, and fear.

Chapter 7 focuses on the moving averages. I explain which moving averages I use, why, and the special clues that they give to help traders anticipate the currency trends. I also introduce the chart time periods I use in my analysis. In Chapter 8, I delve further into trend lines and remembered lines and give examples of the key patterns I look for and what those patterns imply with regard to anticipating and trading trends with more success. In Chapter 9, the focus is on Fibonacci retracements. I go through the derivation, how the levels are set and how the retracements are used within a trend trade or trend correction. Traders need to realize that trends that go one way can reverse and go the other way. Fibonacci retracements allow traders to follow and even trade the countertrend moves (that may transition into a trend).

In Chapters 10 and 11, I look at a specific trend move in the EURUSD that will act as the book's benchmark example on how to attack currency trends. All trend moves have certain similarities that traders can follow as the trend gets started and transitions from leg to leg to the eventual exit. Throughout the example, I apply the clues from three trading tools together along with the three chart time periods (five-minute, hourly, and daily). I show with clearly defined charts how a trader can anticipate a trend, define risk, enter a trade, and then manage the trend trade from start to exit.

Success in trading, as in any business, is about having a mission, having a game plan, following rules, and executing when the risk is controlled, understood, and accepted. It is also about using the proper tools of the trade that will show you how to trade a trend effectively and successfully.

In Part II, you'll learn exactly *how* to attack the currency trends. Are you ready?

CHAPTER 7

Moving Averages

*An object continues in a state of rest, or in a state
of motion at a constant speed along a straight line,
unless compelled to change that state by a net force.*
                                        —Sir Isaac Newton

N ewton's law of inertia is something that most people should know.
I absolutely was not a science guy in high school or college (I was
more of a jock), but Newton's First Law was something that stuck
with me. The law made sense to me. It could be demonstrated. A ball on a
table was not going to move unless I pushed it, blew on it, swatted at it—did
something to it. You exert a force on it, and it moves. The "state of motion"
part was a bit more difficult to get my arms around. After all, if I put a
ball in motion, it would eventually stop rolling. Of course, the stopping was
because of friction. However, since I could not see friction, I had a more
difficult time comprehending what that meant. I learned that just because
you do not see something does not mean you cannot imagine what it should
do. When I think of the movement—or lack of movement—of the currency
market, I think of Newton's law. Maybe Physics class in high school had
some relevance in my life after all.

I have a trading law, which is my cornerstone for anticipating a currency trend. That law states: "There are two types of markets: trending
and nontrending. A nontrending market transitions into trending market.
A trending market transitions into nontrending market."

That sounds a little like Newton's First Law. In financial market terms,
the law could be rewritten as: "A nontrending market will continue to
not trend until it is acted upon by an unbalanced net force." Conversely,

"A trending market will stay trending until it is acted upon by an unbalanced net force."

I imagine when Newton first explained the First Law to his fellow scientists, they collectively said "That makes sense. We know that. How dumb do you think we are?" When I tell traders that nontrending markets transition into trending markets and trending markets transition into nontrending markets, I imagine many traders might say the same thing.

Yet so many traders break the law. They don't recognize that nontrending transitions to trending. I hear things like "The market is range bound" or "I think the market will stay contained," or how about the old, "The summer doldrums will keep the market under wraps."

For me, a nontrending market is like a spring coiling. That coil gets tighter and tighter, and eventually it will explode. I imagine you can say a net force puts the market into motion. It can be something obvious like an economic release, a comment from a central banker, oil or gold going up or down, a natural disaster, a banking crisis, the stock market rallying or falling. Sometimes it is not so obvious. That is, it can simply be the price breaking through a key technical level. I see it happen all the time, if not daily. Of course, the newspapers will give a fundamental reason, but in my mind, an unbalanced number of buyers overwhelmed the sellers.

When the market is nontrending I feel like dressing—figuratively, at least—in my Sunday best. I want to look good because a big old-fashioned profitable trending move either up or down is likely to happen. I may not know which way the market price may trend; however, I do start to anticipate a move higher or lower. I also look for the clues from the tools I use.

This chapter will focus exclusively on the power of a simple trading tool—moving averages (MAs)—and how it can be used to attack currency trends. Moving averages, combined with the price, give a trader clues for the directional bias for a potential trending market in motion.

WHAT IS A MOVING AVERAGE?

In Chapter 6, I outlined the process for calculating a moving average. The calculation defines a moving average level. However, what exactly is a moving average? Let's start by looking at the two words that make up the term.

A moving average is first and foremost *moving*, or in motion. The calculated values that make up a moving average line add a new value after each incremental timed bar. That new value is either greater than, less than, or equal to the previous calculated value.

The first possibility is that the new moving average value for the new bar is greater than the previous bar's value, thus the slope of the moving average line is positive. If the slope, movement, or motion is positive or going up, this can give an idea of the trend. The trend *may* be bullish.

The second possibility is that the new moving average value for the new bar is less than the previous bar's value, thus the slope of the moving average line is negative or going down. If the slope is negative or going down, the trend *may* be bearish.

The third possibility is that the moving average line is going sideways. That is, the calculated new value for the new bar remains the same. In this case, the movement or motion suggests the market is neither bullish nor bearish. It is more neutral or nontrending.

Whenever I can define a market as being nontrending, I get excited because my law says that "nontrending markets transition into trending markets." In Newton's terms, a nontrending market will remain nontrending until influenced by an outside net force. I will delve into this idea later in the chapter.

The other word that defines what a moving average is *average*. An average takes a defined number of values and calculates a single value that becomes a representative for that series.

If you had 100 bars on a chart and wanted to come up with one price that is worthy enough to represent those 100 bars, many traders would suggest the average of those 100 bars is that one price that is most worthy of that distinction. However, when the 101st bar is printed, the first bar drops out, the value of the 101st bar replaces it and the average changes. The new value becomes the representative of the last 100 bars. The average price moves.

Looking at each of the two words that make up the term "moving average" gives traders a firm understanding of what it represents. So what is a moving average? A moving average is a value that is in motion and is a representative of the market price over a specified time period.

HOW TO USE MOVING AVERAGES

We already learned in Chapter 6 that the price, when compared to the moving average, is really the most important relationship for traders to fully understand and follow. If the price is greater than the moving average—or the most representative price over a specified time period—the bias or trend is bullish. If the price is less than the moving average, the bias or trend is bearish.

This is different than the slope of the moving average being positive or negative. The slope of the moving average being upward or positive simply *implies* the market *may* be bullish. Since moving averages are a lagging indicator, the average can take a while to change course or

FIGURE 7.1 Price Moving below MA Line Is Most Important

direction. However, what is *most* important is if the current price is above or below the moving average price. That condition makes the bias unambiguously bullish or bearish.

For example, in Figure 7.1, the 100 bar MA, or solid line in the chart, is positively sloped. However, when the price moves below the moving average line at 1.2973, it turns the bias bearish. The market trends to the downside and bottoms at 1.2838.

The rules are in place for the moving average as a tool for our trading. The question now becomes: What moving average time period or periods should be used?

How Many and What Type

I use two different moving averages in my analysis and trading plan. The reason I use two is because I want one to be what I call the "trigger" moving average and the other to be what I call the "confirming" moving average:

- *The trigger moving average* determines the bullish or bearish bias. If the price goes above the trigger, the bias is bullish. It triggers a buy. If the price goes below the trigger, the bias is bearish. It triggers a sell.

- *The confirming moving average,* for lack of a better word, confirms the trading bias. If the price moves above the trigger, and subsequently the confirming MA, it confirms the bullish trend. If the price moves below the trigger MA, and below the confirming MA, it confirms the bearish trend.

Since the confirming moving average comes after the trigger, it makes that moving average a target for a trend-type move. It becomes an exit on the Bullish or Bearish Highway discussed in Chapter 5 that, if passed, should give the trader added confidence in the trend.

What happens if the price moves above the trigger MA, but cannot get through the confirming MA? That is, what if the price action cannot confirm the trend? If the price cannot get past the confirming MA, the market price will either go back below the trigger MA or remain in between the two moving averages, keeping the bullish bias intact, but the momentum limited. Eventually, the price will breach one of the moving average lines.

Obviously, if the price moves back below the trigger MA, the bias switches to bearish and the "If . . . Should" rule goes into effect. That is, "*If* the price moves above the trigger MA, the price *should* go higher. If it does not—that is, if the price moves lower and back below the trigger MA—get out." The trader should exit the bullish position.

If the price remains above the trigger MA but below the confirming MA, the bias remains positive but the price action is in effect stalled. I like to say the market is not ready to trend higher for the time being. To use a sports analogy, this specific situation is like trading between the goal posts, with the goal posts represented by the trigger (100 bar) MA and the confirming (200 bar) MA. I will discuss this condition, and what it is a prelude to, later in the chapter.

Using a trigger and confirming moving average provides me with the clues I need to enter a trend and confirm a trend move. It is then up to the market to keep that trend moving or in motion.

People often ask me, "Why not use three or four moving averages? Each could be used to confirm the next target." I only use two, because using more adds an additional level of complexity and uncertainty for the trader. Not only does it add more clutter to charts, but there is also the problem of slopes of each line being different, causing confusion. In addition, the short time-period moving averages can be too fast. The longer time periods can be too slow. The combination can make the averages more out of synch with each other rather than making them work in tandem with each other, like a two-period MA can do.

There are just too many filters to sift through from a visual and analysis standpoint. I have tried it. It does not work. It does nothing but increase uncertainty. With increased uncertainty fear is increased. The game plan is to keep fear to a minimum—not add to it.

Two moving averages are simple. They conform to Rule 1: Keep It Simple to be Successful, or the K.I.S.S. principle. Using two MAs allows for one to be the trigger for a trade to be initiated. The other is the confidence booster for the trend-type move. There are plenty of other targets from the other tools I use (i.e., trend lines or remembered lines, and Fibonacci retracement levels). They all work together, and I will outline examples of how that happens over the next few chapters.

Using 100 and 200 Bar Simple Moving Averages

The next question is what moving averages to use. The two that work for me are the 100 and 200 bar simple moving averages.

As already mentioned, I have a tendency to take what is said on the business news channels with a grain of salt. I have already outlined how most commentary on television is focused on fundamentals. Fundamentals can be an ambiguous trading tool, and as a result, fundamentals can increase uncertainty and that increases fear.

Moreover, when experts do talk about markets on television, it is more often than not a blanket reference to unrealistic and shocking targets. This applies to currencies, gold and oil, and even the stock market or individual stock prices. The EURUSD going to parity, gold going to $2,000 or even $3,000 an ounce, and Google going to $1,000 per share are some of the shocking comments that have been bantered about in recent history. It is often based on some fundamental belief. It is rarely a level based on technical analysis or a chart.

What I have found, however, is that if technicals or charts are talked about on television, commentators will mention the 100 or 200 bar simple moving average. Often, it is an afterthought. Some commentators will scoff at the mention—they want to know the fundamental reason the market will move, and a 100 bar MA is not good enough reason for them (it is for me!).

Nevertheless, if a technical level is cited on television, it will most likely be because the 100 or 200 bar simple moving average is breached or being approached.

Why do I recommend these two moving averages? The best I can answer is that a great number of traders from around the globe follow those moving averages, and as a result, there tends to be a keen level of action at the levels. In addition, the smart or successful traders who tend to have the most influence on the market also believe in these moving averages for market bias clues. That is, they will base trading decisions around the levels.

Other reasons are that the two values are round numbers and easily remembered. They also get their share of exposure in other trading books, and they may be simpler to understand versus say Fibonacci values like the 18 bar or 34 bar MAs.

I find that given the volatility of the currency market, a slower moving average like the 100 or 200 bar MA keeps the trader involved without trading too often. Speed of a trigger is not sacrificed, however, since I will apply the moving averages to shorter period charts, specifically a five-minute bar chart. Finally, it is my belief that the market pays attention to simple concepts. The 100 and 200 bar simple moving averages are simple concepts for most traders to understand. It is my strong belief that it is always best to trade with the crowd—not against it.

For me, what is most important is not necessarily why the moving average time period makes sense, but what tends to happen around that moving average value. Successful traders base trading decisions around a level that they feel comfortable as a borderline. The 100 and 200 bar moving averages are two of those levels. As we have learned, if a level is a borderline, the market price tends to either hold that level or break through the level. This allows traders to quantify their risk. They know the bias is bullish if the price is above the 100 and/or 200 bar moving average, and bearish if the price is below the 100 and/or 200 moving average.

As a result, if they buy and the price goes below the 100 bar moving average, they take the loss and close the position. If the price rises, they know they likely have good trade location.

Since traders are able to quantify their risk, their fear is dispersed. Their risk is also limited. When risk is limited to a small amount, the potential exists to earn a multiple of the risk taken. As long as traders are consistent with their risk parameters and risk to reward ratios (i.e., trading near the borderline MA levels) when they lose, the loss will be limited and should be constant. When they win and the market does trend even for a modest move, the win is more likely to be a multiple of the loss.

I have found through my many years of trading experience in the currency market that the 100 and 200 bar MA attract activity. The market finds buyers/sellers against the levels. I like to think of the moving average lines as mirrors that either reflect the price back from whence it came or do the opposite—blast through the MA line, smashing the mirror in the process. Oftentimes, the price does not stay around the level. This further increases the value and importance of the two moving averages as tools for trading and anticipating trends.

Simple versus Exponential

The next question often asked is "Do I use the simple or exponential moving average?" As a review, or for those who do not know, the simple moving average will equally weight all values in the time period for the moving average. So if it is a 100 bar moving average, the closing value for each bar carries an equal weight of 1/100th.

Without getting into details on the calculation of an exponential moving average (EMA), this moving average will weight each value differently. The bars that are further away from the current bar have the lowest weight and influence on the EMA, while the more recent bars have the highest weight and the largest influence.

As a result, the exponential moving average will be quicker to change according to current market conditions. Sometimes that is a benefit. That is, the price crosses the 100 bar EMA first and continues to trend, breaking through the 100 bar SMA later in the trend. Sometimes it is not a benefit. The price breaks through the 100 bar EMA and reverses back down before reaching the 100 bar SMA.

What I have found is that the EMA is less known and perhaps less understood by the market. Saying it another way, "It is not simple." I can explain the math of a simple moving average to most people. I could not explain the math of an exponential moving average to that same sample of people. Some would not understand the calculations. They may understand the concept, but the math would not be simple. I want to trade with the larger herd, not the smaller herd.

The second reason I prefer the simple moving average is with regard to the speed of the EMA to the SMA. I like the pace of the 100 bar MA in the currency market. The currency market tends to have a level of volatility where having too fast a moving average will lead to more trades that get whipped around. This can occur during times the market is nontrending as well as in trending markets. Often, there will be healthy corrections in a trending market that fall below the 100 bar EMA, but don't make it through the 100 bar MA. Although it may be subjective, I "simply" prefer the moving average to be slower and feel most traders feel the same way.

Simple or exponential? Simple gets my vote.

TIME FRAMES FOR ANALYSIS

There are three different time frames that I look at when finding levels to initiate trades: the five-minute, the daily chart, and the hourly chart.

When I speak at seminars, the audience often wrongly assumes that the three periods represent short-term trading, medium-term trading, and longer-term trading time frames. That is, the five-minute chart is used for intraday trading, the hourly is for medium-term trades, and the daily is for long-term position trading. That may be true for some, but not for me. I look at the three for the same reason: to find the best low-risk trading levels or targets that have to be breached (or reached) to either start or maintain a trend-type move.

Nevertheless, I know traders who are strictly focused on the longer-term trends, and they focus solely on the daily or even weekly chart. They do not want to pay attention to the swings in the shorter-term intraday moves. They consider themselves longer-term investors and tend to hold positions for weeks at a time. So they act on those longer-term charts only.

There is another group of traders who will look solely at a more inter-mediate time period. Some like the four-hour chart. Others like the one-hour time period. This group of traders focuses purely on the hourly charts and might consider themselves a cross between an investor and a trader. A "trader" would be someone who does not plan to hold positions for an ex-tended period of time—over intraday to three days. An "investor" typically holds positions for a week or so, but rarely longer.

Finally, there are the strictly shorter-term traders who focus on charts like the five-minute or even the minute charts. These traders look to trade solely intra-day with durations lasting for minutes to hours and positions exited by the end of the trading day.

I do not focus on any one chart, but rather on all three. If I do not have a position, then my goal is find the borderlines that are most dominant for the day from any one of the charts. I want to find the price levels where I can enter a trade with a defined risk that I am comfortable with and have the realistic potential for a two to three times return on the position as a minimum. If it goes further, that's even better.

If I am already in a trade, I am looking for those price targets or exits on the Bullish or Bearish Highway that will keep me on the trend. In order to keep the car moving on a trending highway, the exits need to be reached and passed. If the exits cannot be passed, a consolidation period or a rever-sal of the trend may occur. Finally, if already in a trade, I am also looking for those points where the bias may be shifting from being bullish to being bearish or vice versa. These levels become my stop-loss levels. I am always concerned about my risk.

All these three levels (the entries, the targets on the trending highway, the trade exit levels) are borderlines. I am indifferent to which chart (the five-minute, the hourly, or the daily) the impetus for trade locations come from. However, what I do want to know is what price levels the traders in each respective bucket (short, medium, and long term) are focusing on.

If the five-minute traders are the ones who have a key borderline level to trade against that may exert the force to push the market up or down, then I want to know that level. If the traders who look at the hourly chart have a key borderline level to trade against today, I want to know that level. Finally, if the daily longer-term traders have a key borderline level to trade against, then I want to know that level too.

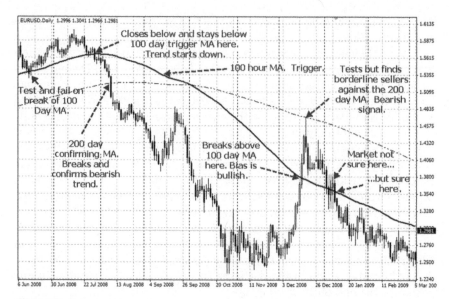

FIGURE 7.2   EURUSD on a Daily Chart

I am indifferent to which bucket of traders is going to control the action. However, I want to know what levels each are following—what simple things all are focusing on—and filter in my mind the most important borderline levels from the tools I and they are using.

The Daily Chart

As an example, in Figure 7.2, the daily chart would be the key chart to follow when the price was trading around the 100 day MA (solid line) or the 200 day MA (dashed line) as it was in June and July 2008. Even if I do not plan to hold positions for weeks on end like a longer-term trader would, I want to be aware when the price is trading around the 100 day moving average. That level (which is at 1.5664) is the most significant borderline level on that day.

NONTRENDING CLUE

A break and close below the key MA level is significant and likely to lead to a continuation of the downward trend—if broken.

If I were to focus solely on the daily chart, a realistic target on a break of the 100 day MA would be the 200 day confirming MA (the dashed line in Figure 7.2). That level is all the way down at 1.5224 or 440 pips away.

That potential move is significant. Even for an intraday trader, knowing the potential target is important. It should at the very least give the trader a bearish bias.

Of course, targeting the profit potential is important, but perhaps more important is defining the risk. I am always concerned about risk. So, what would the risk be if I were solely trading on this daily chart? As with all borderline trading decisions, using unambiguous trading tools like the 100 day MA, the risk is that the price will not stay below the moving average. If the price closes back above the 100 day MA, the trader should close the short position. If this were to happen, the bias would switch from bearish back to bullish.

In this example, that never happened. The price used the 100 day MA as a level to sell against and soon trended to, and through, the 200 day confirming MA eight trading days later. The trend to the downside was just beginning. The trigger was the move below the 100 day moving average.

In my daily commentary for FXDD on July 29, 2008, the day the 100 day MA was broken, the written remarks were simple. The chart was simple. The words rang true to the rules for the 100 day MA, and what I was paying attention to on that day. Figure 7.3 shows that post.

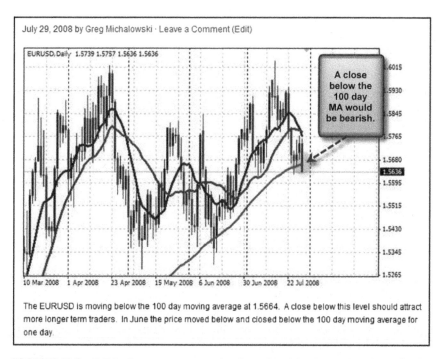

July 29, 2008 by Greg Michalowski · Leave a Comment (Edit)

EURUSD, Daily 1.5739 1.5757 1.5636 1.5636

A close below the 100 day MA would be bearish.

The EURUSD is moving below the 100 day moving average at 1.5664. A close below this level should attract more longer term traders. In June the price moved below and closed below the 100 day moving average for one day.

FIGURE 7.3 FXDD Commentary on the Day the EURUSD Broke through the 100 Day MA

July 29, 2008, was the last time the price traded 1.5664. The price bottomed at 1.2329 on October 28, 2008, for a total trend-type move of 3,335 pips in three months! Traders who were not aware of the daily chart may have missed this key signal that should have solidified a bearish bias—even for shorter-term intraday traders. Traders who recognized the importance of the daily moving average level set themselves up to anticipate a trend-type move to the downside, and, as always, the smart traders, the traders who are prepared and aware, reap the rewards of the knowledge.

Trends are directional. Trends are quick. The EURUSD showed all the characteristics of a market turning from bullish to bearish. The main clue was the price move below the 100 day MA.

Of course, along the way on the longer-term trend down for the EURUSD, there are corrective moves that can be substantial. In September, for example, there was a correction that went from 1.3900 to 1.4800. This is significant and can increase trader fear. Successful traders will therefore look to take advantage of these trend moves as well. Shorter-term chart periods like the hourly and five-minute charts provide clues for intermediate and shorter trends that keep traders in synch with the rhythm of the market.

The Hourly Chart

Oftentimes, the market is far away from key levels, like the 100 or 200 day MA, in a daily chart. In Figure 7.2, in September and October 2008, the price was a fair distance from the 100 day moving average. This is a characteristic of a trending market and moving averages. The price simply moves faster than the moving average when the market trends.

At some point, the market needs to consolidate or correct so that the moving averages can catch up with the price. However, that takes time—especially after a quick and sharp trend move. As a result, traders need to use shorter-term time periods to analyze the short-term swings in the market trends.

During times when the moving averages on the daily chart are not relevant, I look toward the hourly chart and apply the same 100 and 200 bar moving average rules. Like the daily chart, the market tends to be sensitive to the key moving average borderline levels on the hourly chart.

Figure 7.4 is an hourly chart of the EURUSD from June 30, 2010, to July 12, 2010. On July 1, toward the left side of the chart, the EURUSD finds resistance against the 100 hour moving average line near the 1.2271 level (solid line). The price breaks above and triggers a buy. The price moves sharply higher.

FIGURE 7.4 EURUSD Breaks the 100 Hour MA and Starts a Trend Move

On the next hourly bar after the break, the 100 hour MA line (the solid line in the chart) is tested. When willing low-risk buyers enter and support the price, this gives the bulls the needed confidence, and a buying momentum pushes the pair through the 200 hour moving average (the dashed line in the chart at 1.2294), confirming the trend. The risk for the buyers on the break above the 100 hour MA level is simply a move back below the key 1.2271 level plus a 5- to 20-pip volatility buffer (this is dependent on the traders' risk appetite). Risk is defined and limited.

If the market begins to trend, it tends to stay trending until it is influenced by an outside force. In this example, the trend takes the pair from 1.2271 to a high of 1.2612 in a little more than a day. At that point, the market consolidates for a few days as traders take profit, and trend fighters look to short the sharply higher levels. The corrective activity allows the 100 bar MA to catch up to the price.

On July 6, the price starts another leg to the upside that takes the price toward 1.2655. Another correction allows the 100 hour moving average to catch up on July 7. On that date the price got within 23 pips of the 100 hour moving average. When this happens, I like to prepare for a market decision. Either the trend will end and the price will move below the 100 bar MA or the market will find buyers against the MA line and another leg higher will begin. It's decision time.

In this example, buyers enter once again, keeping the trend intact, and the price makes the final push to the high of 1.2723 on July 9. When the price finally falls below the 100 hour MA on July 12, the bullish trend is over. The entire move took place in a span of seven trading days. The move totaled 354 pips. The risk was minimal.

The trend move off the hourly chart began in much the same way as the trend on the daily chart—with the breaking of the 100 hour MA (the trigger). This move was also confirmed by the break of the confirming 200 hour MA at 1.2294. From that point the trend was in motion.

The risk, at the trade's start, was minimal—maybe 20 pips. Buying at the 1.2275 to 1.2280 level above the 100 hour MA would warrant a stop if the price moved below the 1.2260 level. The resulting trend higher more than covered the risk. In fact, if the trade was covered on a break back below the 100 hour MA, the closing level would extend up to the 1.2625 level or 350 pips from entry. Low risk leads to the potential for high reward if the trader stays on the trend. The 100 and 200 hour MA define the trend.

The Five-Minute Chart

The third time period I analyze when looking for trading opportunities is the five-minute chart. Like the daily and the hourly, the same moving average rules apply.

In Figure 7.5 the five-minute chart for the EURUSD is shown for the same day the trend started in the hourly example from Figure 7.4. In the chart, the price is remaining below the 100 bar MA (solid line), which is

FIGURE 7.5 Moving Average Setup on the Five-Minute Chart

a similar setup to that of the hourly chart. The chart also shows the clear floor along the bottom (white circles 1 through 4). Like the hourly chart, the bias remains bearish or to the downside with the price being below the 100 bar MA. However, the failure to fall below the floor keeps the market contained and in a neutral, nontrending mode.

At the point marked with the black circle 5, the price moves above the 100 bar MA but fails to extend above the confirming 200 bar MA (dashed line). As a result, the price dips back down and tests the floor again at the white circle labeled 4. Support holds and the price bounces higher once again.

At this point there are a number of nontrending clues that are being developed:

- The 100 bar MA (solid MA line) is flattening and going sideways between the black circles 4 to 6.
- The 200 bar MA (dashed line) is also flattening.
- The 200 bar MA is converging on the 100 bar MA.

Nontrending markets transition into trending markets. The five-minute chart is giving traders clues that are similar to those received in the hourly chart. The difference is the trigger and confirming levels of the 100 and 200 bar moving averages are at levels that are much lower than the 1.2272 level where the 100 hour moving average was located (the 1.2272 level is at the horizontal solid line in Figure 7.5). In fact, the 100 bar MA on the five-minute chart is at 1.2215 and the 200 bar MA is at 1.2232—both well below the 1.2272 level.

When the 100 bar MA in the five-minute chart is broken at black circle 6, the trend higher starts at 1.2215. Traders anticipating the trend off this chart see the clues. They are anxious to buy. Can they define risk?

Looking at the chart, the risk on the trade can be as low as 1.2293 where the floor and last low is found. It can be higher, perhaps a break of 1.2300 (markets do find more buying and selling action against round numbers like 1.2300). At either point, the risk is defined and contained. If the trader can accept the risk, then fear is dispersed.

The subsequent surge higher above the key 100 and then 200 bar moving averages ultimately takes the price through the 100 hour MA line at 1.2272. This is significant. Why? By trading the five-minute chart and its clues from the MAs, the 100 *hour* MA becomes a target; an exit on the Bullish Highway. For those traders focused solely on the hourly chart, the level is only a trigger. This is why I want to watch both charts. I want to know what the shorter-term intraday traders are seeing. It may give me better trade location. I also want to know what the intermediate traders who follow the hourly chart moving averages are seeing. In this example, the hourly moving averages give me a target and the confidence in the trade and trend when they are broken. The trader who bought at the 1.2215 area, who anticipated a trend, who risked 20 pips, reaped a gain of 56 pips by the time the price is just moving through the 100 hour MA. A 3:1 ratio is nearly already achieved. The ability to hold that level on the subsequent correction down gives the buyers the confidence to continue to force the price higher. The price surges to the upside with little in the way of a meaningful correction. Now that is a low-risk trade, with a huge reward.

ANTICIPATING A TREND

If your local weatherman says it is likely to rain in the afternoon, you can anticipate rain and bring an umbrella and raincoat so you don't get drenched when you go on your scheduled sales meeting that afternoon.

When you go out for the meeting, although it might not be raining, clouds might be rolling in. You begin to anticipate the rain in your mind. So you bring your umbrella and sling your raincoat over your arm. Your work partner looks at the sky and says, "What rain?" and leaves without any protection.

While you make the walk to your customer's office 10 blocks away, you may notice the winds may pick up a bit. No rain yet, but you are prepared. Your partner is not concerned.

You attend your meeting, and it is a huge success. You leave and notice a light drizzle has begun. The temperature has dipped, the winds have intensified. You put on your coat and begin your walk back to the office. Your partner peers nervously at the sky. When the rain starts to fall harder, you open your umbrella. Your partner buys a newspaper and holds it over his head. The rain falls harder and the wind picks up; your partner ducks into a building to wait out the storm. His suit is wet, his hair is wet, and his newspaper is useless. You tell him you will see him back at the office.

As you get off the elevator, your boss is there when you arrive. You tell him of the successful customer meeting, and he invites you to have an early dinner with him to discuss the details. Forty minutes later, your work partner arrives at the building, his suit is soaked, his shoes are soaked, and he is soaked. You are long gone, having a drink with the boss at the bar.

You anticipated an event. You reaped the rewards of that anticipation.

Anticipation is also an important application for trading trends. The most successful traders are able to use tools to anticipate trends. It is not good enough for successful traders to simply buy after the price has already gone up (or after it is already starting to rain). The most successful traders anticipate a trend, and by doing so, they accomplish two important things.

- They are early position takers in the trend, which minimizes their risk.
- They are much more inclined to stay on the trend and reap the rewards.

If you are anticipating a trend, you will be focused on a breakout even when it is still nontrending and quiet. When it does break, you will look for the development of the trend (i.e., the storm) and be in a better position to stay on the trend. You won't be surprised and be left watching or trading against the trend.

Even during corrections that scare most traders out of their position, a trader who anticipates a trend stays on course and is not slowed down. Remember, the most money is made by trading and staying on the trend, but most traders are not able to stay on the trend—they are sidetracked—and, in fact, often find that they start to trade against the trend. The trend gains are needed to pay for the losses that occur when the market does not do what it is supposed to do. It is important to stay on the trend.

Figure 7.6 is the hourly chart showing the first leg up of the trend move higher. Prior to the move higher, the 100 and 200 hour moving averages were sloping down, but at a decreasing pace. Also of note is the price was staying below the moving average lines. In fact there were no *closing bars* above the 100 hour MA. This is bearish bias.

FIGURE 7.6 Clue for Nontrend to Trending: 100 Bar MA Is Flat

On June 30 there was a low at the 1.2193 price. The price moved up from there, trading briefly above the 100 hour MA but quickly failing. The bias remained down, and the price wandered back down to the 1.2193 low level. For seven hourly bars, the price pushed against that low level (the shaded area at the bottom of the chart), but the price could not break below the floor. Although the price is below the 100 hour MA, the failure to push through the floor is certainly not what the bears or traders who are short the EURUSD want to see.

The market is not doing what it *should* be doing. Putting it another way, the floor is a target; an exit on the Bearish Highway. Failure to break below the level or pass by the exit puts into question the bearish bias. The market is more neutral as bullish and bearish tendencies are in place.

The price does not break through the floor but instead moves back toward the 100 hour MA. At this time, the 100 hour MA line is flattening. For nine hours the moving average was virtually flat. There is no slope on the MA line.

NONTRENDING CLUE

When the 100 hour MA is flat, this is indicative of a nontrending market. Non-trending markets transition into trending markets. Anticipate a trend when the market is not trending.

At this point the clues for a trend move are building.

1. The price banged on the floor for seven hours but could not break. This is indicative of a market that is not ready to trend *lower* despite the fact the bias is down (below the 100 hour MA).

2. For the last 30 or so hours, the price has not been able to break above the 100 hour MA. This is indicative the market is not ready to trend *higher*.

3. The moving average is nonsloping/flat. When the average of the last 100 bars is going sideways and the price is near that moving average, it is indicative of a nontrending market.

4. The 200 hour MA (dashed line) is also starting to flatten out, which is also indicative of a nontrending market. It is also converging on the 100 bar MA, another key clue for a potential trend.

Traders who face this market development can confidently anticipate a trend. The question becomes, which way?

In the example, when the price pushes quickly above the 100 hour MA line at 1.2272 area, the bias switches to bullish. A trigger to buy is initiated. Since the clues are for a trending market and the lows have been rejected, trend traders are anxious to enter the market. A buy is executed. The risk is for a move below the 1.2255 to 1.2260 area. If the price goes below this level, the move above the 1.2272 level is a failure. Risk is defined and limited. Risk is accepted. Fear is dispersed. One final test of the 100 hour MA borderline is made and anxious buyers who are anticipating a trend enter. The next hourly bar moves sharply higher and the trend is in motion.

MANAGING A TREND

Traders who are long against the 100 hour moving average level at 1.2272 have great trade location. They know their risk. They do not have any pain from a loss. If they anticipated the trend, they are now getting excited about what may lie ahead. Now it is time to manage the trend.

It is at this point that the real trend traders feast. Figure 7.7 shows the trade's progression.

Initially, the break higher above the 100 hour and 200 hour MAs takes the price up to 1.2343 in two hours. Is that move enough? If we did not know the outcome of the trend at that time, would it be prudent for a trader

FIGURE 7.7 Anticipating a Trend

to take profit at that level? After all, if the risk was 15 to 20 pips at the start, a gain of 71 pips or so can be achieved with little risk, little fear. That is a good, if not great, risk-to-reward ratio. Or is it?

What we know is that a move that starts off a strong floor low, with a flat 100 hour MA line, a flat 200 hour MA, and the first close above the 100 and 200 hour MA for over a day, is saying "Anticipate a trend." Is 71 pips a trend-type move? It may be the end of this leg higher, but is it logical to think the trend is over? No. It is time to be *greedy* (Chapter 5, Rule 5). It is time to take that extra risk. It is time to attack the currency trend and manage the trend-type move, not cut it short.

A trend trader would look to first focus on a new stop-loss level. Where does the bias turn from bullish to bearish? It would be logical to move the stop loss from 1.2260 to the 200 hour MA at 1.2294. Why at the 200 hour MA? If the price moves below the 200 hour MA, it would switch the bias from bullish to bearish.

Of course, because the price has moved away from the lagging MA levels, the borderline stop level is farther away. As a result, the risk a trader has to take when a trend is beginning is often greater than at the beginning of the trade when the price is trading around the borderline level. Over time that will change, of course, as the MA starts to follow the price. Also, there are other tools that can be used to better define a stop other than the MA. We will develop those alternatives later. Nevertheless, 1.2294 is the proper stop-loss level.

In our example, a move from the 1.2343 initial high to the new 1.2294 stop level is a pretty good correction, and certainly more than the 20 or so pips risked at the beginning of the trade. However, the difference is that the trader is risking account profit. If stopped, the trader still has a 22-pip gain. It is not a loss. That is good.

So although a good chunk of the gain would be gone, the reward of a larger trend move is what is anticipated from the clues from the market. Trading trends requires risking some profit for the chance of a much greater gain. Traders have to take that risk to stay on the trends.

Another reason it is important to risk more on early corrections during a potential trend is because it is much more difficult to get back on a potential trend trade after taking profit. Traders who take profit early in a trend—in our example by selling at or near 1.2343—are much more inclined to sell a new trend move high, then to buy new highs on a break. Think about it: If the last trade you did was to sell in order to take profit, and you sold what you thought was a high, when the price goes higher, your mind says "sell" because it is a higher high. You should be buying instead because it is trending higher, but that trade is harder to do.

Traders who anticipate a trend will wait out the corrections—and especially that first move down. They will logically and calmly place a stop at 1.2294 and wait with little fear. A profit of 22 pips is the worst-case scenario. A break above the high and continuation of the trend is the best-case scenario.

What happens? The market corrects from 1.2343 down to 1.2314, but well above the 200 hour MA stop at the 1.2294 level. The 29-pip decline likely attracted some new shorts. These shorts were accustomed to the narrow range and were not anticipating a trend. Sellers also included those who were long and were happy with their gain, so they took profit. They too did not anticipate a trend.

That is good for those who do anticipate trends and is healthy for trends in general. Those traders who are selling will be the ones who will trade against the trend as it develops and be forced to cover when the market rallies higher and higher and higher. They will be the ones who cannot believe the strength of the trend, who will focus on the ambiguous tools like oscillators or perhaps even fundamentals, and will continue to try and sell. They also will be part of the outside net force that will cover after new buyers keep pushing the price to new highs. The combination of short covering and new trend buyers causes trends to be fast and directional.

In Figure 7.7, the market trends sharply higher over the next four hours to a high of 1.2485 (a 213-pip gain). One bar down and the trend moves to the high at 1.2540 (268-pip gain), where the trend starts to show signs of stalling with four lower hourly bars. Trends transition into nontrends. For 16 hours the market price moves sideways.

Risking 20 pips to make 200-plus pips. Anticipating the trend. Managing the profit. Staying on the trend. This is what attacking currency trends is all about. The entire trend move received the influence of an outside unbalanced force initiated by the clues from the 100 and 200 hour moving averages. Those clues gave traders a reason to buy, and once the motion was started, it continued until that time when the friction from the market slowed it down.

MANAGING PROFITS

As the market trends higher, traders should manage the profit by moving the stop higher. Since there is a reason to get into a trade, there also should be a reason to get out of a trade. Traders should look for that borderline that turns a bias from bullish to bearish.

On the hourly chart (Figure 7.7), I moved the stop from below the 100 hour MA up to the 200 hour MA early in the trend's life. At the end of the trend move, I noted how the price had a number of hourly bars that had lower lows and highs. The moving averages on the hourly chart were still lagging well behind, and therefore had no relevance as a borderline or stop level for that trade. So what tools could be used?

FIGURE 7.8 Trending to Nontrending

The other tools I use, such as trend lines and Fibonacci retracements, are often used for stop-loss levels or targets and give borderline clues for exiting a trend trade. I will talk about them more in the next several chapters. What also can be used are the 100 and 200 bar MA lines on a five-minute chart. These moving averages from a five-minute chart are more closely tied to recent price action and therefore react more quickly to recent market moves. A 100 bar MA on a five-minute chart goes as far back as 500 minutes (8 hours and 20 minutes ago). A 100 bar MA on an hourly chart goes back 100 hours. Needless to say, the sensitivity in the 100 bar MA on the five-minute chart will be much quicker than the 100 hour MA on the hourly chart.

In Figure 7.8, the 100 bar MA on the five-minute chart initiated the trade, and after the trend started, the MA followed the price higher. As long as the price remained above the MA line, the bias remained bullish. After the price peaked at 1.2540, the trend higher slowed. The price consolidated and moved sideways. This allowed the 100 bar MA to catch up to the price. When the price moved below the 100 bar MA at 1.2513, there was a reason to exit the position. The bias turned from bullish to bearish.

The trend that started at 1.2215 on the five-minute chart and 1.2271 on the hourly chart ends at 1.2513 when the price goes below the 100 bar MA line on the five-minute chart for a gain of 298 pips. The car on the Bullish Highway ran out of gas. A sideways 100 bar MA on both the hourly and the five-minute charts, and confirmation from the 200 bar MA, got the bullish trend going.

Earlier in the chapter I showed how a flat 100 bar MA was a way to anticipate a trend. The moving average is indicative of a nontrending market and nontrending markets transition into trending markets. In this section, I will introduce two other trade setups using moving averages. I call them "Three's a Crowd" and "Trading between the Goal Posts."

Three's a Crowd

In our examples, the 100 and 200 bar moving averages were near each other, but not necessarily equal to each other. In technical analysis, when two moving averages converge at the exact same price point, it is called a moving average crossover. A number of traders look for a crossover when the shorter-term moving average crosses over a longer-term MA and declare the market bullish if the cross is above or bearish if the cross is below.

Figure 7.9 shows a 100 and 200 hour MA bullish crossover. The crossover occurred at 1.2230. If I were to take this signal, where would the stop or risk level be set? Off the moving averages where the signal is

FIGURE 7.9 Do Moving Average Crossovers Signal a Trend?

generated, the crossover would be way down at the 1.2077 price area. Is that the risk or stop loss? If so, it is too far away for me. I am not interested in risking 153 pips (1.2230 −1.2077 stop = 153 pips) on this bullish crossover at least.

Is there a crossover that will allow me to trade trends and keep risk to a minimum? Before exploring crossovers, I want to introduce an idiom.

Idiom is defined at www.dictionary.com as a "Group of words whose meaning cannot be predicted from the meanings of the constituent words." An example of an idiom is "It is raining cats and dogs."

There is another common idiom that says "Two's company, three's a crowd." This idiom is intended to refer to people. I like to think that it has particular relevance for a romantic couple. If two people are on a date, a third person is simply not welcome. That third person needs to go away. Is it really a crowd? Not really, but idioms are not meant to be literal, they just need to be understood.

The "three's a crowd" idiom can be a good descriptive phrase for a trend setup that I look for in my chart analysis. It is the phrase I use to describe the situation when the 100 bar MA and the 200 bar MA converge with the market price. When the three key pieces converge, it is another clue the market is nontrending. When it happens, I like to think the market is completely balanced. It is a market that is at rest. A market at rest will stay at rest until it is influenced by an outside net force.

NONTRENDING CLUE

When the 100 bar MA and the 200 bar MA converge with the price, it is a "three's a crowd" situation. It is also indicative of a nontrending market. Nontrending markets transition into trending markets. Anticipate a trend when the market is nontrending.

When the "three's a crowd" sets up, I start to anticipate a currency trend move. If I can anticipate a trend, I am in position to attack.

In Figure 7.10, at the far left of the graph the 100 bar MA (solid line) for the EURUSD is already showing signs of nontrending. The moving average is going sideways for an extended time period. The price range around the MA is narrow (38 pips). The 200 bar MA (dashed line) is meanwhile still rising but approaching the 100 bar MA. At the 1.3282 level the two key MAs converge with the price, creating a "three's a crowd" trading clue. At this point, it is time to anticipate a trend type move either up or down.

Initially, the market price makes a break to the upside. Is it correct to be a buyer? Yes, it is. The market is nontrending and the "three's a crowd"

FIGURE 7.10 Three's a Crowd Is a Clue for a Trend Move

condition exists. However, the price is not able to move above the previous high and retreats below the two moving averages. This is not what the market *should* do (the "If . . . Should" rule), so the trade should be exited.

Even though the trade failed and a small loss may have occurred, the "three's a crowd" situation still exists, and a trend-type move should still be anticipated. When the price moves back below the 1.3382 level and moves down toward the floor at 1.3268, a short should be established. Even if a short was made on the way from 1.3282 to 1.3268, the risk is limited. Traders should have confidence in the move, especially after the failure on the last move higher. When the market breaks lower and stays lower, confidence in the trade is increased. The risk is if the price moves back above the MA lines at 1.3282. It is often wise to give a cushion of a few pips above the MA line. That is the stop area for the trade.

The price moves lower and consolidates, allowing for the 100 bar MA to catch up at the 1.3232 area. This is the first real test. At this time, I like to say the market has a decision to make, "Will it go higher above the MA or continue the trend with a new leg down?"

On the first real test of the 100 bar MA, I typically will often be more patient after a "three's a crowd" setup. Since I am anticipating a trend, I want to give the trend a chance to develop. A 50-pip move does not make a trend in the EURUSD. It is time to be greedy. I also realize that trends are partly fed by buyers on dips who do not anticipate a trend-type move.

As a result, I will tolerate a move above the 100 bar MA on the first test, and instead move the stop down to the 200 bar MA level and accept the consequences should the market reverse and cash me out. It may be hurtful to watch, but it is important to be patient when anticipating and attacking a currency trend.

In the example, the 100 bar MA is tested three separate times. However, when the MA holds, the market has only one way to go—down. Sellers enter against the MA and push the pair aggressively to the downside. This leg is where the trend move starts to pay off and the price reaches a bottom of 1.3134. Although there are signs the trend is over, the trend move is officially over at 1.3173 when the price moves above the 100 bar MA line. The risk is 15 pips while the reward is around 95 to 110 pips.

The setup from "three's a crowd" tends to anticipate trend-type moves in the other time-period charts I monitor. For example, the GBPUSD surged higher off the hourly chart after a "three's a crowd" setup.

In Figure 7.11, the "three's a crowd" occurred at 1.5246. In this instance, the chart formation never strayed from the bias. The 100 and 200 hour MA converged. The price touched the moving average lines. The price action at the start of the trade was also a clue for a potential trend move with the high-to-low range contained. Those who trade the GBPUSD as a currency pair know that it does not stay still for long. So there was really no reason to have a bearish bias and enough reasons to anticipate a trend move higher. The move higher, which lasted 10 to 13 days, covered anywhere

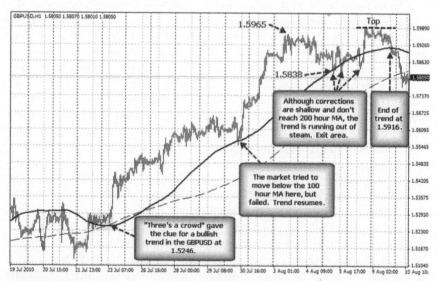

FIGURE 7.11 Three's a Crowd Off the Hourly Chart

from 592 pips (exit at 1.5838) to 670 pips (exit at 1.5916). There was one hourly bar that dipped below the 100 hour MA, and that bar did not close below the moving average line.

Not all currency trends over the course of a trading year or trading month or trading week are so profitable. Obviously, there are more trends similar to the one shown in the five-minute chart example. On the other extreme, there are also some trends that are even more profitable than the hourly example.

Traders who anticipate a trend, attack that trend, and stay on the trend can book a big gain like this example with very little risk. Remember "two's company, three's a crowd" and start booking those trend gains.

Trading between the Goal Posts

Most people have a visual of goal posts. Hockey has goal posts, football has goal posts, soccer has goal posts, rugby has goal posts, lacrosse has goal posts, field hockey has goal posts, and water polo has goal posts.

Trading currency also has goal posts. You may not have known it, but in my book and in my trading mind, trading certainly has goal posts. The goal posts in currency trading are represented by the 100 and 200 bar MAs.

In the last section, the "three's a crowd" setup included the 100 and 200 bar MAs. This occurred when the price and the 100 and 200 bar moving averages all converged.

What about when the 100 and 200 bar MAs are not so close and the price moves above (or below) the 100 bar MA, changing the bias from bearish to bullish (or bullish to bearish), but cannot get through the confirming 200 bar MA? What happens when the price breaks through the confirming 200 bar MA but then fails and crosses back over the 200 bar MA? I call these situations "trading between goal posts" because the price is literally between the two defining boundaries. One post is the 100 bar MA; the other is the 200 bar MA.

With "three's a crowd," the 100 and 200 bar MAs converged. This implies that the market is nontrending or consolidating. What does it mean when the 100 and 200 bar MAs are not close together and the price crosses through the 100 bar MA, reversing the bias?

When this dynamic happens, the market action prior to the move was likely trending in the opposite direction of the current directional move. We know that markets transition from trending to nontrending. What about when the market goes from an uptrend to a downtrend without nontrending? Eventually, the market will transition to nontrending, but it is possible to go from one trend to a trend the other way. When this dynamic happens, the moving averages remain a distance apart. They form the goal posts.

FIGURE 7.12 Trading between the Goal Posts

As a result, when the price breaks the 100 bar MA, the distance to confirm the trend by moving through the 200 bar MA can be a distance away. The farther away, the stronger the trend reversal needs to be. Sometimes, that distance becomes too big a challenge for the market given the current bias. As a result, a move below the confirming 200 bar MA runs out of momentum and instead of confirming the trend move, the price reverses back through the 200 bar MA. The market is just not ready to trend. It needs to consolidate first.

For example, in Figure 7.12 the USDCAD was trending higher toward the left portion of the chart. The 100 bar MA slope is moving higher, indicative of a bullish market. The 200 bar MA slope is also moving higher, but lagging, also indicative of a bullish market.

At 1.0675, the price tops and reverses lower. Instead of consolidating the trend, like what typically happens after a trend, the price quickly moves below the 100 hour MA at the 1.0612 level, triggering a sell. The price trends lower, like it should, and even falls below the 200 hour MA at the 1.0518 level on its way to a low at 1.0484. However, the move down from 1.0675 to 1.0484, or 191 pips, runs out of momentum, and the price rebounds back above the 200 hour MA and the break fails. The price moves between the goal posts—between the 100 and 200 bar MAs. The market action is saying, "We've gone too far too fast."

When the market crosses back above 200 bar MA and moves back between the goal posts, the short position in the example should be closed.

Traders start to use the 200 hour MA as support. A move back to the 100 bar MA—the other goal post—becomes a target. In addition, the market has two triggers now. One is a break back above the 100 hour MA. The second option is a fresh break below the 200 hour MA. A break of either goal post should lead to a trend move in the direction of the break.

In the example, the price does move up to test the 100 hour MA at 1.0605. This is a selling opportunity, and low risk sellers enter and push the market back down. The 200 hour MA is broken once again at 1.0534. This time the market is ready to trend, and the market moves sharply lower.

Trading between the goal posts is another formation that I look for to anticipate and attack currency trends using the clues from the 100 and 200 bar moving averages. The setup can be found in five-minute, hourly, or daily charts, and because of the distance between the two moving averages, can provide multiple trading opportunities while the price remains between the goal post as well as when the price finally makes the break through either of the moving averages.

THE PUSH THAT GETS THE MARKET GOING

By now, you've probably memorized our mission statement: To make the most money with the least amount of risk. And you know that the mission statement is fulfilled when we stick to our game plan: Trade the trends and keep fear to a minimum. Looking for the clues from the moving averages, such as a flat 100 bar MA, three's a crowd, and trading between the goal posts, allows traders to anticipate trends. If trends can be anticipated, traders can attack and stay on them.

Currency markets at rest will stay at rest until acted on by an unbalanced force. The clues from the moving averages provide the push that gets the markets going, if you know what to look for. Be aware. Be prepared and catch currency trends.

CHAPTER 8

Trend Lines and Remembered Lines

Most traders know about trend lines. However, a number of retail currency traders use them only as a secondary trading tool. After all, surely there are more "advanced" trading tools that are better. Let's face it: Trend lines aren't the most intellectual of trading tools. Connect the dots by drawing a straight line. Even a preschooler can do it, right?

The idea of advanced versus beginner trading strategies or tools tends to get me a bit perturbed. Phrases like "Let's have an advanced trading seminar to attract a higher clientele of traders" or "Let's focus the webinar on advanced trading tools and concepts" just make no sense to me. If I teach something that is advanced, it is not simply because it is advanced, but because it satisfies my mission statement.

There is a right way and a wrong way to approach and trade the currency market. Your approach to trading is determined by your mission (and in this book, the mission is defined as making the most money with the least risk). So-called advanced trading tools and sophisticated strategies are not a requirement for either. Too many retail traders complicate trading, which increases uncertainty and, with it, fear.

Trend lines are probably the simplest of trading tools but effective for traders who want to execute low-risk trades that often lead to a trend with defined risk. They are also beneficial in targeting profit levels after a trend-type move. Trend lines are visual, they are intuitive. I look at a chart and immediately draw the most obvious trend lines. I also *believe* in the most obvious lines. Why? Because the most obvious trend lines are the ones that the most traders from around the globe see, including the large institutional traders who have the muscle to push the price through a trend line, or who may cause the price to bounce off a trend line.

Since trend lines are also an unambiguous trading tool that gives a bullish bias if the price is above the line and a bearish bias if the price is below the line, they define risk. With risk defined, trader fear is automatically lessened. This chapter will outline the main trend line patterns that I use and discuss how they can help anticipate and attack currency trends.

BULLISH TREND LINES

The main utility for a trader using trend lines is to define a trend. If a trend line is drawn by connecting any two points on a chart and the slope is to the upside, this is indicative of a bullish trend line. If the price is above a bullish trend line, the bias is, well, bullish. I did not say it was difficult. That is not the point. The point is, "Is it effective?" Let's look at a typical example.

Figure 8.1 shows a bullish trend line. After the lows at points 1 and 2 are established, a bullish trend line can be drawn. The price moves steadily higher with higher highs and higher lows. Near the 1.3101 area, the trend begins to stall and the first major correction begins.

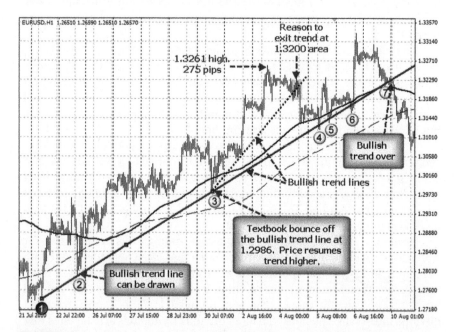

FIGURE 8.1 Bullish Trend Lines Lead the Way Higher and Define Risk

The subsequent correction sees the price fall below the 100 hour MA line (solid line in Figure 8.1). At this point, the bias is negative (below the 100 bar MA triggers a negative trading bias) and exiting any long position for a profit is appropriate. The breaking of the trend line (at 1.2986) becomes the next target to breach (at point 3) to keep the bearish bias.

What happens? Instead of bearish momentum pushing the price below the bullish trend line at point 3, buyers emerge against the line. Risk can be defined, and the risk is low. Traders are happy to buy against the trend line with a 10- to 15-pip stop below the line. If the price can move back above the 100 bar MA, the bias higher is confirmed. This is what happened, and the bullish trend to the upside is reestablished.

Anticipating Trends

After the trend line is tested at point 3 and the market bounces, is it appropriate for traders to *anticipate* another leg in the trend? Absolutely!

Whenever a trend line holds like it did in this example, be confident that the market saw what you saw. Expect that the market will be encouraged by the bullishness from that test. Ask yourself, "What is the worst that can happen?" The risk is that the price can go below the trend line and you book a small loss.

Alternatively, what is working for the trade?

- The trend is up.
- The price corrected from the first major leg up.
- The risk is very limited.
- The chance exists that the trend extends to new highs.

Reward clearly outweighs the risk. Successful traders focus on the low risk and the potential reward. They are also looking for those clues that the trend is continuing. The market moved off the trend line because the trend is bullish. Believe it.

On the next leg higher, another trend line can be drawn (dotted line in Figure 8.1). This line can act as a profit-taking borderline for the move higher. At the shaded area the price moves below the steeper bullish trend line at the 1.3200 area, and the trade can be exited with a profit of over 200 pips. The price falls with the main trend line coming back into focus as the next target.

Tiring of the Trend

At points 4, 5, and 6, the market starts to show some tiring of the trend. At each of these points the price dips below the trend line by 8 to 12 pips.

However, each time, momentum to the downside could not be sustained and the price rebounded back above the trend line. The momentum is starting the fade, but the bias remains bullish.

The dips below the trend lines at each point ignite the "If . . . Should" rule. That is, "*If* the price moves below the trend line, the price *should* go down." However, on each move below, the price did not develop any downward momentum. The price moved back above the trend line a few bars later. Traders who went short on the break looking for selling momentum should look to cover the position at a small loss. The market simply did not do what it should have done (i.e., go down).

Would it be appropriate to buy or go long when the price moves back above the trend line? Answer the following questions:

- Is the trend still up? Yes.
- When the price moves above the 100 hour MA, does that confirm the trend? It sure does.
- Can risk be defined and is it low? Yes, risk is a move back below the MA or trend line.

Even if buying is not done, what is certain is that there is no reason to sell or become bearish as long as the price is still comfortably above the trend line and the 100 bar MA. Eventually, a more meaningful break lower or bearish clue will occur where risk can be defined. However, until then listen to what the trend tools are saying.

The End of the Trend

The price continues higher and the peak is reached at 1.3333 (see Figure 8.2). From there the price starts its retreat back lower. When the price moves below the trend line and then the 100 hour MA (solid line), the bullish trend is officially over. In fact, the break is a selling opportunity (10–20 pips risk) with multiple reasons for a short:

- The trend line is broken.
- The 100 bar MA is broken.
- The 100 bar MA is going sideways and looking like it wants to slope down.
- The market has enjoyed a 600-pip rally and is ready for change.

Overall the trend from the low to the high lasted for 12 days. The trend line was in place by the second day. The trend line was tested five times. A total of seven hourly bars traded below the bullish trend line, and of those, only three had closing prices below the trend line. The total number of bars

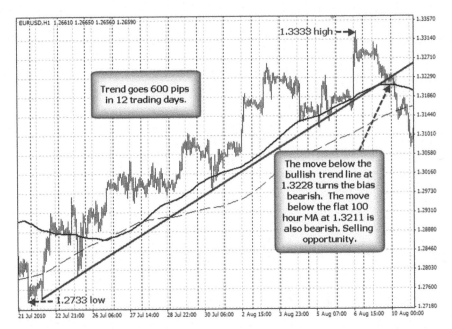

FIGURE 8.2 Bullish Move Ends and Bias Turns Bearish

in the trend was approximately 300 (97.6 percent of the bars were above the trend line).

Are trend lines too simple to ignore? Not if you are interested in making the most money with the least amount of risk.

BEARISH TREND LINES

Needless to say, the bearish trend line has the same dynamics as the bullish trend line, except in the opposite downward direction. In Figure 8.3, two trend lines are drawn. One comes off the high near point 1 on the chart. The second downward trend line starts at point 3.

In this example, I would like to outline not only the clues from the trend lines, but also the clues given by the 100 and 200 bar moving averages. By using the tools in combination, it helps confirm the trend and define the risks. They also can be used together to find profit-taking opportunities.

The trade and trend starts at point 1 at the 1.5558 level. Note how the 100 and 200 bar moving averages represented by the solid and dashed lines are converged with the price. This is the "three's a crowd" setup that was outlined in Chapter 7. As we learned, this formation is often a precursor to

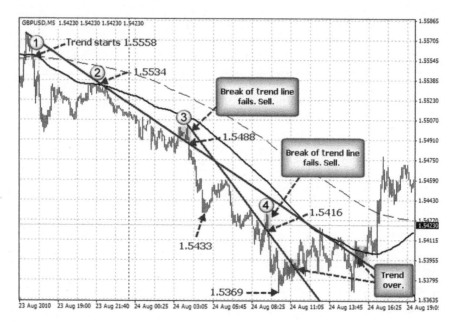

FIGURE 8.3 Bearish Trend Lines Follow the Downward Path

a trend move. When the price falls sharply below the two moving averages at point 1, the bias is bearish and to the downside. Traders should sell at the trigger area of 1.5558. The risk is a move above the 100 and 200 bar MA. A trader could put an initial stop 10 to 20 pips above the two moving average levels to account for any volatility at the outset.

The price does what it *should* do and moves lower and consolidates. The market gives a second sell opportunity at point 2 at the price of 1.5534. As discussed in previous chapters, traders who have the fear of success typically cover their shorts after a small profit and can push the market to test the 100 bar MA line (solid line). They make a small profit and likely cannot wait to tell all their friends on the message boards about their good fortune.

Meanwhile, while the quick profit traders buy at point 2 in Figure 8.3, the smart, trend-anticipating traders sell with great joy as the risk is low and defined and the trend is likely just starting. Both moving averages are now sloping down, the correction is testing the 100 bar MA, and the 200 bar MA at 1.5549 (dashed line) is not far above. The 200 bar MA would be the logical risk or next stop level (15 pips). The new stop is never approached as the 100 bar moving average line holds; the price moves lower and the trend down resumes.

After the moving average holds the correction at point 2, the bearish trend line can be drawn. That line—in conjunction with the moving averages—is now in control of the bearish trend. If the price remains below the trend line, the bias is down. If it stays below the 100 bar MA as well, the bias is down. This defines the trend and also defines the trader's risk or stop-loss levels along the way. In essence, the trader has two stop levels from the two tools.

With risk defined, the price continues its way lower. At point 3, the first major test of the trend occurs as the bearish trend line is broken. The trader has a decision to make. The price is above the trend line, turning the bearish bias to bullish. However, the price is still below the 100 bar MA at the 1.5509 price level. This keeps the bearish bias for the moving average.

With one tool switching to bullish and one still bearish, would it be acceptable to cover the short position when the price crosses above the trend line? The answer is yes, it would be acceptable, but it is not necessarily the right trade to do. A gain of 70 pips is a good gain. However, if any profit is taken, I would argue for only partial profit. There are several reasons for this trading judgment.

One, since the trend is fairly new (70 pips), and the clues at the start of the trade were that the market was nontrending and therefore likely to trend, taking the full profit is probably not warranted until the price moves above the 100 bar MA at the 1.5509 level.

The second reason is that in terms of risk, the worst-case scenario if nothing is covered is a profit of 49 pips (short at 1.5558 − stop at the 100 bar MA at 1.5509 = 49 pips). That is still a good profit and a multiple of the initial risk on the trade. It is not great, but it is good, and most importantly, it is a gain. Traders who get in the position to manage gains, and are not forced to manage losses, are ahead of the game.

However, the traders who are *most* successful know that trends can run longer than 70 pips. They also know that corrections can gather even more downside momentum if the price can test key levels, but hold the level and maintain a bearish bias.

Thinking of it another way, if you started your trading day at point 3 and saw the price testing the 100 bar MA, would you be more inclined to sell or buy at that point? I would be more inclined to sell against a stop above the 100 bar MA (risking 10 to 12 pips), and I think the smart successful traders would concur.

I want to trade trends, and so do the smart traders. Just hours before the trend started, the market was nontrending. Little money is typically made in that type of market. Traders are paid to make money. You as a retail trader have a mission to make the most money. Nontrending is not a good way to make the most money. The most money is made in trending markets.

The smart traders want the price to trend in a directional way. If they have a profit, can define their risk, and use part of that profit as seed money for a bigger profit, they will do it. They will attack currency trends and make profit happen when the time is right. No one knows for sure what is going to happen at point 3, or even point 4 in Figure 8.3, which is the same scenario but comes after the trend is more established. The price could have reversed to the upside, broken above the 100 bar MA, and stopped the trade out. That is trading. The market does not always do what it is supposed to do.

However, the more likely outcome is what actually happened. Risk was defined, the trend had started from a nontrend, the correction was modest, and the overall bias remained bearish. Attack the currency trends. Stay on the currency trends. Use the clues from the tools just like the smart, successful traders do. Everyone has the same opportunity to sell against a borderline like a trend line and moving average and benefit from a subsequent trend. It is a matter of recognizing those opportunities and taking advantage of the power of a trend.

In summary, the gain on a bearish trend move down, with little risk, should have been around 140 to 160 pips. There were a total of 12 bars that traded above the two trend lines (at point 3 and point 4). The price did not trade above the 100 bar MA until after the trend lines were broken and the market started the obvious consolidation phase. The bearish trend lines and the two MAs provided the clues for entering the trade and defining the risk, and provided the clear path lower for the pair to follow.

The next few sections will outline other sloping trend line patterns that can be used to stay on trends and anticipate trend moves. The chapter will end with a look at nonsloping trend lines I call remembered lines.

CHANNELS: HIGHWAYS TO RIDE THE TREND

A channel draws two parallel trend lines that connect lows to lows and highs to highs. The purpose is to define boundaries for a downtrend or an uptrend. I like to think of them as a highway with guardrails for the trend to follow. The market will use the lines to create a borderline to take profit or to initiate a trade along the trend. Since both lines are borderlines, they also define risk. With risk defined, fear is dispersed. The game plan of trading the trend and controlling fear is maintained.

In Figure 8.4 following the chart from left to right, the trend is down for the AUDUSD. A bottom trend line can be drawn between the white circles 1 and 2. With the line in place, a parallel line can be drawn that uses the

FIGURE 8.4 Bearish Trend Channel

black circle 1 as the anchor. The price corrects higher and the borderline is defined at black circle 2. The price holds the line and moves back lower. The trend remains between the guardrails.

Toward the bottom of the chart the price tries to break below the trend line (shaded areas) and through the guardrail. What should a currency trader looking to attack the trends be thinking when the market breaks the floor?

The trend is down, the pace of the decline is steady. The lines are nei-ther too steep nor too flat. A general rule that some use is if the slope of a trend line is 10 to 4 on a clock for a downtrend (or 8 to 2 for an uptrend), then that is just right. In this trend, it is 10 to 4 o'clock. The pace of decline is just right.

What traders need to always guard against is getting out of the trend or trading against the trend. At the shaded area below the bottom trend line, a trader who is short from higher levels should remain comfortable being short. The price is breaking the trend line floor. The price could accelerate to an even lower level on the break of the trend line. The reason is that "wrong-way traders" who trade against the trend have too much fear when the trend line is broken, and they liquidate their positions.

On the other side are the "right-way traders" who are short, making money, and are anxious to take some profit. The move from the black-circled 2 to the first shaded area was a relatively steep descent of around

FIGURE 8.5 Failed Breaks of the Channel Often Lead to Quick Corrections

60 pips in a little more than an hour's time. The trend has moved from a high of 0.8990 to 0.8832 in less than a day. The price fell below the 100 bar MA at around the 0.8840 level, which is where the first shorts were triggered. The bottom trend line is a borderline level. Taking profit or some profit is prudent. Nevertheless, when the price breaks the trend line, having some short is still the smart and preferred decision. There is no reason to not be anything but short below the bottom trend line. Being long would be trading against the trend.

However, what all traders should guard against is the failure on a break of a trend line or any borderline level. Figure 8.5 takes a closer look at the breaks. Note that in each instance, the price trades below the trend lines but only for a brief period. In the first instance, there are only two closing bars below the line before the price moves back above. The second instance also has two five-minute bar closes below the line before popping back within the confines of the channel.

When the price moves back above the trend line after failing on the break, the trend-following bearish traders with profits in their accounts reverse their bias to bullish and take profit or even buy for a quick rebound. The trend is somewhat mature. In addition, the failed break reestablishes the trend line support at the floor, and therefore the trader can define risk (i.e., if the price breaks the trend line again, then sell). Traders should anticipate—when this happens—the urge to take profit by the winners often leads to a bounceback rally. It may be temporary and limited, but it is a good opportunity to benefit from a quick move against the trend.

I will often look to buy or cover some of the short position. I tend not to be too greedy. On the bounce back, I will look for realistic targets and also look for the move to happen fairly quickly. The longer the rebound takes to develop, the more disinterested I become in trading against the trend.

In Figure 8.5, the first two failed breaks of the trend line had modest corrective moves of 30 pips once the price moved back within the channel. The third failed break saw the rebound move much quicker. It provided much more "you are right" feedback. In 25 minutes the price had rebounded from 0.8803 to 0.8867 or 64 pips (see Figure 8.5). The correction moved above the 100 bar MA, it moved above the upper trend line, and it stalled at the 200 bar MA.

Let's look at another example, this time a bullish channel.

An Example of Bullish Channels

Figure 8.6 shows a bullish trend channel. Notice that at the black circled 3 that the price moves above the channel guardrail and fails. This is the equivalent of the example in Figure 8.5. The subsequent move lower, against the trend, takes the price down from 1.2283 to 1.2166—a significant correction of 117 pips. At point 4, the price found resistance again at the upper guardrail for the channel and corrected down to test both the trend line and 100 hour MA at white circle 3. The subsequent move back higher was quick after that test of the trend line, and the 100 hour MA level held support. This is fully expected as risk is defined. Risk is limited. There are plenty of traders who see the line and will assume the limited risk to get on the trend.

The trading lesson is that channels provide a nice highway with guardrails to travel between. They provide both floors and ceilings. The goal is to stay on the trend and use the clues from the borderlines to execute low-risk trades. When a defined channel is in place, be on the lookout for failed breaks because they can either lead to an acceleration of the trend or provide clues for quick bouncebacks with defined risk. When risk can be defined, there are ways to profit even on moves against the trend. However, be sure to look for the rebounds to be quick. If not, remember to err on the side of trading with the trend because the most money is always made with the trend, while the most money is always lost trading against the trend.

FIGURE 8.6   Bullish Trend Channel

FLAGS AND PENNANTS

There are other line patterns that I will use to help attack a trend and stay on a trend. Classic technical analysis looks for flags and pennants as trend continuation patterns.

A flag is formed after a trend move higher or lower. We know that trends transition into nontrends, and it is during the nontrend period that a flag is formed. The characteristic of a flag is a parallel countertrend move. The countertrend should be shallow when compared to the initial trend move. Once the flag formation is broken and the trend resumes, traders will look to measure a target using the initial trend or flagpole.

Figure 8.7 shows a bullish flag being formed. In the example, the EURUSD moved up from a low of 1.1876 to a high of 1.2467 for a move of 591 pips. The price consolidated/corrected from 1.2467 to a low of 1.2151. A flag was formed with a shallow downward channel containing the bottom correction. The second move lower to the 1.2151 low provided a low-risk trading opportunity for traders. The reasons included the following:

- The channel support came in at the level.
- The bullish trend up from the low remained firmly intact.

FIGURE 8.7 Flags Can Lead to a Trend Move

- The market had corrected for seven trading days.
- Risk could be defined.
- Risk was limited.

Traders who bought near the flag's lower trend line low had that line defining the risk. Confirmation of the likely trend continuation would be on a break of the flag's top trend line (at 1.2356). It was time to anticipate a resumption of the currency trend, and that is what happened in the example.

Once the flag trend line has been broken, as it was on July 1 in Figure 8.7, technicians have a heuristic for measuring flag formation targets. The first thing to do is measure the distance from the low to the top of the flag (or flagpole). Once the bottom of the flag formation is determined, adding the distance of the initial trend move to the bottom of the flag gives the target measurement.

For example, in Figure 8.7, the initial trend move of 591 pips was added to the low of the flag at the 1.2151 level. The topside target of 1.2741 was reached 10 days from the low. Not a bad trend trade.

Of note in the example is that the trend continued much higher before correcting back down to the 1.2732 level. It is important to understand that just because a measured target is met, like the 1.2741 level, it is not a reason to start thinking that the trend is over. The market surge higher continued from 1.2741 all the way to the 1.3029 level, or 288 pips more. Selling at the measured target (at 1.2741) without a defined reason is trading against the trend. It is acceptable to measure a target, but be sure to let the trend develop until there is bearish reason to sell.

What is also important to realize is because there is a measured target, it does not automatically mean that the target will be met. Too many currency traders correctly uncover a flag formation, measure out a target, and stubbornly wait for it to be reached. When it does not happen, they ignore the countertrend clues and wonder why they book a big loss.

For this reason I will use tools like moving averages, Fibonacci retracements, trend lines, and remembered lines to map out the targets or exits along the way. If it ends up that the trade gets to the measured objective, all the better. If, however, the price was to fail and the bullish bias turned to bearish, I would exit the trade.

In this example, the clues from the formation signaled a trend-type move higher and indeed that is what the market provided. The total move higher from the bottom of the flag to the top encompassed a stellar 877 pips. The flag trend line support held like a charm, giving the smart traders a low-risk buying opportunity at the base of the flag near 1.2151. The risk was clearly defined. Could traders anticipate a trend-type move? Sure. A break of the top flag trend line would confirm the bullish bias. From there it was a matter of the market's continuing to give bullish clues from the hourly and the five-minute charts. Surely, there would have been instances when the price corrected in the shorter term and the bias may have turned bearish for a day or so. However, when the trend was reestablished, the market trended higher.

Overall, it took 14 days to cover the 877 pips, with five down days and nine up days. That is a trend I want to anticipate, catch, and stay on as long as possible.

FINDING THE GOLDEN TICKET

I can imagine that most retail traders might dismiss the notion of staying in the trend for 877 pips as not being realistic. Some common justifications for not being able to stay on the trend include:

- The risk during releases is too great.
- It's impossible to trade 24 hours a day.
- Not wanting to take weekend risk.

All have merit. I have a risk phobia myself. However, successful traders are able to see certain opportunities and are able to seize them when they

FIGURE 8.8 The Trend Move Higher Starts Innocently, Then Surges

arise. What is most valuable in catching and staying on any trend is trading near the borderlines and getting not just good, but great trade locations. Once that great trade location is had, it can be like having the golden ticket. It's the ticket that everyone wants, but you have; the ticket that will make or break the subsequent trend for you.

In the example, the initial surge higher occurred on July 1. It was on this day that the price broke the upper flag trend line that paved the way to the upside surge of 877 pips. It paved the way for the golden ticket.

What was that day like? Was there a big gap move (or moves) as a result of some news event that made the trade good on paper, but unrealistic in real life? To the contrary. In fact the day got off to a very sleepy start. Figure 8.8 shows the five-minute chart from that day. There were not any gaps from unexpected major news events.

However, there were a number of clues from the market that paved the way for the bullish surge higher.

Clue 1: *Nontrending market.* The market was in a narrow 51-pip trading range for the first 11 hours of the trading day (shaded area). If the day ended with a range of 51 pips, it would have been the narrowest trading range in years. An extension of the nontrending trading range could be anticipated. The extension could be to the upside or downside. It wasn't necessarily known until Clue 2.

Clue 2: The price moved from below the 100 bar MA to above after failing to make new lows and extending the downside. If a range extension is anticipated, the downside has failed. The trigger is to buy when the price goes above the 100 bar MA. Buy at 1.2215 with a 15- to 20-pip stop loss.

Clue 3: The price confirms the trend when it moves above the 200 bar MA at 1.2232. The high for the day is 1.2243. If a normal day is anticipated, a move above that level of 50 to 70 pips can be expected.

Clue 4: The price not only moves an additional 50 to 70 pips above the old high, making the day's range normal, but the price has no problem moving through the flag trend line level at 1.2356 (from Figure 8.7). This confirms additional bullish bias.

For the rest of the day, the market trends with very little in the way of correction, but more in the way of lost momentum. Finally, at the end of the day, the price moves below the 100 bar MA on this five-minute chart, and the trend line and the short-term bias turns bearish in the short term.

The gain for the 14 hours is 295 pips. The trade that got the ball rolling was a typical setup. The risk was normal, 20 or so pips. The subsequent trend was larger and faster than most. Is the 295 pips from the five-minute chart in Figure 8.8 comparable to the 877 pips from the daily chart in Figure 8.7? No, but it was the golden ticket that should have set up the next 12 days—as long as you traded with the trend, that is!

Anticipating Trend Moves

Pennant formations are another trend line formation that happen from time to time and give clues for a trend-type move in the currency market. The pennant is supposed to work just like a flag, except instead of parallel lines, a triangle forms. Like a flag, technicians will measure a target equal to the initial trend move (the flagpole). Although it is a target, I will always look at my other tools for clues when the trend ends.

Often a pennant will form after an event (i.e., economic release, interest rate decision, comment from central bank figure) that surprises the market. The formation allows for traders to jump on a trend with defined risk and often without event risk. As a result, fear—all traders' worst enemy—is much lower.

Figure 8.9 shows a bullish pennant formation in the USDJPY five-minute chart initially formed after a surprise economic release. The price moved sharply higher, creating the flagpole. I will rarely look to buy the initial reaction off a surprise event. Corrections can be brutal, and risk from the event is still working its way out of the market.

The flow of the market will almost always provide an opportunity to get into the trend-type move through the correction mechanism. There

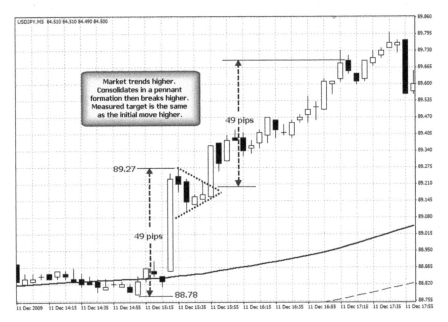

USDJPY,M5 84.510 84.510 84.490 84.500

Market trends higher.
Consolidates in a pennant
formation then breaks higher.
Measured target is the same
as the initial move higher.

49 pips

89.27

49 pips

88.78

FIGURE 8.9 Bullish Pennant Formation; Look for a Break and an Extension Higher

are usually traders who will take profit too early and allow risk-conscious traders—who avoid the extra event risk—to take advantage of the trend. Remember the goal is to make the most amount of money with the least amount of risk. If random event risk can be avoided, avoid it.

Defining Risk

Although support may be defined from the trend lines of a pennant, I will often look toward other support options to define risk. Applying a Fibonacci retracement or drawing a more common flag trend line are ways to more confidently define risk after a sharp directional move.

Figure 8.10 shows the Fibonacci retracement and the parallel flag trend line. These lines in aggregate give traders a more flexible risk area. When the market moves quickly like it did in the example, increased market volatility may require more wiggle room than what the pennant formation provides. It is why of all the formations, pennants happen much less often than flags. The market is excited about moving but it needs some room to move—even on the corrections.

By using the pennant, the flag, and the Fibonacci retracement lines, traders can hone in on the risk, especially after a sharp move higher that surprises the market. In the example, the risk/stop level was to the

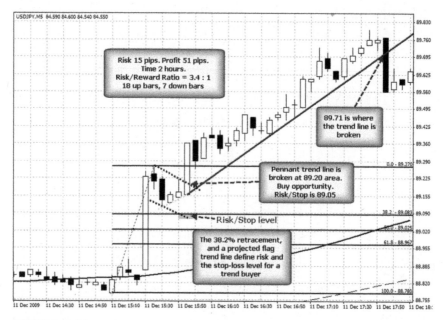

FIGURE 8.10 Defining Risk off a Sharp Move Using Pennants, Flags, and Retracements

89.05 level (see Figure 8.10). This is where the 38.2 percent retracement and the flag trend line could be drawn. The pennant lines remain, but I will tend to look toward the more flexible stop loss levels.

In the example (Figure 8.10), the price broke higher at the 89.18–20 area. The risk is defined to 89.05 or 13 to 15 pips. The subsequent rally experienced only 7 down bars and 18 up bars over the next two hours. The move took the price from 89.20 to a high of 89.80, or 60 pips, before correcting more substantially and falling below the clearly defined bullish trend line. The price broke the trend line at the 89.71 level, where the bias turns from bullish to bearish. This is a reason to exit the trade, and the profit should be taken.

The gain on the trade would total 51 pips. The risk was 15 pips, so the risk/reward ratio would be 3.4 to 1 (51/15 = 3.4). The pennant formation set up the trade, and the market trended.

Pennants and flags incorporate simple trend lines, but in the process they define risk and reduce fear. They also provide the clues that will allow traders to attack currency trends. The mission statement and game plan are achieved by trading the pennant and flag formations.

Let the market tell you what to do and when to do it, but above all, be aware and prepared to attack currency trends by using the simple lines that connect lows to lows and highs to highs.

REMEMBERED LINES

In Chapter 6, I introduced what I call remembered lines. I defined a remembered line as a horizontal line (or narrow area) that connects highs to highs, lows to lows, or highs to lows.

The important word in the definition is *horizontal.* A normal trend line connects highs to highs and lows to lows, but it is assumed that there is a slope to that line. Remembered lines tend to not have a slope, or if they do, the slope is negligible.

I call the lines remembered lines because they tend to be at levels that the market ... well ... remembers. It is a place the market visited before that may have reminded the market of a good time or even a bad time. It may be the price at which a trader who had a bad position got the corrective reprieve back to the breakeven level he desperately needed. It may be a price where a trader panicked and closed a losing position before having the price bounce back. Perhaps it was originally an old Fibonacci retracement level from the three months prior that the market bounced off, or the 100 bar MA on the five-minute chart from six months ago. It could just be a level that, after a sharp fall, found buyers and surged higher, or a price after a sharp rise that found sellers and plunged lower.

They are extremes. As a result, the next time the market revisits these levels, they often become obvious places to execute a trade with a stop below. In other words, the levels become borderlines that give a bullish bias above and a bearish bias below.

The more times that a remember line holds either as support or resistance, the more accepted it becomes as a borderline to trade against. Eventually, however, the price will break through the remembered line and support will become resistance (if a break lower) or resistance will become support (if a break higher). In other words, the floor becomes the ceiling or the ceiling becomes the floor.

When a market is nontrending in a range, remembered lines often become key support and resistance levels that the market uses as stepping stones. There may be multiple remembered lines within a larger range, and the price will bounce from one remembered line to the next. If price can get through that level, it will jump to the next line. It may then reverse and head back to the original remembered line above.

Eventually, the coiling of the energy within the nontrend will lead to a break away, a move away from the remembered lines. Often, there will be clues from the remembered lines that the nontrend is fading and a bias is developing. As such, remembered lines also tend to be launching points when the market does start to trend. Knowing and recognizing these levels can give traders clues for anticipating a trend. What we know is if a trader can anticipate a trend, he has a better chance to stay on a trend.

However remembered lines are used, they are points of support or resistance or both. As such, they become key borderlines that traders can use to define risk, control their fear, and even trade trends (even if the trends might be small). They also can be the gift that keeps on giving as they can work time and time again over a nontrending trading period. So be aware and look for remembered lines—then remember them.

Finding Remembered Lines

Finding remembered lines is sometimes like trying to see the trees through the forest. They do not always just pop out to the untrained eye.

When I look for remembered lines, however, a clue is to look for low or high prices that start a V-like or upside down V-like bounce higher or lower. These moves are actually mini trend-type moves and provide opportunities on a short-term basis. In Figure 8.11, looking at any one of the numbered or lettered points is the start of an up or down trend-type move (take some time; look at the points). The problem is the trends don't last long—a day or two—before they reverse and go the other way. When the market does this, even once, the next time it goes to that V price will often solicit a market reaction. The price can bounce off the level or perhaps move sharply through the level. That price has significance to the market, which remembers it.

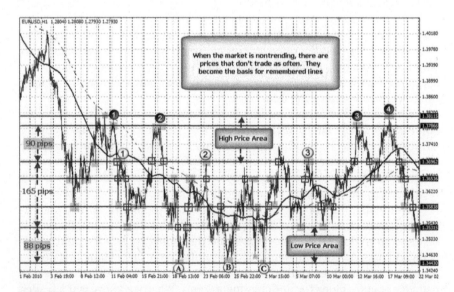

FIGURE 8.11 Remembered Lines Provide Low-Risk Clues for Trend-Like Moves

The main characteristic of a remembered line is that the price usually does not trade for long at the line. That is, the price is either going to find support or resistance at the level, or the price is going to zip right through the level. In Figure 8.11 if you were to follow from left to right along a remembered line, the shaded areas are levels where the price found support or resistance. The boxed areas are where the price moved through the remembered line without spending time there. Very few times the price trades for an extended period at the line itself (go ahead, take a look).

Now, if you were to focus on the numbered or lettered areas in the chart, follow the trend moves up or down that the price makes in each of the instances. For example, black circle 2 moves from the highest remembered line to the bottom of the middle range before correcting to a higher remembered line.

Traders who are able to isolate the lines can use the levels as borderlines with bullish above, bearish below. So following the trend from black circle 2, the price zips through three of the borderline remembered lines before bouncing. Since the price moved through the lines, it confirms the trend for the trader who is short. Stay on the trend as long as the targets are reached and passed. If the price stops at a remembered line, look for a reversal and get out.

Remembered Lines in Range-Bound Markets

The currency market will trend. Then the currency market will not trend. Sometimes it does both. In Figure 8.11 the EURUSD is in a nontrending market. From February 4 to March 22, 2010, the price traded mainly between 1.3443 and 1.3786 or 364 pips. The inside range where most of the trading took place was between 1.3531 and 1.3696 or 165 pips. In fact, only *two days*, February 4 and March 17, did not trade at some point between the 165-pip inside range. The extremes, which border the inside range, had as a high price area the 1.3696 to 1.3786 range (see Figure 8.11). The low price area extended from 1.3443 to 1.3531.

Looking at the chart by focusing on the high and low extremes shows the price action is symmetrical. There are two high extremes to the left (black circles 1 and 2), three lows in the middle (A, B, and C), and two high extremes to the right (black circles 3 and 4).

Admittedly, this is more coincidental than a pattern that normally forms, but is important to realize from the symmetry is the market's willingness to use remembered highs and lows as points of support or resistance. I like to think of them as points of reflection. That is, the price has a tendency to reflect off imaginary mirrors positioned at each extreme.

What is also noticeable is the middle section (the 165-pip low-to-high range) where the majority of the trading bars are found. There are clear remembered lines that I drew in at 1.3696 on top and 1.3532 on the bottom.

The reason these lines form is during a nontrending period the market or smart money needs something to define risk. It needs to create a borderline in a nontrending market that is different than the 100 or 200 bar MA. Lows and highs become those borderline levels.

Although I don't throw the moving averages out in their entirety during nontrending times like these, they do become less important. The market will still move away from them, but they can act differently than when in a trend move.

Notice that in Figure 8.11, when the price is still trending lower along the left half of the chart, the price still uses both the 100 and 200 hour MAs as borderline levels. However, toward the middle, the MA lines become less important. This is not a failure; it just is a symptom of a nontrending period. Similar to all three tools I use, remembered lines supplement moving averages, and moving averages supplement remembered lines. They all are borderlines that traders can lean against to trade.

Moving into a Larger Trend

Figure 8.12 is another example using a remembered line in a nontrending market. In this case, from left to right, the price corrects to point 1 at the 1.5079 area and rallies to 1.5226 (2). The price stalls and reverses back to the 1.5079 level (3). The 100 hour MA (solid MA line) is at the level as well, which gives two reasons why the level finds willing buyers. Risk is defined and risk is limited.

As early as this point the bottom remembered line can be drawn. The market bottomed at 1 and it bottomed at 3.

The market rallies off point 3, and less than a day later the price is testing the high at 1.5226 at point 4. Once that extreme holds, another remembered line can be drawn. The pattern continues with moves down to the 1.5079 and back up to 1.5226 at point 6. Talk about predictable!

By this point, the market seems more intent on not trending. Whether it does or not is not necessarily important. What is more important is there are now two remembered lines that are also borderlines that can be used to lean against for trading opportunities and defining risk. Eventually, one of the remembered lines will give way, and it is off the break that traders can anticipate a continuation of the trend.

In the example, at point 7 it looks as if the price is making a break higher. All indications point toward higher levels with three prior highs at the ceiling of 1.5226, and a shallow correction off the point 6 peak. The fourth time surely must be the charm! What happens, however, is that the

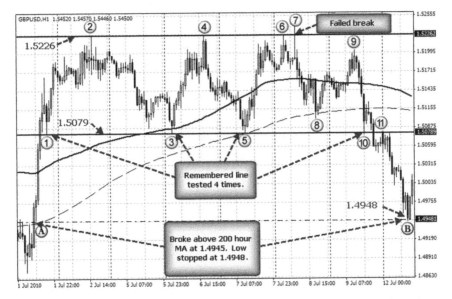

FIGURE 8.12 Remembered Lines and MAs Combine to Provide Trend Trading Clues

price extends briefly but fails. Traders are angry. The break did not gather upside momentum. They take their frustrations out by remembering the "If . . . Should" rule (the market did not do what it should do), and they sell the long and go short—pushing the price back down. The failure creates a low-risk selling opportunity. The subsequent move down stalls at the 200 hour MA at point 8 with another 100-pip gain from a low risk defined trade.

What Happens When the Range Narrows

When the price tests the 200 hour MA at point 8 in Figure 8.12 and bounces, the price is able to move above the 100 hour MA (solid MA line) on its way to point 9. Note, however, that the distance from point 8 to point 9 is a narrowing of the prior range that saw the price move consistently from remembered line (1.5079) to remembered line (1.5226). Up to this point, there were five moves from remembered line to remembered line (from 1 to 2, 2 to 3, 3 to 4, 4 to 5, and 5 to 6).

When the price stalls short of the remembered line at point 9, I start to expect that the market at rest—in a nontrending narrow range—will instead look to transition into a trending range with an expanding range. In Chapter 7, I introduced the "First Law of Trading" whereby a nontrending market will remain nontrending until it is acted upon by an unbalanced outside force. It is time to expect that unbalanced force to push the market. It is time to focus on the clues the market is giving, and they are bearish clues.

The first clue is the move through the 100 hour MA (solid line). This initiates a sale at the 1.5160 level. Shortly thereafter, the price move is confirming the trend through the 200 hour MA (dashed line) to the low remembered line at 10. A quick test of the 200 hour MA is followed by a resumption of the downtrend and finally a break of the 1.5079 level at point 11. Momentum from this break is for real (the market was likely excited about doing something different) and a quick move to the 1.4948 ensues (point B). The price stalls there. Ironically, or not, the low corresponds to the point where the market broke above the 200 hour MA way back at Point A. I told you the market remembers.

Trading Nontrends

No one ever said that trading nontrending markets is easy. It takes a real focus on the swings that occur and requires flexibility. One day you have to be a bear; the next day you have to be a bull. Too many retail traders can get frustrated with that idea. They feel they need to have conviction with their position. They might ask themselves "Are you a bull or a bear? Make up your mind and stick with it."

Don't fall for that feeling. Pay attention to what the price and tools are telling you. If the market price is going sideways in a ranged area, with remembered prices helping to guide the moves, that means the market (i.e., the smart money) is not sure of the trend either. It has a right to not know what to do too. When the market is ready, the clues are usually there for all to see, and the breaks, lower or higher, will occur.

For someone like me who looks for trends, it requires discipline, and an eye to see the trees through the forest, to trade these non-trends. However, that discipline is still rooted in the price and the tools I use. The 100 bar MA is a tool, a borderline, and it gives a risk-defining price. The 200 bar MA is a tool, a borderline, and it gives a risk-defining price. The remembered line is a tool, a borderline, and it gives a risk-defining price. Those tools, combined with the "If . . . Should" rule, can be used to benefit from what the price action is saying.

Lasting Relevance

The remembered lines outlined so far have been over a current defined time period. The price action was in a defined range or ranges, and the price kept using the same levels of support or resistance over and over again.

FIGURE 8.13   EURUSD Bottoms in June 2010 at 1.1876

I have also found that remembered lines can be relevant months and even years later. In Figure 8.13, the chart shows the EURUSD in a strong and prolonged trend move to the downside. The down leg shown takes the pair from a high of 1.3690 in early April 2010 to the low on June 7, 2010, at 1.1876.

While the market was selling off quickly, the pair had moved through multi-year lows. The 2009 low reached 1.2456. The 2008 low was breached at 1.2329. Prior to 2008, the last time the EURUSD traded as low as the current values was July 2005 to March 2006.

Figure 8.14 shows the daily chart for that period in 2005–2006. During that time, there was a remembered area from 1.1858 to 1.1876 that contained a number of lows. When the market broke through that remembered area, the price used the area as resistance (middle section of the chart). The last three low daily bars before the market broke and trended higher were at 1.1867, 1.1872, and 1.1859. The low in 2010 found support at 1.1876.

The remembered area of 1.1858 to 1.1876 from 2005–2006 gave traders a reason to trade in 2010. The risk was defined. The fear could be dispersed. The low was reached at 1.1876, and *two months later* a corrective top of 1.3333 stopped the rally—that was a move from the low to the high of 1,457 pips. It started at a remembered price from 2005/2006.

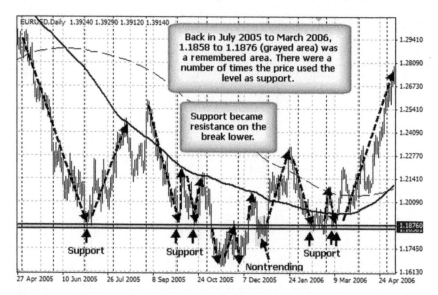

FIGURE 8.14 Remembered Lines from the Past Are Remembered in the Future

SIMPLE BUT EFFECTIVE

The currency market is simpler than people tend to think. It even likes and reacts to simple things like lines. No matter how simple lines on a chart may be, they are powerful and effective tools for successful traders.

Trend lines that slope upward define a bullish trend, providing traders with a borderline that defines risk. Trend lines that slope downward illustrate a bearish trend, define risk, and keep fear contained. Lines that form channels and provide a guardrail for bullish or bearish trends define risk and give traders reasons to trade. Flags or pennants are precursors to trend moves and define risk. Even horizontal remembered lines form borderlines for nontrending periods or can help pinpoint a top or bottom for a trending period.

The main reasons why all these lines are important tools for traders looking to trade currency trends is they can help define a trend, they all define risk, they give an unambiguous trading decision that is either bullish or bearish, and they all are able to keep a trader's fear to a minimum. They also are plain and easy to draw and see. Do not discount the power of lines. They will lead the way as you attack currency trends.

The next chapter will take a look at the final tool I use, which is the Fibonacci retracement. This tool helps define corrections within trends, and in doing so, also give clues where traders can reenter trends (or even think about the reversal of a trend).

CHAPTER 9

Fibonacci Retracements: The Hybrid Tool

D efining trends. Anticipating trends. Attacking currency trends. Trends. Trends. Trends and then nontrends, but nontrends transition into . . . yes, trends. Trends are great, but I often get a lot of questions from retail traders about the painful corrections—those times when the market reverses the trend and corrects 100, 200, 300 pips, or even more.

We all know that the market's price action does not go up (or down) in a straight line, but in steps. Two or three steps up and one step down. When the steps correct, they can be the killer moves that get traders out of synch with the market. Traders need the most help during these corrective moves. When the market is trending and a trader is on the trend, fear should be reduced. Profits are accumulating, the trend is directional. Trading is about targeting the next levels that keep the trend moving in the direction and managing the profit—not managing a loss.

The fear starts to surface when the trend starts to correct. All of a sudden the profits are being depleted and there is uncertainty as to how far the correction can go. How can fear be controlled during these times?

Tools like moving averages (MAs) and trend lines are in place to flash the warning signs of a potential correction. If the price is trending higher and the price moves below the 100 bar MA on the five-minute chart, the short-term bias turns negative, and the uptrend has a chink in its armor. If the price moves below an upward-sloping trend line, the uptrend has a chink in its armor. The MAs and trend lines provide profit-taking clues for the trend traders. When they change direction, traders should evaluate the position and look to exit or take some profit.

Doing this will preserve profit and hopefully accumulate additional equity over time. However, corrections are, by definition, just a temporary anti-trend move. That is, the trend should be reestablished at some point.

If your mission is to make the most money with the least amount of risk, it would be great if the corrections could be measured and defined. If they could, then traders could anticipate when the correction is over and look to reenter the trend at that time. Since the correction is measured, risk could also be defined. With risk defined, fear is kept low.

Furthermore, if a correction can be measured, and the bias is the opposite of the major trend, could a trader benefit from the corrective move? That is, could the trader trade against the major trend and take advantage of the profit potential of a significant correction—or what is called a countertrend—in the opposite direction?

The good news is all of the above can be done.

There are ways to measure corrections and anticipate when a correction might end, with defined risk. There are also ways to trade significant corrections and to measure profit potentials for those moves. If done, money can be made not only trading the trend, but also trading the corrective countertrend. The way this is all done is through the third and final tool I use to attack currency trends. The tool is what I call a hybrid tool; a tool that is a jack of all trades and does a little of everything. That tool is the Fibonacci retracement.

INTRODUCTION TO FIBONACCI

As mentioned in Part I of the book, Fibonacci was a thirteenth-century Italian mathematician who developed a sequence of numbers used to estimate the growth of a rabbit population (believe it or not). Whether the equation worked, or was even provable over an elapsed time period, I do not know. However, the sequence, along with its relationship to a mathematical constant, has certainly stirred the thinking of many scholars, scientists, engineers, artists, and yes, even financial technicians.

You might recall a relatively recent use of the Fibonacci sequence in Dan Brown's bestselling book and blockbuster movie *The Da Vinci Code.* In the book (and movie), the protagonist uses the Fibonacci sequence to open the glass scroll that provides the clues for the whereabouts of the Holy Grail. As a trading tool, Fibonacci retracements may also be a Holy Grail for traders.

Fibonacci sequences can seem mystical at times. However, the sequence does show up in ordering many things in nature. Trees exhibit the sequence in their branch and leaf patterns. The human body composition, as an example, utilizes the Fibonacci numbers 3 and 5. There are:

- Five appendages of the human body: the head, two arms, two legs
- Five fingers
- Five toes
- Three parts of the arm: shoulder, elbow, wrist
- Three parts of the leg: ankle, knee, hip
- Three divisions to each finger

The financial markets, through Elliott Wave theory, have also incorporated the Fibonacci sequence in their analysis to predict the movements of the stock market.

Elliott Wave technicians plot wave patterns that utilize the Fibonacci sequence. For example, there are thought to be five waves up for the major trend, and three waves down in a correction (those 5 and 3 numbers again!). The five up and three down combination keeps the trend moving in the intended upward direction. Within the waves there are similar numbered sequences.

If you ever see an Elliott Wave technician's charts, they are filled with lots of numbers that count the 1-2-3-4-5 waves and then the letters A-B-C, proxies for the three wave corrections.

Part of the idea of using the 5-3 sequence in financial markets is that a market, like the stock market, is a subset of the overall world around it. So, for instance, if the world is growing in population (people populate like rabbits, but at a slower pace), there are similar growth patterns in the economy. That translates into a similar growth pattern in the value of the stock market. Hence, in a very simplistic analogy, stock prices rise along with this pattern of growth in the population and along the same progression.

That is a theory, at least, and to the proponents of Elliott Waves, it helps explain movements of markets like the stock market over long-term periods.

The Fibonacci Sequence

The Fibonacci sequence is the basis of Fibonacci retracements. The Fibonacci sequence is a progression of values that follows a discernable numerical pattern. Table 9.1 shows the start of the sequence of values.

TABLE 9.1 The Fibonacci Sequence

F_0	F_1	F_2	F_3	F_4	F_5	F_6	F_7	F_8	F_9	F_{10}	F_{11}	F_{12}	F_{13}	F_{14}	F_{15}	F_{16}
0	1	1	2	3	5	8	13	21	34	55	89	144	233	377	610	987

The Fibonacci sequence starts with zero and 1, denoted by F_0 and F_1 in the graph. To get the next number, you add these two numbers together to get 1 again $(0 + 1 = 1)$. These are the first male and female of the rabbit population. The sequence is now 0, 1, and 1. Adding the last two numbers in the sequence $(1 + 1)$ yields the next number, 2, and takes the sequence to 0, 1, 1, and 2 (F_3). Summing the last two digits again $(1 + 2)$ yields the next value, 3. Continuing with the pattern yields $2 + 3 = 5$. So we can now see the derivation of the digits 3 and 5 as Fibonacci numbers.

After 5 the numerical progression continues with the following sequence: $3 + 5 = 8$, $5 + 8 = 13$, $8 + 13 = 21$, $13 + 21 = 34$, $21 + 34 = 55$, $34 + 55 = 89$, $55 + 89 = 144$, and so on. As you can see, the birth rate of rabbits grows rather rapidly (not surprising).

A mathematical mysticism in the sequence is seen when you take two successive numbers—say 144 and 233—and divide the larger number by the smaller number. The value approaches the decimal from what is called the *golden ratio*. The golden ratio, or phi (as it also referred in mathematical terms), is a mathematical constant just like the more popular pi $(3.14159265\ldots)$. The constant for phi, however, is approximately 1.6180339887.

So, taking successive Fibonacci sequence values such as 144 (at F_{12}) and 233 (at F_{13}) yields the following value,

$$144/233 = 0.61802575\ldots$$

Taking another two successive digits like 377 (at F_{14}) and 610 (at F_{15}) yields a value of

$$377/610 = 0.6180327\ldots$$

The farther out you go in the Fibonacci sequence the closer the ratio approaches to the $0.6180339887\ldots$ decimal from phi (not that these numbers are not close already).

The Golden Ratio

Although there is an equation that is used to calculate phi, and plenty of written discussion on phi or the golden ratio in books and on the Internet, this book is really not the platform to explore too deeply into it as a derived value. In fact, to those of us who may be challenged mathematically, like me, it can be well over our heads.

However, what financial technicians have realized through time is that the golden ratio has been able to bring some order in many disciplines outside of trading. Perhaps it can do the same thing for trading.

A chart of any financial instrument can seem chaotic to the untrained eye. There are moves up, then smaller moves down if the instrument is in

FIGURE 9.1   The Golden Ratio of 61.8 Percent Provides Support for the EURUSD

an uptrend. The moves down are called corrections. The overall move up is of course the trend.

Since market trends do not (usually) go up in a straight line but instead go up, correct, go up, correct, market technicians looked for ways to make sense of the corrections. That sense was manifested in Fibonacci retracements. The golden ratio of 0.618 or 61.8 percent was one of those retracements. It helps bring order to traders' chaotic charts.

For example, Figure 9.1 shows the EURUSD on an hourly chart. The price trends to the upside from a low at 1.3537 and makes a high at 1.3796, before starting a correction to the downside. A Fibonacci retracement overlay from the low at 1.3537 to the high at 1.3796 is placed on the chart. The price moves back lower and stops the fall after testing the 61.8 percent Fibonacci retracement level (the golden ratio) at the 1.36359 level (low reaches 1.3639). From there, a move back to the upside begins.

The Fibonacci retracement at the golden ratio point provided a definable target for the corrective move. It gave a low-risk borderline that traders could buy against, and when it held, it gave the trader a clue the trend was resuming. It took chaos and made sense of the move.

The 38.2 Percent and 50 Percent Levels

The golden ratio is not the only retracement level used by traders. Note in Figure 9.1 that there are other Fibonacci retracement levels plotted in the

TABLE 9.2 The Fibonacci Sequence

F_0	F_1	F_2	F_3	F_4	F_5	F_6	F_7	F_8	F_9	F_{10}	F_{11}	F_{12}	F_{13}	F_{14}	F_{15}	F_{16}
0	1	1	2	3	5	8	13	21	34	55	89	144	233	377	610	987

chart. The financial market tends to use two other retracement levels for market trends. Specifically, the 38.2 percent and the 50 percent levels are key levels to monitor.

The 38.2 percent Fibonacci retracement is also derived by the Fibonacci sequence. However, instead of using consecutive numbers in the sequence, the derivation of this value skips over one value, then divides the smaller number into the larger number. The subsequent number yields a value of approximately 0.382 or 38.2 percent.

For example, taking the Fibonacci sequence number 89 (at F_{11} in Table 9.2) and dividing it by 233 (at $F_{13,}$ skipping F_{12}) equals 0.38197 or 38.2 percent (rounded up).

$$89/233 = 0.38197 \quad \text{or} \quad 38.2\%$$

Try taking F_{14} (377) and dividing it by F_{16} (987). Do you get 0.382 or 38.2 percent? Of course you do. In fact, you get 0.38196555, or .382 rounded up.

Going back to Figure 9.1, note that on the way down from the high at 1.3796, the market decline stalled as the price approached the 38.2 percent retracement level at the 1.3697 level (low reached 1.3701). After the test, and the modest move higher, the resumption of the corrective move down broke through the 38.2 percent Fibonacci level on its way to the low at 1.3539. This is not a coincidence. The market will often look to use the Fibonacci numbers as borderline targets (i.e., exits on the Bearish Highway).

The final Fibonacci retracement level that I use in my analysis is the 50 percent retracement level. The midpoint of any low-to-high range has traditionally been a level the market pays attention to as a level of support or resistance (a borderline level). The digits 1 and 2 are also Fibonacci numbers, but unlike the consecutive numbers further in the sequence that when divided together yield a value approaching the golden ratio, dividing 1 by 2 yields 50 percent. This is another reason why 50 percent is included as a Fibonacci level—and borderline—for traders.

PLACING RETRACEMENTS ON A CHART

The Fibonacci sequence, the derivation of the golden ratio, and the Fibonacci retracement levels are certainly worth knowing and understanding. However, what is more important to understand is how and when to apply Fibonacci retracement lines on your charts.

Typically, when a market trends higher, the trend is characterized by higher highs and higher lows. Whenever a trend starts from a low, reaches a peak, then starts to come down (or corrects), this is grounds for putting Fibonacci retracement lines on a chart. This describes a bullish Fibonacci retracement.

When the market trends lower, the trend is characterized by lower highs and lower lows. Whenever a trend starts from a high, reaches a low, then starts to move back higher (or corrects), this is grounds for putting bearish Fibonacci retracement lines on a chart. With the lines in place, traders can measure and anticipate what prices the correction can target. Those targets become borderlines and exits on the correction highway.

Bullish Fibonacci Retracements

When the market trends higher, peaks at a high, and starts a correction lower, the Fibonacci retracement lines should be drawn on the chart. Most technical charting packages have this functionality as a standard tool. At FXDD (my firm), we use the MetaTrader charting and trading platform, and the Fibonacci lines are drawn automatically by anchoring the cursor on a low (or high) and dragging the cursor to a high (or low).

Figure 9.2 shows the EURUSD on a five-minute chart. Fibonacci retracements can be drawn on any time frame chart (i.e., five-minute,

FIGURE 9.2 A Bullish Fibonacci Retracement Correction

one-hour, four-hour, daily, weekly, or hourly) to show the start of the trend, the end of a trend, and the expected Fibonacci retracement levels.

The first step to set a bullish Fibonacci retracement is to define a low. In Figure 9.2, the low is at point 1. This is where the bottom of the Fibonacci is anchored.

The next step is to define a high. In the example, the EURUSD broke above the 100 and 200 bar MA levels and accelerated higher. At point 2 the momentum fades, and a corrective move lower begins. When a low and high are clearly defined, set the Fibonacci retracement lines from point 1 to point 2.

When done, the chart shows three corrective levels. The 38.2 percent line comes in at 1.30115 (point A). The midpoint or 50 percent retracement line comes in at 1.30045 (point B), and the 61.8 percent Fibonacci retracement comes in at 1.29975. The three are now targets for the corrective move lower.

The minimal, or smallest, completed correction of the trend move would pause at the 38.2 percent line. The middle, or medium, correction move would stop at the 50 percent line, while a larger, more substantial, correction would go all the way to the 61.8 percent line. The length of the correction of the trend typically gives a clue as to the strength of the trend.

In our example, the correction falls to 1.3010, just below the 1.3012 38.2 percent Fibonacci retracement level (point A). The price stalls briefly at the level before moving higher. The trend picks up steam after the break of the old high at 1.3034 level.

The correction was small (to the 38.2 percent level), and this led to a strong move back to the upside. If the correction extended to the 61.8 percent line, one could expect that the move back higher might not be as robust. Note, however, that this is not always the case. So be on the lookout for less momentum, but if the trend picks up steam do not be surprised either.

Bearish Fibonacci Retracement

The setting of a bearish Fibonacci retracement is the exact opposite of the bullish alternative. In this case, the major trend is down or bearish for a currency pair. Lower lows and lower highs define the bearish trend. When a bottom is formed and there are reasons to expect a meaningful correction higher, a Fibonacci retracement can be placed on the chart. The process starts by defining a high extreme, then defining the low extreme.

Figure 9.3 shows the GBPUSD as it trends down from point 1 to point 2. The trend move down takes the pair from a 1.4741 high (point 1) to a low (point 2) of 1.4387 (or 354 pips). Along the way, the price falls below the

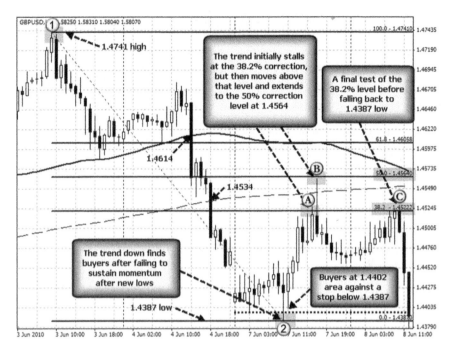

FIGURE 9.3 A Bearish Fibonacci Retracement Correction

100 hour MA (solid MA line) at the 1.4614 level and the 200 hour MA (dashed MA line) at the 1.4534, securing a firm bearish bias. A new low is made on the break of 1.4399 but can only reach 1.4387 (at point 2). The quick correction off the new low moves the price back above the 1.4399 level. Since the low was rejected so quickly, traders might expect a correction higher.

If a correction is anticipated, applying a Fibonacci from the high at point 1 to the low at point 2 is appropriate. The Fibonacci retracement levels are 1.4522 at the 38.2 percent level, 1.4564 at the 50 percent level, and 1.4606 for the 61.8 percent level.

The correction takes the price up from the lows to test the 38.2 percent Fibonacci retracement at 1.4522 (point A) in six hours. The price finds sellers against the level initially. This is an acceptable place to sell to reestablish a bearish trend position. Risk is defined (10 to 15 pips is all that is needed initially), and the market is stalling at the level. The trader should look to target a move back to the lows at 1.4387.

The price sells off from point A at 1.4522, but finds buyers below at 1.4485 area and rotates back higher. The failure to move lower says the market is not ready to trend lower just yet.

When the 38.2 percent retracement level is broken at 1.4522, a sharp move higher pushes the price to the 50 percent Fibonacci target at the 1.4564 level (point B). Like the 38.2 percent retracement level, the 50 percent level finds sellers who are looking to reestablish a short position with risk defined and limited (a stop above the 50 percent level can be expected).

This time, the price trends farther down. A final test of the 38.2 percent retracement level at point C finds aggressive sellers, which ultimately leads to a move back to the 1.4387 lows. Whether a bullish Fibonacci retracement or a bearish Fibonacci retracement, the dynamics for setting the levels are consistent:

- Find the trend high (or trend low).
- Find the trend low (or trend high).
- Overlay a Fibonacci extending from the high to low (or low to high).
- Target the 38.2, 50, and 61.8 percent Fibonacci retracement levels for the corrective move.

The next step is to understand the uses of this versatile trading tool.

USING FIBONACCI RETRACEMENTS

As we learned in Chapters 7 and 8, following the tools like moving averages and trend lines will provide clues for bullish or bearish bias. If the price is above the MA or trend line, the bias is bullish. If the price is below the MA or trend line, the bias is bearish.

The Fibonacci retracements are not the same type of tool. They have a role in trends and defining trends at times. Other times they are important in defining the countertrends or the moves that are against the trend. This gives them a role as a hybrid tool. Not quite fully a trend-defining tool, not quite fully a corrective-trend-defining tool, the advantage is they do both.

There are two distinct uses for Fibonacci retracements. Each addresses different market dynamics related to corrections and trends:

1. They measure targets for corrective or countertrend moves. In this role, they do not define a trend, but define a move opposite the trend. By defining the targets for the corrective moves, they provide traders with the ability to anticipate when the trend will be reestablished. In this role, the Fibonacci retracement is a way to attack the currency trend, but from a corrective level.

2. They can be used to target a profit level for a countertrend trade. After a large trend move, a correction can take the currency pair hundreds and sometimes thousands of pips in the opposite direction. There are times when traders can anticipate a countertrend and trade that corrective move with limited risk and a high profit potential. In this type of strategy, the Fibonacci levels become profit targets for those countertrend trades.

As a hybrid tool for traders, Fibonacci retracements complete the toolbox for attacking currency trends.

Reestablishing a Trend Position

Remember our game plan: to trade trends and keep fear to a minimum. Well, it is hard to trade the trends when the market is correcting. So what can a trader do during these times to keep the game plan intact? Proactive traders will look to exit trend positions when the bias turns from bullish to bearish or bearish to bullish in anticipation of a correction. Then, when the correction has run its course, traders will look to reestablish the trend position at a more favorable level. This is the first major use of Fibonacci retracements.

Remember that corrections are excellent opportunities for the market to refuel for the next leg of the bullish (or bearish) trend. As a result, traders that take advantage of the Fibonacci retracement levels to get back on a trend are actually attacking currency trends from a better price level. They also should benefit from a juiced up market that is ready to continue the major trend.

In addition, Fibonacci retracements may also be a way for traders who are not on the trend to get on it. The fact is, we cannot all be trading when a trend starts. Some may be at work. Some may be on vacation. Maybe some are running an errand or even asleep. Some may simply not pull the trigger when the trend begins. If the start of a trend is missed but the trader wants to participate in the trend, I encourage traders to wait for a time where risk is defined and limited. Fibonacci retracements provide those borderline points where getting on the trend is at a more favorable level with lower defined risk.

So although corrections run opposite the trend, and Fibonacci retracements define corrective levels, the levels that are defined are actually at points where traders look to attack currency trends. They also define risk because each Fibonacci level is a borderline where the bias is bullish on one side and bearish on the other. As such, fear should also be minimized. Reestablishing positions using Fibonacci retracements is a key require-

FIGURE 9.4 NZDUSD Trends Higher and Corrects to the 50 Percent Fibonacci Retracement Level

ment for attacking currency trends. It also is very much a key tool for maintaining our trader's game plan.

An Example: NZDUSD Figure 9.4 shows the NZDUSD on an hourly chart trending to the upside. The initial trend move takes the price from 0.7156 to 0.7238 or 82 pips (from A to B). At point B the price makes a new high but closes near the low and down versus the previous bar. Traders who are long may anticipate a correction and exit their long position.

A Fibonacci retracement overlay can be placed on the chart from the low (at A) to the high (at B). The following Fibonacci retracement levels are calculated and targeted as potential corrective borderline levels:

- 38.2% = 0.382 × .0082 = .00313 pips: 0.7238 − .00313 = 0.72067
- 50.0% = 0.500 × .0082 = .00410 pips: 0.7238 − .00410 = 0.71970
- 61.8% = 0.618 × .0082 = .00507 pips: 0.7238 − .00507 = 0.71873

The initial move down stalls at the 38.2 percent level at point a (38.2 percent = 0.7207). Although the price dips below the Fibonacci line (to 0.7205), the next two hourly bars (after a) hold support against the 0.7207 level. This is a bullish signal and presents a low-risk borderline opportunity against the Fibonacci level. The following trade should be executed:

Trade 1

Trade: Buyers, looking for a resumption of the trend higher, buy at this Fibonacci level (at 0.7207).

Risk: Since the 38.2 percent and the 50 percent level are close (10 pips), risk can be defined at a level below the 50 percent at the 0.7197 (c).

Since it is the beginning of the trend, a move to the 61.8 percent would not be welcomed. I prefer to see the first correction of a potential trend stall at the 38.2 or 50 percent levels.

Initial Target: When buying against the 38.2 percent retracement, the initial target is for a move back and through the high at point B since a reestablishment of the bullish trend is the goal. Of course, a further move higher is expected.

Result: In our example, the move higher stalls at point b (at 0.7231) before reaching the initial target at the old high at 0.7238. When this happens, the buyers at the 38.2 percent retracement level become impatient that the price cannot extend back to the old high (i.e., to the target), and they exit their positions.

With the sellers still in charge after the upside failure, the focus for buyers will now be on the 50 percent level at 0.7197 (point c) for the next possible trade opportunity. When the price reaches the level, the bounce off the borderline is convincing and strong. This is a clue the market is now ready to continue the trend higher. The price rallies at c and closes the hourly bar back above the 38.2 percent level at 0.7207. It is time to reestablish a trend position.

Trade 2

Trade: With buyers more confident, there is a green light to enter the market once again, looking for a resumption of the trend higher. Another purchase between 0.7197 and the 0.7207 level is a low-risk trade.

Risk: Risk is defined and limited to a move back below the 50.0 percent retracement level at 0.7197.

Result: This time, the anticipated move back above the old high at B happens. The market trends from 0.7197 to 0.7284 or 87 pips, without much hesitation (from points C to D).

Be aware and prepared for the Fibonacci retracements to provide low risk targets to reenter the main trend. Using the respective Fibonacci lines as borderlines, define risk in the same way as a MA or trend line. The difference is that there are three borderline levels instead of one when using Fibonacci retracements.

When the move off a retracement line stalls before reaching the extreme level (i.e., the old high or low), be aware for a rotation back to the Fibonacci level. However, with risk defined and limited, fear should be dispersed. In most cases, the trader will either be rewarded with a trend move (in this case 50 to 80 pips), or penalized with a small loss (10 to15 pips). This type of risk-to-reward profile is what all successful traders are looking for to increase their account values.

Trading Countertrends

The second use for Fibonacci retracement levels is as targets for countertrend trades. I define a countertrend as a move that has the potential to be more substantial in terms of pips than a normal correction. Typically, a substantial correction will come after a larger-than-normal trend that reaches an exhaustion point. That trend could be in terms of months. However, it could also be in terms of days or even hours.

In general, a substantial correction on a daily chart can be thousands of pips. A substantial correction off an hourly chart can be measured in terms of hundreds of pips.

The Fibonacci retracements help define the countertrend possibilities and as such, give profit targets for countertrend moves. Perhaps even more importantly, they highlight the significance (in terms of pips) of the potential countertrend move. Being aware of where the market could go gives traders confidence in trading the countertrend.

For example, if a key bottom of a substantial downtrend is thought to be found, and a Fibonacci of that move targets a 38.2 percent correction that is 500 pips higher, that type of move would be something most traders would be interested in trading (or not trading against). The move is significant. It has profit potential, but it has loss potential as well. Like a trend, a countertrend can be fast and directional, and trading against it can lead to quick losses.

It does not matter so much if the price gets to the 500-pip target; the tools like MAs and trend lines will guide you along that way. What does matter is the shift in thinking from what has been a strong bearish trend to the bullish corrective countertrend. You need to reprogram your brain from bearish to bullish thinking. The Fibonacci retracement values help make that transition. Not all corrections fit the mold of a potential countertrend. The next section will help define those that are most likely.

Anticipating a Countertrend We all know the trend is your friend, but we now need to understand that the countertrend move can be a pretty good friend as well. How can a countertrend be anticipated?

As an example, from November 2009 to June 2010, the EURUSD trended lower. The high for the pair was 1.5144. The low extended to 1.1876. That is a substantial move of over 3,200 pips. Along the bearish trend, there was little in the way of a meaningful correction. The longer a market goes without having a meaningful correction, the better the chance that one will occur. The EURUSD in June 2010 was a candidate for a meaningful correction. In fact, it was a candidate for a meaningful countertrend move.

An Example: The EURUSD When the price bottomed in June 2010, near the height of the Greek banking crisis, talk of parity permeated the newswires and the demise of the euro as a currency was getting headlines.

Despite the bearish fundamental backdrop, whenever a trend is well established in terms of time and overall high-to-low trading range, and there is no correction of the major trend of more than 38.2 percent, anticipating a more significant correction is always a possibility.

In the case of the EURUSD, the following was known:

- The trend down took the price from 1.5144 to 1.1876 or 3,268 pips. This range easily surpassed the previous trend move higher (2,688 pips). The move down also took the price to the lowest level since February 2006.
- Apart from the initial correction at the outset of the trend, there was not a correction of significance during the entire move down. The largest correction was a 21.8 percent retracement, which took the price from 1.2510 (point 2 in Figure 9.5) to 1.3093 (point C) in two trading days before heading back lower.
- There were 28 weeks from the high to the low. Only 5 weeks were positive week on week. There were no two successive weeks that were positive.

From a fundamental perspective:

- Although there were bearish debt implications in Greece and the other weaker members of the European Union, the currency had already devalued by 22 percent from the high. Currency changes are self-correcting for an economy. That is, a weaker currency will make exports cheaper and therefore act as a stimulus to an economy that has growth issues domestically. Although the weak sisters of the Eurozone

FIGURE 9.5 EURUSD Trend Had Limited Corrections of the Overall Trend

were suffering, the relatively healthy economies, like Germany, were enjoying an export boom. The weaker euro was a stimulant.

- Sentiment was overwhelmingly bearish for the EURUSD. Even though the price was at the 1.1900 area, sentiment had the EURUSD going to parity. A move from 1.1900 to parity would imply another 16 percent decline in the value of the EURUSD on top of the 22 percent decline from the peak. Such a change has implications not only for Europe but also the United States. With 10 percent unemployment in the United States, another 16 percent appreciation would make exports that much more expensive and would likely lead to further employment pressure. This would not be a welcome development for the United States or the global economy.
- Central bankers are there to do all they can to solve problems and find solutions. If a solution for Greece is found, such as a sharp austerity package and debt relief, there is a reason for a rebound.

Even though each of these items is a reason to think a correction may take place, it is not a reason to buy. In fact, these items demonstrate the trend's bearish characteristics.

However, the strong trending characteristics are a warning that should the market bottom—should it find a reason or reasons to trade higher from a key technical perspective—there is a potential for a substantial corrective move in terms of pips.

Successful retail traders tend to know the potential for correction exists. They will look to measure a correction with Fibonacci retracement. The final step is to look to trade in the direction of the countertrend if and when the winds of change blow in the market and the bias turns from bearish to bullish. Any extended trends that do not have a substantial correction within the trend are candidates for a countertrend move to the 38.2 percent retracement (at least) once there is a reason to correct. Be on the lookout for these candidates, and be in position to trade the countertrends for a profit.

Measuring Countertrend Targets

While the EURUSD is trending down, the smart traders will be thinking in terms of "What if the market were to start a meaningful bullish corrective move in the EURUSD from the lows of 1.1876? Where can the market correct to? What are the Fibonacci retracement levels?"

Figure 9.6 shows that a normal 38.2 percent Fibonacci correction would take the EURUSD from 1.1876 to 1.3124 (represented by the shaded gray area in Figure 9.6). This is simply the minimal and normal correction that could take place. Although it seems far, far away and nearly impossible to imagine, it is the market's place—not yours—to determine whether a move is possible.

The market does not have go to these levels tomorrow, or in the next week, or even ever. After all, the market had corrective chances in the past along this trend and never came close to targets like the 38.2 percent Fibonacci retracement.

However, in currency trading anything *could* happen and as long as risk can be defined, as long as there is a key reason (or reasons) to be bullish (in the example), and the technical bias remains bullish in the eyes of our trend defining tools, a trader who is comfortable with risk, can trade the countertrend with confidence.

Market Perception and Countertrends

Traders' bullish or bearish bias perception is important for trading countertrends. In our EURUSD example, targeting Fibonacci levels helps change the trader's perception of the market bias from being overly bearish to being bullish. This is a key point.

FIGURE 9.6 The 38.2 Percent Fibonacci Retracement Targets 1.3124

Retail traders—despite the fact that they have a difficult time trading trends—will often get caught up in the trend at the wrong time. For example, they may recognize the start of the correction (or countertrend), but instead envision a shallow correction that reverses quickly. In the EURUSD example, they suddenly are enamored with the idea of things like parity, and those ideas cloud their judgment.

As a result, they will tend to ignore the risk of a potential countertrend move that can be substantial. This tends to put them on the wrong side of the market momentum. That is, they are looking more closely at selling rallies. Meanwhile, the smart successful traders are looking to buy the dips and trade on the side of the countertrend move. The retail trader tends to be out of step with the market's true rhythm during a significant countertrend.

Measuring where the market can go and saying (or at least thinking), "This market has the potential to have a normal correction to 1.3124 if the bullish bias continues," is a healthy, risk-conscious thought process for traders. It helps reprogram the trader's brain to think in terms of trading opposite the trend that has been prevalent for an extended period of time.

It sounds obvious, but to trade any countertrend, you need to know that the market has the potential to countertrend and that it has the potential to go to a specific level. Without that target, without that level in mind, the focus is often on doing the wrong trades. That is, selling when you should be buying or buying when you should be selling.

Why Trade the Countertrend?

Of course, I will never prescribe trading against the major trend without having a firm reason to do so. Without a firm technical reason that gives a bullish (or bearish) bias and that defines risk, there is no reason to change the major trends bias. Trends are your friend as long as the technical bias is in the direction of the trend. I use the MAs and trend lines to define that bias in a trending market.

In our example, there needs to be a clear technical reason to buy the EURUSD. Figure 9.7 shows a few important market levels that traders who may be anticipating a corrective countertrend will focus on. They become the basis of the countertrend move.

- The 1.2150 level is the key level. Until the break in early June, this level had the potential to be the low for the trend move down. Traders were buying off the initial double bottom in mid May, and the triple bottom toward the end of May. However, when that floor was broken on June 4, the remaining longs were closed at a small loss, and the

FIGURE 9.7 A Normal Fibonacci Correction of Trend Move

price moved to the new trend low of 1.1876. After the break, the floor at 1.2150 became a ceiling at the same level. The level also became a key remembered line.

- The move higher off the 1.1876 low has traders selling against the 1.2150 ceiling for two consecutive days. This was a low-risk trading level for bearish traders (and the bias was firmly bearish). Selling against the key remembered line at 1.2150 defines the risk. A move above the line would be the stop on the trade. The reward would be yet another new wave to the downside. Is there a reason to expect a countertrend at this point? No. The key level to get through is clearly the 1.2150 level.
- When price moves back above 1.2150, the smart traders have that key reason to anticipate a bottom is in place (see Figure 9.7). They now can say the bias is bullish as the price moved above a key remembered line. They can now define risk with a stop 20 pips below the 1.2150 remembered line. They now need to target a profit potential.
- A Fibonacci is applied and the target 38.2 percent Fibonacci retracement from the high at 1.5144 to the low at 1.1876 targets 1.3124.

A move from 1.2150 to 1.3124 implies a potential and substantial 974-pip countertrend correction. Is it time? Can it really happen?

Deal in What Is Real

Admittedly, on the days following the trend bottom in June, I am not thinking we are going to correct straight to 1.3124. That would be unrealistic—nearly a fantasy—and in fact, puts me in the bucket of those analysts who are forecasting parity.

If the countertrend is going to materialize, it will have its share of moves and corrections. The hourly and five-minute chart analysis will provide the clues for the shorter and intermediate trends along the journey. They are the tools that will be relied upon to show the bullish way. A bullish move will still rely on maintaining a bullish bias from those tools.

However, when the price moves above the 1.2150 level, the reality is this:

- The price is above the 1.2150 key remembered line.
- The risk is a move back below 1.2150 (with a 20-pip stop loss).
- The potential exists for a substantial correction because the market had an even more substantial fall of 3,268 pips. A normal correction could target 1.3124 (974 pips from 1.2150).

- Even if the market only corrects one-third of the 974 pips, that still represents 325 pips higher. Would I take 100 or 200 pips? Sure. The point is there is room to move higher, and the risk is minimal and defined.
- Although the correction may not have any fundamental reason yet, it has a *key* technical reason. The market will always find a fundamental reason over time. I like to tell traders that "Tomorrow's newspapers will give the explanation as to why the market did what it did today." For me, the reason is the price moved above the 1.2150 level. My explanation will not sell any newspapers, but it is a reason that defines my risk (and does the same for other currency traders as well!).

Reality or fantasy? I always deal in what is real. What can be defined? What is the potential? What is the risk and then let the fantasy either happen or not happen. Unsuccessful traders will let the fantasy control their emotions and forget about the reality. Take note of that important difference.

We can all have our fantasies but they have to be realistic when trading. Listen to what the market price and the tools tell you. They will never lie. And be cognizant of what could happen if the conditions are right. It will allow you to trade the trends and the countertrends.

How did the countertrend turn out? Figure 9.8 shows the move higher after the break of the 1.2150 level. The price initially moved to test the high

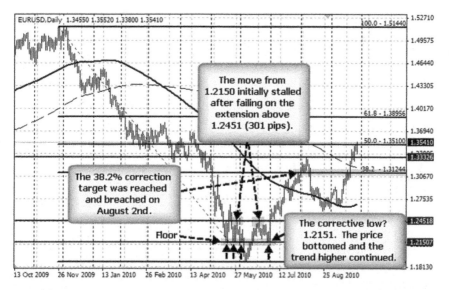

FIGURE 9.8 EURUSD Uses 1.2150 Area as a Key Reason to Countertrend Higher

from May 28 at the 1.2451 level, six days from the trade date, and a full 300 pips from the trade level (high reached 1.2467 on June 21). Profit takers entered after the failure above the May 28 high and pushed the market down to the familiar 1.2151 remembered line (floor level from May). Once again, traders had reason to buy with the same defined risk of 20 pips. The key borderline held once again (with risk defined and limited) and the price surged higher. Remembered lines are remembered for a reason! Use them!

The fantasy of 1.3124 became the reality on August 2, less than two months after the low was reached (on June 7). The momentum pushed the price to a high for the countertrend of 1.3333 on August 6. Two months and 1,457 pips later, the price found a top for the countertrend move.

Does Trend Direction Really Matter?

Figure 9.9 shows the EURUSD daily chart from the low in early June 2010. The countertrend higher is indeed a trend move. The low was 1.1876. The high reached 1.3333. The low-to-high range was 1,457 pips! Countertrend or trend? Does it really matter? 1,457 pips is a significant move that traders need to be on. It is also a trend they do not want to trade against.

FIGURE 9.9 EURUSD Countertrend Exceeds Fibonacci Retracement Target and Moves Even Higher

What is most important is to realize that corrections in the currency markets can be substantial. Trends in currency are indeed your friend. However, when there is a trend in the market that does not correct to the 38.2 percent Fibonacci retracement, measuring the potential retracement level and anticipating a significant countertrend cannot be ignored.

In order to trade the countertrend, follow these steps:

1. Have a key technical reason to trade against the trend.
2. Define the countertrend target using the Fibonacci retracement.
3. Realize that the potential exists for the countertrend move.
4. Ensure the countertrend directional bias remains intact by using our other technical tools like the 100 and 200 bar MAs, trend lines, and remembered lines.

Following these steps will define your risk, help change your market perception, and keep you in the trend, even if it is the countertrend.

TRADING SHORTER-TERM CORRECTIONS

The previous example focused on a longer-term countertrend move that offered some nice clues to anticipate the countertrend and target the corrective move while keeping risk and fear to a minimum. Can the same be done over shorter-term trend moves?

In general, all charts show similar patterns over time. They just use different trend scales. For hourly charts, the moves are going to be smaller. There will not be a 1,457-pip countertrend move off an hourly chart. There can be a 100-, 200-, or 300-pip move (or more), however, and those gains can be a nice boost for your trading equity.

Our general trading rules still apply when looking at shorter-term countertrend opportunities. If there is a technical reason from one of our trading tools that turns the bias from bullish to bearish or bearish to bullish, and risk can be defined and accepted, trading a corrective move—especially when it has the potential to be significant—can be an extremely positive move not only for the equity in your account, but also for your trading confidence. There is nothing like trading a trend and then trading a countertrend too.

For example, Figure 9.10 shows the EURUSD on an hourly chart. At the far left of the chart, the EURUSD begins the trend move higher after a breaking above the 100 hour MA trigger at the 1.2272 level. A buy at the 1.2272 area should be executed. The bullish move higher is confirmed after the 200 hour MA is broken and the trend to the upside begins in earnest.

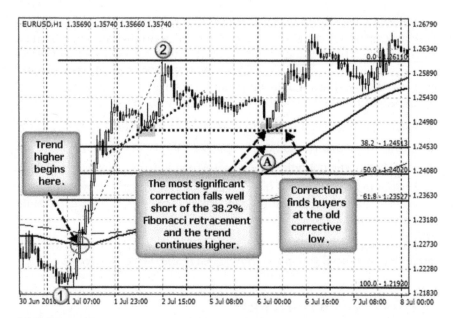

FIGURE 9.10 EURUSD Trends Higher but Corrects Modestly

The most significant correction occurs after the move from point 1 to point 2. The trend higher had moved from a low of 1.2192 to a high of 1.2611. A top is in place (at 2), and a trend line is broken. This signals a correction is likely. Any bullish positions should be closed. The correction targets become previous consolidative lows, and the 38.2 percent Fibonacci retracement at the 1.2451 level.

The subsequent correction finds support at the previous corrective low, but falls well short of the 38.2 percent correction level at point A. The failure to move lower leads to a continuation of the trend move higher. Traders could reestablish long positions with risk limited to the correction low.

Figure 9.11 shows the continuation of the trend move. The trend remains above the 100 hour MA, but momentum is starting to fade as the price approaches the new high at 1.2722.

We learned from the daily chart example that if a significant trend move does not have a correction of 38.2 percent, the conditions exist for a potential countertrend move.

The same logic can be applied when looking at an hourly chart. In our example, the EURUSD trended higher with no significant corrections of 38.2 percent or more. The price remained above the 100 hour MA, keeping the bullish bias, but momentum seems to be fading. The slopes of the trend lines are flatter; the ranges are smaller.

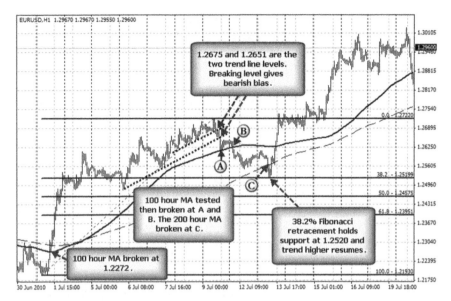

FIGURE 9.11 Trading the Countertrends

Nevertheless, as long as the bias remains bullish, traders should not sell. If the bias moves from bullish to bearish, however, there is a technical reason to trade. With a reason to trade, risk can be defined. Traders should explore the idea of trading the countertrend.

In Figure 9.11, there are several reasons to anticipate a correction and potential countertrend move:

- The low to high move took the price up 529 pips from 1.2193 to 1.2722 in seven trading days. This is a significant move for the time period.
- There are trend lines (dashed lines in Figure 9.11) that have been developed over a few trading days, giving them borderline significance. A move below the trend lines changes the bias from bullish to bearish.
- Risk from selling against the trend can be defined by using the trend lines. A sale on a break of either of the trend lines gives a reason to do the trade and a reason to get out. If the price moves back above the trend line, the short countertrend position should be closed.

Another thing that can encourage the countertrend trade is the map of the targets on the downside. In this trade example:

- The 100 hour MA is a target (at point A).
- The 200 hour MA (at point C) is the next target.
- The 38.2 percent Fibonacci retracement level is the third target.

All the targets line up, one after another, giving the trader a step-by-step progression. The steps provide confidence along the countertrend, and stop levels should the market reverse back to the upside. If, for instance, the price moves below the 100 bar MA but reverses back above the MA line, the trader has a reason to exit the short position.

In addition, since the trend has not had a significant correction of 38.2 percent for the entire trend move higher, a move toward the 38.2 percent retracement at 1.2520 is anticipated. This would target a potential countertrend profit of around 130 pips.

Trade 1

Trade: A countertrend sell is established on a move below the second trend line at 1.2651. The first trend line was already broken at 1.2675, giving a bearish bias. The second line being broken is a confirmation of the bias.

Risk: Risk is limited to a move back above the upper trend line at 1.2675 (24 pips). Risk can get moved down as targets are passed.

Targets: The 100 hour MA at 1.2614 (at A) and the 200 hour MA at 1.2562 (at C) are the first two targets. The main countertrend target, since the trend higher has not had a significant correction, would be the 38.2 percent Fibonacci retracement at 1.2520. Below those levels, the 1.2480 (low from July 6) and 1.2458 (50 percent retracement) are other downside targets.

Result: The market price ends up testing the 100 hour MA level and finds initial support (A). This is the first major test of the key MA since the bias turned bullish at 1.2272. True to form, the price bounces 35 to 40 pips off the MA level. However, the move cannot extend back to the trend lines, and when the price breaks below the MA at point B, this increases the trader confidence in the countertrade. From there the next target becomes the 200 hour MA at 1.2562 (point C). The price moves easily below this target. From there the market tests the key 38.2 percent retracement at 1.2520.

Is there a reason to buy against the Fibonacci retracement borderline level and reestablish the trend trade? Yes, of course there is. Reasons include:

- The corrective move down covered 202 pips in the span of two trading days. The correction was orderly but not overly aggressive. The trade yielded a maximum profit of 131 pips (from 1.2651 to 1.2520). Initial risk was 24 pips.
- Although the price was below the 100 and 200 hour MA, the trend higher was still the major trend.

- The two MAs also could provide confidence in the move back higher just like they provide confidence in the countertrend. Getting above the 200 hour MA negates the bearish bias, and moving back above the 100 hour MA puts the bulls fully back in charge.
- Risk was clearly defined against the 38.2 percent Fibonacci level. If the price were to move back below the Fibonacci borderline level, a new short could be reestablished with the next target being the 50 percent retracement level.

Trading countertrends can be done on any chart time frame. Any trend move of significance in terms of time and direction that has not corrected 38.2 percent during that trend is a candidate for a countertrend move. Be aware and the rewards of the trends and countertrends can be yours.

USING THE TOOLS TO YOUR BEST ADVANTAGE

If you can attack the major currency trends higher or lower, you will do very well as a trader. If you can avoid the pain of the corrections and reestablish trend positions at low-risk borderline levels, you will do even better as a trader. If you can anticipate a countertrend and target profit levels and profit from the trading against the trend, you will be a star of currency trading.

Fibonacci retracements are the hybrid tool that allows traders to use the corrections in a trend to their advantage.

I have now outlined the major tools I use for attacking currency trends. The book's final two chapters will put the pieces together and show how each tool supports the others in the trend-trading process.

CHAPTER 10

Preparing for the Trade

A ttacking currency trends successfully is all about having a firm foundation that includes a mission statement and a game plan. Secondary to having those, you need rules and tools in place to support your mission statement and game plan. It is about understanding what the market is telling you. Is the market trending or nontrending, and what do those things mean? How do corrections fit in the picture? How can you benefit when a market corrects? How do you enter or exit a trade and why? What do you look for when the trade blotter is blank?

Clues to help answer these questions have already been presented throughout the book. In the next two chapters, we'll bring the pieces together. How do the three charts—five-minute, hourly, and daily—work and complement each other? How do the three tools—100 and 200 bar MAs, trend lines, and Fibonacci retracements—work and complement each other? How do we define risk and manage trades along the way? How do we dance the dance of a trend trade? Along the trend journey, I will show what signals to look for, what the good entry points are, how to manage the trade, what the good exit points are, and when it's a good time to reestablish a trade.

There is no set step-by-step process for how a trade may progress from start to finish. The markets are simply not that consistent, nor static. What is most consistent in trading currencies is that the focus should be on controlling and defining risk. Understanding risk is the most important thing a trader needs to know. If risk is understood, fear can be controlled.

From there the focus turns toward attacking currency trends. In order to attack the trend, you need a risk-defined entry. Your tools are meant to show where that entry point exists. Furthermore, it's important that you use unambiguous tools that tell you bullish on one side and bearish on the other. Manage the trend so you can stay on it and know when it is time to exit. Hopefully, the exit will come when the account is nice and fat.

At the very least, following these steps will prevent you from blowing through account equity. The best scenario is that you will ride and attack the currency trends. Not all trades will be nice trend trades that accumulate vast fortunes in your trading accounts, because markets don't always do what you think they should do. However, you can limit your losses and improve your gains if you are well prepared to trade the trends.

FIRST THINGS FIRST

Like anyone, if I do not have a trade on, I am searching for one. Trading successfully is about being patient. The good news is I do find there are opportunities most days to define risk, keep risk to a minimum, and execute successful trades that might not trend for a long time but still provide decent returns. I outline those on my commentary pages and in my daily video e-mails for FXDD each day.

The real money, however, is made trading the longer trends. Trends are fast and directional and make traders the most money with the least amount of risk. These are the trades that will make or break your year. There are three steps you must take at the outset of any trade and they are to define the direction of the trend (is the trend transitioning into a nontrend or vice versa?), choose the currency pair you want to trade, and pick which time periods (or charts) to use.

Defining the Direction of the Trend

Typically, a trend trade sets itself up to trend. It does this by nontrending. The nontrending market will transition into a trend market. It still is the best way I know to *anticipate* a trend. If a major league baseball player can anticipate a fastball and get it pitched where he wants it, he has a better chance of hitting a home run. The same is true for traders. Nontrending markets are a way to anticipate a fastball.

Not all trends last for hundreds and even thousands of pips. I never know when a trend may end. I may trade a trend that only lasts a day or even less. Even on the longer trends, there are of course periods of corrections on the five-minute charts that can take you off the trend highway for a period before putting you back on that road again.

You prepare for a trend. You anticipate a trend. Then when you get on a trend, the job becomes staying on the ride for as long as you can go. Be greedy and watch the account balance fatten up like a pig. Then, when the market cannot go any farther, when the pig cannot get to the trough for his food, slaughter the position and *get out*. And start looking for the next opportunity because trends do transition into nontrends.

Choosing a Currency Pair

My approach to my charts is the same every day. There are no changes. The toolbox has the same tools in it each day. I look at three charting time periods for clues: five-minute, hourly, and daily. I plot the 100 and 200 bar simple moving averages (MAs), trend lines, and most relevant Fibonacci retracements on each. I look for the clues the market is giving, and if something stands out as a favorable risk/reward opportunity, I will look to act. Once I'm in the trade, the task becomes managing. Then exiting.

Since the EURUSD is the most liquid currency, I will use it as the currency for the trend-trading demonstration. Note, however, that the same analysis can be used on most any currency pair.

I do use the EURUSD for a purpose, though. In addition to being the most liquid, it has a good high-to-low trading range of about 100 to 130 pips per trading day, and its bid-to-ask spread is the narrowest; it is the benchmark for all other currency pairs. Since the United States and Eurozone are similar in economic makeup, the economic bias tends to alternate from one to the other. Sometimes it favors the Eurozone; sometimes it favors the United States. However, the economic trend tends to stay the same for a while. This allows the pair's price to trend one way, then when the economic bias changes, reverse and trend the other way. For these reasons the EURUSD is the best currency pair for my mission statement. If you don't focus attention each day on the EURUSD, you should.

How many currencies should you trade or follow? Trade and follow are two different things. You should look to trade around three, but they don't have to be all at once, and you can switch around. There are currencies where the economic story is more in focus. I want to concentrate on them. As a result, I will *follow* more currencies than I trade. If there is a commodity story, watch the technical trend of the AUDUSD. If there is an oil story, USDCAD can be a pair to focus on.

If the U.K. has inflation, and the Bank of England has to go on a tightening spree, pay attention. If the U.K. has inflation but growth is slowing, it may not be the best time to trade the GBPUSD. The USDJPY may be under pressure because of the inherent trade balance issues, but if the Bank of

Japan intervenes (or threatens to intervene), the currency pair goes off my radar because it carries too much risk.

If risk is increased and a surprise attack or counterbalancing events might make a currency chart look more like an EKG graph, be smart and follow the currency pair, but don't trade it.

Picking Your Charts

As discussed earlier in the book, I look at three time periods, or charts, when I trade: the five-minute, hourly, and daily charts. Some people mistakenly think that the five-minute chart is used to scalp intraday, the hourly is for intermediate-term trading decisions, and the daily is for long-term position trading, but that is not the case.

I look at all three in tandem so that I can follow the key levels in each. Those key levels are borderlines where risk is defined and limited. Those borderlines become the points where trades are entered. They become the targets on the trend that the market price must pass to keep the trend momentum intact. They become exit levels as well.

Why bother with all three time periods and not just focus on one? Well, other traders do, but I don't. There are traders who focus only on the five-minute chart. I want to know where they are executing their borderline trades and what levels are important to them. There are also traders who focus only on the hourly chart. If the price is approaching the 100 hour MA on their chart, I want to be aware of that key borderline. Finally, there are traders who focus only on the daily chart. I want to know when the trend line of the chart they are looking at is being broken.

I want to see what each group of traders is focused on when it looks at the charts for the EURUSD, GBPUSD, USDJPY, USDCAD, and so on. Failure to do so ignores groups who may be influencing the market action at a price. Have you ever wondered why the price stopped cold at a certain price level? It is usually some key technical level that a group of traders defended.

So the purpose of looking at all three time periods is to be aware of the key borderline levels for each one. Then when I do my trade analysis, I will be more in touch with the best level for a profitable trading opportunity. That level may just be the start of a trend.

ANALYZING THE CHARTS

I will start my analysis of what I look for when preparing to enter a trade by looking at each of the time period charts: the daily, hourly, and five-minute.

As mentioned, I will use the EURUSD as the currency of choice. The charts are all from September 10, 2010. The same questions will be asked each time: What trades are developing and why? What are the risks, and ultimately, what trades are entered into and why?

From there, I will map out the how to manage the trade and how to look for exits along the way by looking at key points along the trend. The analysis will bring together the tools and key concepts outlined in the book.

Trading successfully is about using tools in tandem with each other. The 100 and 200 bar MAs, trend lines, remembered lines, and Fibonacci retracements all work together along with the three chart time periods to define the trend, keep risk under control, manage the trade, and give reasons to exit the trade.

The Daily Chart

The daily chart typically has two purposes. One is to give a macro view of a currency pair's direction and bias. The second purpose is to provide key borderline levels that a trader can use to target, enter, or exit trades.

Figure 10.1 shows the typical macro view of a currency pair using the daily chart. The chart also includes a typical chart setup I may include on the chart. All the charts in the analysis in this chapter and the next will be set up in the way I would set them up if I were trading them live.

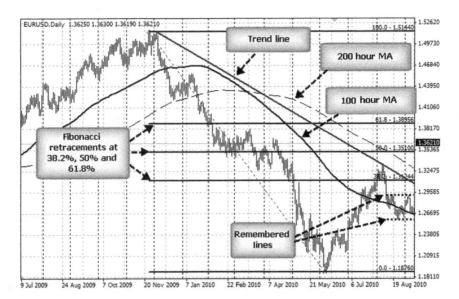

FIGURE 10.1 The Longer-Term View of the EURUSD Is Looking More Bearish

The Fibonacci retracement is plotted for the major trend. The 100 and 200 day simple MAs are included. I will draw relevant trend lines and re-membered lines.

When the downtrend ended in early June 2010 and the countertrend started, the setup from Figure 10.1 helped guide the countertrend move higher. The 100 day MA was an upside target. The market stalled at that MA line (solid line in Figure 10.1), trading above it and then below it before breaking to the upside to the high.

A Fibonacci retracement was drawn at the start of the countertrend higher that went from the high at 1.5144 to the low at 1.1876. The 38.2 per-cent Fibonacci retracement targeted what seemed like an impossible 38.2 percent retracement of 1.3124 (at least at the start of the countertrend). However, the market made its way to the level and beyond. A high was reached at 1.3333 on August 2, and the price started to move to the down-side. The countertrend higher was over—for the time being, at least.

Reversing the View   With the significant and impressive 1,457-pip rally over, it was time to reverse the bias and view. In this view I needed to reverse the Fibonacci retracement from the high to low in Figure 10.1, and instead have it go from the low to high (see Figure 10.2). I needed to target Fibonacci levels in the opposite direction so I could better map the move and targets on the downside.

FIGURE 10.2   The Current Trend for the EURUSD Is More Bullish

In Figure 10.2, I zoom in and focus on the EURUSD daily chart from a current perspective. This chart starts by showing the countertrend move higher from the June low to the August high and the subsequent correction of that move. The Fibonacci retracement overlay is reversed and goes from the 1.1876 low to the 1.3333 high. The Fibonacci retracement lines come in at the following levels:

- 1.2776 for the 38.2 percent
- 1.2604 for the 50 percent
- 1.2432 for the 61.8 percent.

From the high, the price moves lower, stalls at the 38.2 percent retracement at 1.2776 and the 100 day MA line just above that level (see start of boxed area in Figure 10.2). The price finds support and tries to trade back higher but fails. The move to the low stalls near the 50 percent target level at 1.2604. Support is found against the key midpoint. Over the next 13 days, the price trades in a narrow range. It moves from the low at the 50 percent retracement level back toward the range high at the 1.2915 to 1.2931 area (this is the boxed area in Figure 10.2). From the high, sellers reenter against the level and push the price back down. The price stalls once again at the all important 100 day MA line. The market is mired in a clearly defined range and is waiting at the 100 day MA until it decides its next move.

A Tale of Two Trends: One Down, One Up When looking at the two daily charts, we have a tale of two trends. In Figure 10.1 the trend seems to be to the downside. The EURUSD price fell from a high of 1.5144 to a low of 1.1876. The correction higher (or countertrend higher) took the price up to 1.3333 above the 100 day MA, above the 38.2 percent retracement at 1.3124, but stayed below the 50 percent and the 200 day MA. The move higher, although quite substantial at 1,457 pips, looks like a correction from a distance. The current move back to the downside at the 1.2600 area could be the start of the reestablishment of the trend down.

In Figure 10.2, the macro picture is different. The trend moves to the upside in this chart, and the subsequent correction takes the price down through the 38.2 percent correction and the 100 day MA, but pauses at the 50 percent retracement at the 1.2604 level (the low was 1.2586, but that low was quickly rejected).

At this juncture, the macro view of the daily chart has me (and likely the market) in a quandary. There is a reason to lean to the bearish side if you are looking at Figure 10.1, while Figure 10.2 might sway you to be more bullish. Does it matter to you as a trader?

To be honest, no. Those people who say the EURUSD is going to parity might have an interest. You might be interested in the debate whether the EURUSD is bullish or bearish in the long term from this point.

Don't get me wrong, I am interested in longer-term trends from the charts, but what is most important to me is what clues the daily chart is giving me now for a trade. I'm most interested in what key borderline levels the chart is giving me that will allow me to enter a trade, define risk, manage a trade, or exit a trade. As a result, the second chart is my focus. Since we have no position, let's explore the trade entry clues.

Trade Entry Clues   If Figure 10.3 looks familiar, it should. It is the same chart from Figure 10.2. I show it because I want to focus on what it is telling me. I want to pick out the key borderline levels in the chart. Those border-lines will provide clues for a trade and help define risk in the process.

- *The 50 percent retracement is a key borderline (1.2604 bullish).*
  The first key borderline is the 50 percent retracement level. The level comes in at 1.2604. On the way to the downside (see inside the boxed area), the market moved below this level on its way to the low at 1.2586.

FIGURE 10.3   The Boxed Area Shows All the Clues I Need to Know from the Daily Chart

Does this break of the Fibonacci level change my perception of the market bias? No. The break below the 1.2604 level was brief and quick; the price did not close below the level. Sellers below the 1.2604 level (including me) closed the position for a small loss when the price moved back above the 1.2604 level a short time later. The price did not do what it was supposed to do ("If . . . Should" rule). What is of note from the chart is that the day after the 1.2604 was broken, the price low was 1.2608. Buyers used the level as support and the price moved higher. Hmmm, a clue. With the price above the 1.2604 level, the bias is bullish off of that borderline.

- *The 38.2 percent retracement level is a key borderline (1.2776 bearish).*

The 38.2 percent retracement area from 1.2763 to 1.2776 is a key borderline level, too. Look at the boxed area in Figure 10.3 and start from the left edge and go to the right. There are seven days that got within 13 pips of the level and found support or resistance. The market seemed to want to be above it or below the level. So not only is the area a Fibonacci level, but I would also define it as a remembered line (or area). The price is currently below the 38.2 percent retracement, which gives a bearish bias.

- *The 100 day moving average is always a key borderline (1.2657 bullish).*

Although the price moved above and below the 100 day MA throughout the boxed area, what is significant to me is the last four days of trading in the chart. The first day had a low of 1.2676, which was the 100 day MA level. The second day went to a low of 1.2658 versus the 100 day MA at 1.2669 but closed above the line. The third day had a low of 1.2663, which was exactly on the 100 day MA, and the fourth day had a low of 1.2643 with the Fibonacci at 1.2657. However, the day closed well above the level at 1.2709.

The failure of the last move below the 100 day MA and the move back up to 1.2709 is a bullish development—a bullish clue.

- *The high-to-low range is at its narrowest since October 2007.*

The final clue from the daily chart is found in the high-to-low trading range. The boxed area represents 22 trading days. Assuming a 30-day calendar month and four weekends per month, 22 trading days is a proxy for a month of trading. The low for the month was 1.2686; the high for the month was 1.2931. The total high-to-low trading range was 345 pips.

That does not sound all that bad, does it? In reality, the high-to-low trading range for the EURUSD was the lowest range since October 2007. Figure 10.4 shows the running 22-day range going back to that time. To put the range into perspective, the average 22-day range over

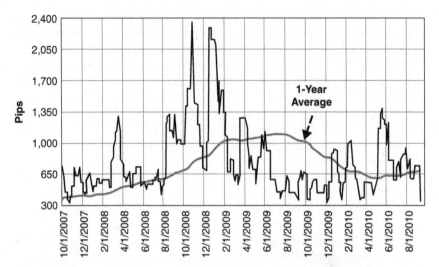

FIGURE 10.4   The 22-Day High-to-Low Trading Range for the EURUSD

one year on that date was 685 pips. In other words, with the current range at 345 pips, the price has room to extend the high-to-low range by 340 pips to get to the average.

The question is, "Will the extension go to the upside or to the down-side, or even both?" Looking at the daily chart, the bias is favoring the up-side because the price is back above some key borderlines like the 100 day MA and the 50 percent retracement. However, a move above the 38.2 per-cent retracement/remembered line at the 1.2776 would be needed to help confirm the bias. Also, a move above the 22-day high at 1.2931 would also be needed to confirm green lights for a bullish trend. Needless to say, a move below the 100 day and 50 percent would take the wind right out of any bull's sale and instead target a bearish trend.

The next step is to look at the hourly chart for clues and key borderlines.

The Hourly Chart

With the key borderline levels uncovered on the daily chart, I will now fo-cus on the key levels in the hourly chart. Figure 10.5 shows a broad picture of the EURUSD over the narrow trading range that has kept the price con-tained over the last month.

What you might notice is that the chart setup I used takes a lot of clues from the key levels in the daily chart and puts them in this chart. I have

FIGURE 10.5 The Hourly Chart for the EURUSD from August 11 to September 10

added a horizontal line placed at the 38.2 percent Fibonacci retracement line at 1.2776. I have done the same at the 50 percent Fibonacci retracement line at 1.2604. I put a horizontal line at the current 100 day MA at 1.2657. Finally, horizontal lines mark the ceiling over the last 22 trading days at 1.2931 and the floor at 1.2586.

I strongly recommend that when you set up your three time period charts, if there is a key level in play, like the 100 day MA, put a horizontal line at that price level in your hourly and even five-minute charts. This way you are aware of the level when you are focused on the other time period charts.

Of note in this chart is that I did not include a Fibonacci retracement. The market has been nontrending for a month and the inclusion would simply clutter the chart. What trend is there to retrace if the market is nontrending? Trend lines are also not effective when the price is moving up and down like it has been doing in a nontrending pattern. Horizontal and remembered lines tend to be king in a nontrending environment.

Trade Entry Clues   There are three important borderline levels when looking at the broader view of the hourly chart. The first is that the ceiling of the trading range is really an area from 1.2915 to 1.2931. There were a total of four separate highs that were rejected at that price area. This increases the importance of the area as a key borderline. The level should solicit selling interest as it is approached and buying interest on a break above.

The second borderline level of interest is the 1.2657 level. Note that the two most recent peaks at the 1.2915 area ultimately made their way down to the 1.2657 level. I will look at this area more closely in the next figure. Finally, what I find interesting is the way the market used the four horizontal lines/areas as "pit stops" during the moves up and down. Those levels came in at the 38.2 percent and 50 percent Fibonacci retracements from the daily chart, the high ceiling area, and the 1.2657 level.

If you follow the moves up and down on the chart, the market was very orderly as it moved from borderline to borderline to borderline. The hourly chart puts an exclamation point on the importance of each of those key levels.

- *1.2657 is a key remembered line, borderline, and entry level.*

    As mentioned in the last section, the 1.2657 level is a key borderline level worth taking a closer look at. In order to do that, I have zoomed in to look at the period from August 20 to September 10. Figure 10.6 shows that trading period.

    In the chart, the numbered circles show the number of times the price tested the 1.2657 level as support or resistance (mostly support). There were no fewer than 12 separate occasions. The more times a specific price (or contained area) is tested, the greater the significance as a key borderline level. The market remembers the level and typically will react on breaks to the downside or upside. If the price is above, the bias is bullish. If the price is below, the bias is bearish. Most of the times the market came down to the level, the price moved higher.

    On September 10, the 100 day MA was at the same level as the 1.2657 remembered line. The market price moved below the line at 1.2657 (point 12 in Figure 10.60). This should have led to a sharp move lower for the pair; in fact, I sold in anticipation of further downside momentum. Instead, the market price moved to a low of 1.2643 and stalled. Although the market stayed below the key borderline for 95 minutes, no further selling ensued and the price moved back above the 1.2657 level. I closed out the sell with a small loss.

    This reluctance to move lower after breaking the 100 day MA and the remembered line is a clue the market is not ready to sell off. At least not yet.

- *The 200 hour MA is a key borderline at 1.2657.*

    The other key focus from the hourly chart in Figure 10.6 is the reluctance to move above the 200 hour MA. Focus again on the boxed

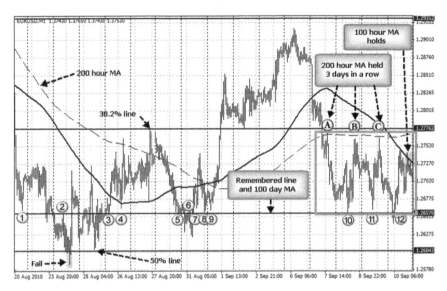

FIGURE 10.6 1.2657 Is a Key Remembered Line for the EURUSD

area in Figure 10.6. On September 7 the price trended sharply lower, falling through the 100 and 200 hour MAs (at point A), and the 38.2 percent retracement at 1.2776.

The next day, after bouncing off the ubiquitous 1.2657 remembered line, the price moved back up to test the 200 day MA (at point B) but fell short, finding sellers against the level. On September 9, the market tested both the floor (at point 11) and the 200 hour MA in the same day (at point C). This time both the floor and the ceiling kept the price contained.

For three days the market waffled between the 200 hour MA (dashed line) and the 1.2657 level. Like the other borderlines at the Fibonacci levels, the remembered line and the high area, the 200 hour MA can be added to the list of key indicators that the market will pay attention to on any break or failed break. With three successive tests in three days and the flatness of the line, it has the characteristics of a remembered line and trend line. Any upside break of the level going forward will be a clue for a bullish move, while any test and failure to get through the level will be a bearish clue. It is a key borderline.

- *The 100 hour MA keeps the sharp rebound under wraps.*

It seems that all major levels were in play off the recent action in the hourly chart. The key 100 hour MA is not the exception (see solid MA line in Figure 10.7).

FIGURE 10.7 The 100 Hour MA Ends the Rally Higher and the Price Closes the Week below the 100 Hour MA

On September 10, the 100 hour MA was the perfect profit-taking point for traders who purchased the EURUSD on the failed break below the 100 day MA and the key remembered line at 1.2657. The sharp rally took the price within 2 pips of the key MA line (high reached 1.2745 and the MA was at 1.2747). Later, another attempt higher moved the price above the line (by 6 pips) but was quickly rejected. Subsequent tests failed, keeping the bearish bias intact as the trading week came to a close.

The key levels are also the key reasons to trade. Moving through the levels will give the clues for a bullish trend or a bearish trend.

Low Range Equals Nontrending   Although the range over each of the last three days has been so-so, with the September 8 range being 103 pips, September 9 being 101 pips, and September 10 being 98 pips, the range for the three days in aggregate has been only 122 pips from the high to the low (1.2643 to 1.2765).

There have only been five trading days going back to January 2008 with less of a trading range (and most were around a major holiday like Christmas or the Fourth of July). The average for a year comes to 247 pips. Like the narrow range from the daily chart, the nontrending characteristic over

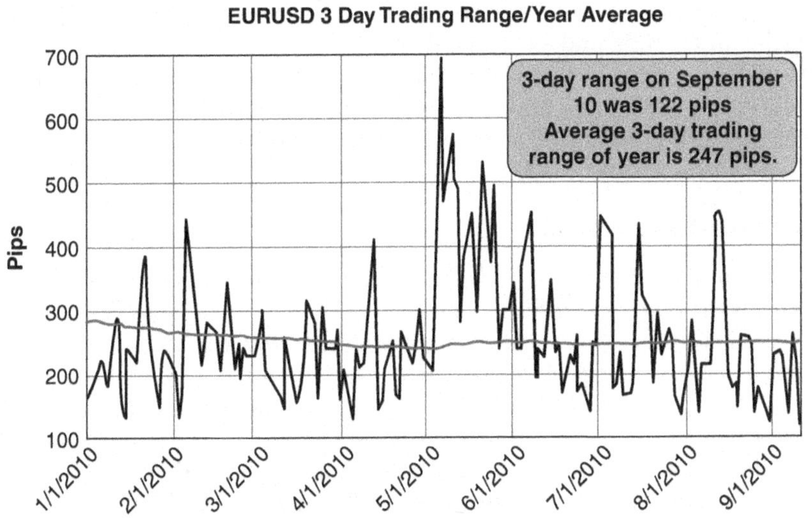

EURUSD 3 Day Trading Range/Year Average

FIGURE 10.8 The Three-Day High-to-Low Range Is at Low Levels, Suggesting a Move Soon

the last three days is also a precursor to a trend-type move ahead (see Figure 10.8).

A Mix of Bearish and Bullish Clues   There are some bearish clues and bullish clues from the hourly chart that keeps all traders happy (or confused).

- The failure below the key remembered line at 1.2657 and sharp rally was bullish, but . . .
- Staying below the 100 hour MA off the rally is bearish. The price tested that level all the way into the close and the market could not sustain momentum above it.
- In addition to the reluctance to move above the 100 hour MA, the 200 hour MA had its share of tests and failures during the week. Although the level did not come in play on this day, the prior three days' failure to break above the key level increases the importance of it as a key borderline going forward.
- The coiling of the market is obvious with the bulls and bears fighting it out. The key levels are being respected, but the ranges are contracting in what already is a narrow trading range (for the month). The hourly chart—like the daily chart—suggests a trend move is likely going forward.

It is simply a matter of time before the market chooses the direction for the entry trade and subsequent trend. The clues from the hourly chart are all lined up to put traders on red alert for the imminent move. The next section will take a look at the five-minute chart. Does it give any new clues that will tip the scales to the bullish side or the bearish side?

The Five-Minute Chart

When I am looking at the five-minute chart, I am looking for momentum clues. If the market is trending intraday, the five-minute chart will often be the guide for the trend. The price will simply follow the MA, staying above it if the trend is bullish or staying below it if the trend is bearish.

Figure 10.9 shows the activity of the five-minute chart over a day and a half. The setup is consistent with the other charts. The 100 and 200 bar MAs are shown. I added a horizontal line at the 100 day MA and remembered line at 1.2657. I added a line at the 100 hour MA line at 1.2747. This is the area where the market peaked against the 100 hour MA earlier in the day. I also added the Fibonacci retracement from the low to the high for the day to see if there were any clues from it.

The price coming into the day was below both the 100 and 200 bar MA on the five-minute chart, giving a clear bearish bias (solid and dashed MA lines in the chart). The subsequent break below the key support at the

FIGURE 10.9 EURUSD Five-Minute Chart Is Showing More Neutrality

1.2657 remembered line and 100 day MA gave green lights to be short the market.

The move below the key support line should have led to increased momentum and a trend-like move to the downside. Instead, the market stalled. For 95 minutes the price traded in an 18-pips range from 1.2643 to 1.2661. This is *not* what I would expect on a break. Figure 10.9 shows the lack of activity below the 1.2657 level. It certainly was uninspiring, to say the least. Note that it is only by looking at the five-minute chart that we can truly see the lack of market momentum.

When the price moved back above the 1.2657 level (and my short trade was covered for a small loss), the five-minute chart shows the momentum I was expecting to the downside. Buyers used the 1.2657 level as a level to buy against (see point A in Figure 10.9).

Is it a good trade to buy on the failure and move back above the 1.2657 level? Sure. Risk is defined and limited to a move below the 1.2643 level. Often, the failure of a key borderline to break ends up being the start of a good trade. In this instance, the price moved through the 100 bar MA but stalled before the 200 bar MA. Eventually, however, the price broke above the 200 bar MA and surged to the highs for the day.

The trend move looked to be on its way until it ran into the resistance from the 100 hour MA at the 1.2745 level. The trend move stalled, and although the move from the 1.2657 level provided some bullish clues (and a nice trade gain for the buyers), the price stalling at the 100 hour MA took the bullishness out of the trade and a rotation back down ensued.

The day (and week) ended with the two MAs converging on each other (7 pips separated the 100 and 200 bar MA), and the price settled between the two. How uncommitted to a bias can you get!

Ending the Week Neutral   With the price between the 100 and 200 bar MAs on the five-minute chart, and the two MAs within 7 pips of each other, it is suggesting the market is nontrending and unsure.

Like the hourly and the daily charts, the nontrending characteristics of the five-minute chart are pointing to a move. All three charts are in agreement. The market is nontrending.

A COMPOSITE VIEW OF THE CLUES

When multiple charts are nontrending, do not forget the implication of that dynamic. Typically, the nontrending clues come via the five-minute chart or the hourly chart. When the daily, hourly, and five-minute charts are all nontrending, it is *really* time to take note. We know nontrending will transition into a trending market.

In our example, the clues are building for a trend-type move. The basis for a move is in the nontrending characteristics of the market. Below are some of the clues the market is giving from each of the charts I monitor:

Daily Chart

- It is the narrowest month-long trading range (345 pips) since October 2007.
- 100 day MA slope is relatively flat and flattening.
- Market is still moving up and down within a narrow range, suggesting the market participants are unsure of the direction.

Hourly Chart

- Three-day trading range is only 122 pips (only five other times since January 2008).
- 200 hour MA has no slope.
- 100 hour MA is flattening.
- Market price is still moving up and down in a narrow range, suggesting the market participants are unsure of the direction.

Five-Minute Chart

- Both 100 and 200 bar MA are flattening.
- The two MAs are within 7 pips of each other.
- Price is between the two MAs, waiting for a clue to buy or sell.

I know the market is nontrending. I have analyzed each of the charts. Each of the charts has bullish and bearish characteristics. However, I know there are some key borderline levels. These borderlines mainly come from MAs, remembered lines, and Fibonacci retracements. Since the market has not been trending, a normal trend line has not been a major tool, but that does not mean it won't play a role as the trade progresses.

On September 10, 2010, the market closed at 1.2709. The key borderlines above and below from the respective charts include the following:

Daily Chart

- Month low price: 1.2586
- 50 percent Fibonacci retracement: 1.2604
- 100 day MA: 1.2657
- CLOSING PRICE:1.2709
- 38.2 percent Fibonacci retracement: 1.2776
- Month high price range: 1.2931

Hourly Chart

- Remembered line: 1.2657
- NY low: 1.2685
- CLOSING PRICE:1.2709
- 100 hour MA: 1.2726
- High from Friday: 1.2745
- 200 hour MA: 1.2769
- Month high price range: 1.2915–1.2931

Five-Minute Chart

- 100 bar MA at 1.2716
- 200 bar MA at 1.2709

"IS IT A BOY OR A GIRL, DOC?"

On Monday, September 13, in Australia, the currency market will open. With key borderlines known and in place, the trade decision is dependent on whether the market moves lower or higher. Which key level will be breached first, and when one is broken, will there be momentum buyers or sellers?

As a trader, I really do not care which way the market goes. When the market is in such a state of confusion, it means the market does not know which way it wants to go. Typically, at this point people will get the loudest and pound their chest on the business news channels saying things like, "The EURUSD is going to test the lows," or, "The dollar is going to get hit in the last quarter." Then you will get those who will say, "We are in a range-bound market. I expect the market to stay between 1.2600 and 1.2900."

Yeah, right. Traders are paid to make money. The most money is made in a trending market. Even if it is 300 to 500 pips, the chances are it will trend. For me, my response is "Whether it is a boy or girl, I will love it." In other words, let the market decide. It is not up to me. I am just a follower. But I will love whichever way it goes.

If the market is going to trend lower, the price needs to break below the NY low at 1.2685, the 100 day MA and key remember line at 1.2657, and the 50 percent retracement at 1.2604. Then I target and map the next levels lower.

If the price is going to go higher, the price needs to break the 100 hour MA at 1.2726, the 200 hour MA at 1.2769, and the 38.2 percent retracement at 1.2776, and then ultimately the high range at 1.2915 to 1.2931. Then I target and map the next levels higher. "Is it a boy or girl, Doc?" Hopefully, the decision will come soon.

The next chapter will go through the trade entry and trend trade progression. The triggers will be triggered, the risk will be defined, and the targets will be set. How far the trend will go will depend on the strength of the trend and the ability to keep the bullish or bearish bias intact. What we do know is the market is ready to move.

See the Webinar: "Trading Forex in a Non-Trending Market"

In September 2010, I gave a webinar at FXStreet (www.fxstreet.com) and later for customers at FXDD (http://forex.fxdd.com/webinars) titled "Trading Forex in a Non-Trending Market" (both can be found archived on those websites).

In the webinar, I talked about the 345-pip high-to-low trading range. I looked at the different charts and focused in on the key borderline levels. I spoke of what needed to happen to push the market out of the nontrending quagmire that had gripped the currency markets for a month's time. I gave the bias at the time from what the clues were saying and knew that a break below the 100 day MA was needed to start the process to the downside, while a move above the 200 hour MA was needed to get things going on the upside. The message was clear, "I don't know where we are going, but we are going somewhere."

CHAPTER 11

Executing the
Game Plan

T he snap cadence of football quarterbacks everywhere goes something like this: "Blue 52. Blue 52. Hut. Hut." That snap cadence gives clues to the offensive linemen, the running backs, and the receivers, who remain motionless as they await the snap of the ball. Sometimes the quarterback's snap cadence will change the play. Sometimes its intention is to confuse the opponent's defense. In all situations, during the snap cadence the players coil like springs. Then, when the ball is snapped, the spring explodes and the players execute the play. Each play is a part of the team's game plan. The play should support the team's objectives set up by the game plan. Sometimes the play does what the team thought it would do, and a good gain is achieved. Other times it does not, and a small loss or gain is made on the play.

In currency trading, there is no quarterback calling out a cadence; the market does give clues that often ignite a "play." That play is a trade, and the trade is part of the game plan. Our game plan—to trade trends and keep fear to a minimum—should be a requirement of all our trades. Sometimes the trades do what is expected and the market trends. A good gain is achieved. Other times it does not, and the trade is closed for a small loss or gain.

In Chapter 10, the snap cadence for a trend trade was developed. It was the market's cadence to the trade. The market clues from the five-minute, hourly, and daily charts all pointed to a potential trend move—to a good gain. To be successful in attacking the currency trends you need to see and recognize the clues from the market. Recognize the cadence that the market provides to traders.

Once that is done, it becomes a matter of executing what you have been preparing for—the game plan. If the market does not do what you think it should do, you adjust by exiting the trade. Sometimes you will put together a few nice trades in a row and have a sustained profit drive. This is the equivalent of a trader's touchdown. Other times you may have some losing trades, which are the equivalent of allowing the opposition to score. However, just like in any athletic competition, you try not to make the mistakes that will kill you or cause you to lose the game. Ultimately, if you are able to anticipate the trend and stay on that trend, and the profits start to accrue, you will be successful, a winner. It is time to celebrate.

By now we know the mission statement. We know the game plan. We can define the borderlines with our tools. By doing so, we understand the risks. We will look to not make the big mistake but understand that there will be losses. You cannot trade and not have losses. It is just part of the business. It is a business. It is all business. Anyone who trades currencies is going against the market, the big boys.

In order to win and be successful at trading, you have to think like the market. Anticipate the trend by following the clues. If the market is not trending, look for it to trend. Look for the sustained trend trade—the equivalent of the long drive in football. When you are on the trend, stay on it. Make those who are trading against the trend pay. Stay on it until you reach the end zone. Then after the position is closed out and the market starts to correct, give yourself a high five, be happy, and start to prepare for the next series, the next trend trade.

"Blue 52. Blue 52. Hut. Hut." It is time to execute the trade and look for the trend.

THE KICKOFF: THE ENTRY TRADE

In the initial hour of trading on September 13, the market went to a low of 1.2703 and a high of 1.2718. The range was narrow. The market was quiet. The second hour had the same low price but extended to the 1.2724 high.

In the third hour the market made its move (see Figure 11.1). The price moved above the 100 hour MA and triggered a buy at the 1.2725. There is a key reason to trade. Risk can be defined by the closing price from Friday at the 1.2709 or 16 pips. The anticipation of a trend move propelled the market higher. The buyers were there. The market was seeing what I was seeing. The initial risk was never threatened.

Is this trade realistic? Or is it a made-for-TV script where everyone lives happily ever after? Needless to say, I know how the trade developed and ended in this example, but that does not mean that what happened is not

FIGURE 11.1 The EURUSD Breaks above the 100 Hour MA at 1.2725 and Gets off to a Great Start

replicated at other times in the currency market. When the trend clues are lined up in the market, when the borderlines are evident and clear, they are clear for everyone. It is no secret formula. It is a combination of lines, moving averages (MAs), and Fibonacci retracements—simple things that everyone can see, and that often lead to trend moves!

If I know a nontrending market will eventually trend, a break of a 100 bar MA will solicit a reaction from me. If the price breaks the 100 bar MA, goes up 15 pips, and goes back down below it, I lose a little. It does not make it a wrong trade. Trading successfully is not about being right all the time. It is about being *really* right when you are right, and when you are wrong being wrong by only a little.

The first few hours after major surgery, the anxious moments after a rocket launch, the first offensive series in a football game—those beginning moments are often critical to success or failure. Trading is no different. All traders want to see the market do what it is supposed to do during the first few hours after the trade. A profit right away is a tremendous boost to confidence (and ego), but like many other things, you don't know until that initial time is over.

In my trade, it got off to a good start (see Figure 11.1). The market price trended higher and broke the 200 hour MA at the 1.2769 level. It broke the 38.2 percent Fibonacci retracement at 1.2776 soon after that. The m happened in the first several hours of trading.

FIGURE 11.2 The First Trend Leg Should Hold the 38.2 Percent Correction; Be Patient.

The next key levels to target are the 1.2915 to 1.2931 levels, which are the month-long high price. That is a big jump from the 1.2776 level, but it is the trade's first major target. If reached, the trade would yield nearly 200 pips. Not a bad return for 16 pips of risk.

There is going to be some resistance along the bullish journey, but there are ways to manage it. There is still the risk that market could turn around. But that is trading, and I have the tools to know if the trade is wrong. If I am wrong, I will get out. If the market does not do what it is supposed to do, I don't mess around. My focus, however, is on a trend. The trend is my rocket launch and the first few hours look good. The market price goes to 1.2794, the profit is up to 68 pips, and the market finds some profit takers (see Figure 11.2). What am I now thinking as a trader?

MANAGING THE TRADE

Managing the trade requires using all of our tools together. It is also about using the five-minute, hourly, and daily charts to find key borderline levels that give entry signals, confirm the trend, give exit signals, and provide clues for retracements and the resumption of the trend.

The entry trade has been done, and the market has done what I expected it to do (i.e., climbed to 1.2794). It has trended higher away from the key initial resistance. In outlining the progression and management of the trend trade going forward, I will step through the initial legs of the trade. The initial major target will be the 1.2931 level. That is where we want to go. The only way to get there is to stay with a bullish bias. Let's see how the trade progresses.

The First Leg: Risk Profit for Rewards

When I manage a trend trade, the goal is to stay on the trend as long as possible. In order to stay on a trend I need to *risk profit*. By this I mean that there may be a correction within the early part of the trend that can take unrealized gains from an account. However, if the trend is truly a trend, and a trend is anticipated, the directional move will be reestablished before the bias is changed from bullish to bearish (or vice versa). The potential return is the rewards from a sustained, directional trend move.

Note the words *risking profit*. When you are on a trend there should be profit from having a position with the trend, even if it is toward the start of the trend. As a result, the risk that traders need to take is in the form of investing some of the profit in the trade, not a risk of loss from the trade.

Think of a retail business. Most retail businesses invest some of their profits in their business. The hope is that the money invested will lead to greater rewards. It is no different in the trading business. If you anticipated a trend trade and you have an early profit in that trade, you will need to make an investment of some profit in the trend when the market corrects. The best investment traders can make when attacking currency trends is risking profit when a trend trade is anticipated.

If the trend is anticipated and the market appears to be obliging, be sure that you do all you can to stay on that trend. You want to be greedy because if this is a trend, the market will go higher.

I often feel that the first leg of the trend is often the most difficult. There is a quick gain, and there tends to be a quick correction too. This is because those traders who are happy with 20, 30, 40, 50 pips come in and sell. There is also a group of traders at the beginning of a trend who are so used to the nontrend that when the price goes higher, they are like Pavlov's dog. The bell rings and they sell simply because the price is higher.

This is normal, so let them sell. The first correction should be a healthy correction, and the correction will often tell you about what may lie ahead for the trend. By this I mean that you will often find out if the move has support from the market and in particular the big boys, the most successful traders. They are the ones that matter the most and carry the most influence for a trend-type move.

Where you find if they are participating is usually at any key technical level that lies below the current spike high (there usually is at least one borderline from the five-minute, hourly, or daily chart that can be pinpointed). In addition, the 38.2 percent retracement level of the move from the low to the high (see Figure 11.2 Fibonacci retracements) is also a level that, if held on a correction, gives confidence for the trend type move. The 38.2 percent retracement is the shallowest of the Fibonacci retracements, and holding it is indicative of good buying interest from smart traders. If the first correction can hold those levels, the potential for a currency trend is looking good.

In the trade, the 200 hour MA (or confirming MA on the hourly chart) was at 1.2769 today. This was the line that held the tops the prior week for three successive days (look back in Chapter 10 at Figure 10.6). Using the "If . . . Should" rule: If the price breaks the 100 hour MA trigger (which it did) and the confirming 200 hour MA (which it did), the price should go higher. If it does not, think about getting out. Since the current price in Figure 11.2 is above the 200 hour MA line, this is a level I want the market to stay above on a correction.

My getting-out point (or stop loss) in this trade is actually down to the 38.2 percent line at 1.2759 since that is below the 200 hour MA line. If the 200 hour MA line was at 1.2755 instead, I would put my stop below 1.2755. With that stop loss in place, I am saying that I am willing to risk a move below the 200 hour MA and down to the 38.2% retracement at 1.2759 (from 1.2794). That is a 35-pip investment. You are probably wondering why I was willing to risk so much. The answer is that at the start of the trade I was initiating a position at the borderline. I did not have profit. I had nothing. I was anticipating a trend, but I did not know it was going to trend.

Now I have profit. I also have some clues that the market should trend. I want to stay on the trend because I know that the gain will be much greater than 70 pips if it is in fact a trend. I also know the hardest thing to do is get back on that trend trade once the position is closed. I am willing to invest 35 pips of profit in anticipation of a trend move. I also do not want to scare myself out of a trend trade early—especially since I expect a trend. I worked hard to catch the trend, and I want to stay on it. I am willing to reinvest profit.

The trade progressed and the big boys held support (low came in at 1.2773) against the 200 hour MA at 1.2769 and the 38.2 percent retracement at 1.2759. The second leg of the trend has begun.

The Second Leg: Temptations to Take Profit

The second leg of the trend trade starts to take shape (see Figure 11.3). The upward momentum is slowing a bit, but the price still works its way up

EURUSD,M5 1.37770 1.37790 1.37770 1.37790

1.2783 is the 38.2% retracement. Buyer also bought here earlier.

0.0 - 1.28330

38.2 - 1.27833

50.0 - 1.27680

61.8 - 1.27527

100.0 - 1.27030

The stop-loss zone is now 1.2783 to 1.2768. 1.2768 = 200 bar MA, 200 hour MA, 50% retracement, and where the big boys bought earlier.

13 Sep 2010   13 Sep 02:00   13 Sep 03:20   13 Sep 04:40   13 Sep 06:00   13 Sep 07:20   13 Sep 08:40   13 Sep 10:00   13 Sep 11:20   13 Sep 12:40   13 Sep 14:00   13 Sep 15

FIGURE 11.3   The Second Leg of the Trend Should Still Find Buyers on Dips

to the 1.2833 level from the 1.2773 corrective low. Is it time to take profit? After all, 100 pips can be locked in on the trade. There is another temptation to book a profit and get out of the trade, but does it make sense? Is there a reason?

In my opinion, it is still too soon to take profit. The reasons include:

- The market has only moved 108 pips from 1.2725 entry level. If this is a trend move, it will have more room to roam.
- I am up 108 pips on the trade, but in order to make trend profits, you need to risk trend profits. Give me a better reason to sell. That is, give me a reason that says the bias is bearish.
- The first leg support held like a charm. There is likely to be support from the big boys below.
- There are logical stops below that, if triggered, would mean there is something very wrong with the idea of a trend and the bias would be bearish.

For this leg higher, I have moved the stop up modestly. The new stop loss zone is between 1.2768 and 1.2783 (see Figure 11.3). The reason I have a range for the stop is that it gives an option. I like to do this early in a trend move when the market is still influenced by quick profit takers and countertrend traders.

The top stop level is a more conservative stop. Maybe I take partial profit? Maybe I am still not sure of the trend (although all reasons point to a trend)? Maybe the level is of significance?

In the trade, the 38.2 percent retracement of the move up from the low is still a level that should hold support early in a trend move. Note that at the level there were some buyers earlier, so there should be a good base of support at the level.

If I were to decide to stop myself out at the higher 1.2783 level, but the price holds the bottom stop zone price at 1.2768 levels, I would look to purchase at least part of my position back when it goes back above 1.2783. The reason is that it is still early in the trend, and the holding of the 1.2768 level should be encouraging to the market. Stay on the trend as long as you can!

The other lower stop level I set is at 1.2768. This stop level is what I like to call the "This is not a trend; I want out" stop level. The level corresponds with four separate borderlines: the 200 bar MA on the five-minute chart, the 200 hour MA, the 50 percent retracement, and it is also where the big boys bought earlier.

Is the level significant? Yes, it is! Needless to say, if the price goes below this level, I get out. I make 43 pips on the trade, I risked 16 pips initially, and I go back to the drawing board. It is not my fault. It is the market's fault for not wanting to trend!

There will always be a level that makes you doubt the trend and consider bailing. These levels are obvious. The stop at 1.2768 is obvious. There are four reasons why the price should not go below that level. The old saying goes, "If it walks like a duck, quacks like a duck, and looks like a duck, it is a duck." Find the ducks that say *stop* and regroup. The good news is you still are likely to have a profit on the trade, and you can regroup with a clear, fear-free head.

Be prepared for some chinks in the armor, but don't panic. Note in Figure 11.3 how the price fell below the 100 bar MA (solid MA line) on the five-minute chart. Is that a worry? Not really. I am still more focused on the 38.2 percent as being more of a worry. The trend is still young. The 1.2915 to 1.2931 level still is our minimum target. There are better levels of support below. Remember, be patient, especially early in the anticipated trend. Look for reasons to stay on the trend.

The Third Leg: Exiting with a Reason

If you have made it this far, the rewards are about to start getting more serious. We are also now talking about a trend day (see Figure 11.4). The

The third leg moves nearly 100 pips higher and is approaching 1.2915–31 target. Time to take some profit?

FIGURE 11.4 Third Leg Higher Surges Nearly 100 Pips. Is It Time to Take Some Profit?

market has been trending higher with little in the way of corrections (higher highs and higher lows). The price has moved comfortably back above the 100 bar MA on the five-minute chart after the minor drops below it earlier. The stop levels on the last leg were not threatened and the price surged to the upside.

On this leg up there should not have been any fear. Sure, the price moved up and corrected below the previous high (see gray line), but it had a V reversal well before it even got to the 100 bar MA. The price peaks at the 1.2891 level, tacking on nearly 100 pips from the last corrective low. I am long at 1.2725 and the price is at 1.2891. All is good with the trend. However, with the price approaching key resistance at 1.2915 to 1.2931 (the month-long high-ceiling level), it is time to think what lies ahead and plan the next trade. It is time to think about a *temporary* exit.

It may have seemed unlikely at the start of the trade and the day, but the high area for the month of trading at the 1.2915 to 1.2931 level is within sight. This is a level that is likely to lead to some profit taking, selling on the first test.

The smart traders who anticipated the trend, and who have 165 pips of profit, will likely sell and take profit or partial profit against the level, with the knowledge that if the price goes above the 1.2931 level, they will buy. This is simply sound money management and makes logical trading sense. The traders who have been selling (and are short) as the market goes higher and higher and higher will also be selling against the level. In their minds it is time to have that correction that gets them back to breakeven. Don't be one of these traders!

If the price does find sellers and moves lower, buying and reestablishing at a lower support level is what should happen. In order to take profit (or exit), I always need a technical reason to sell. Selling because you have a profit is not a good reason. However, selling against the key resistance at 1.2915 to 1.2931 is a good reason to sell. It is a key borderline. Borderlines give us reasons to trade. Are there any other reasons to sell at this area other than the 1.2915 to 1.2931 level? After all, 1.2891 is still 40 pips away from 1.2931.

Because I am always looking ahead and my charts are dynamic, not static, there are three options for exiting.

Option 1 Sell against the top trend line (point A in Figure 11.5). When the market is trending higher (or lower), it is not only important to draw the bullish trend line by connecting the higher lows, but it is also important to connect the highs in the chart to higher highs.

FIGURE 11.5 This Leg Higher Is Starting to Approach Resistance Levels Where Profit Taking Is Likely

In Figure 11.5, while the shorts were covering one last time, they were pushing the price right up to the top trend line that connected the earlier highs for the day. That level came in at the 1.2891 level. Is that a low-risk selling borderline? Yes!

What is my risk selling against the top trend line borderline? I do have risk because I am taking myself out of a trend that I want to be on. My risk at this point is if the price goes higher above the trend line and breaks above the month-long high at 1.2931. If this happens, I need to buy on that break. So, by selling here I forgo 40 pips of profit and have to buy a new break.

I can define my risk another way. I can sell against the trend line at the 1.2891 area, but simply buy my position back if the price goes above the top trend line by 7 to 10 pips (at 1.2898 to 1.2901). If it goes above the trend line by that amount, there should be additional short covering buying that should push the price up to the 1.2931 level really quickly. If I buy again at the 1.2900 area, I simply put my stop 5 to 10 pips below the trend line at the 1.2885 area. The logic is that if the price breaks this obvious trend line, then fails, the correction down will likely start from that point. So I risk 12 to 20 pips by taking profit at the trend line with this option.

This is an option I cannot refuse. I am trading against a borderline, I have defined risk, and I have a defined plan. I can reestablish the long position at a more favorable level if the market corrects lower or buy back on the trend if the market does not correct and continues higher. I book a profit of 165 pips and have all my options open to reestablish the long position. These are the rewards of being on the trend. It just makes logical sense. No fear, just happiness for a trend well traded.

Although Option 1 is taken, there are two other options if I were to decide to stay with the position.

Option 2   Do nothing, but be prepared for a sharp fall. If the market peaks and falls sharply from the high, eye the upward-sloping trend line and the 100 bar MA as a level to exit (at point B in Figure 11.5). Then look to reestablish a long when risk is more defined and the selling is abated. This is an option you don't want to face since it increases fear, but it preserves profit.

Option 3   Stay with the position and see what happens. If the price goes higher, sell against the 1.2915 to 1.2931 level. If it goes to the Option 2 point I get out. If it wanders and eventually moves below a key technical level or levels from the tools I use, then I get out.

If I took this option, what eventually happened is the market consolidated into the day's close and allowed the 100 bar MA to catch up with the price at the 1.2871 level (see point C in Figure 11.5). The bottom trend

FIGURE 11.6 Exit at 1.2871 Is Also the 38.2 Percent Fibonacci Retracement of the Move Down from 1.3333

line also came into play and converged with the MA level. A trend line from a pennant formation also converged at the borderline level. As if that was not enough, the 1.2871 level also corresponds with the 38.2 percent retracement of the move down from the 1.3333 high to the 1.2586 low on the hourly chart (see Figure 11.6). The hourly chart comes into play too! Needless to say, it provided a nice third profit-taking option that turned the short-term bias from bullish to bearish.

Even though there were good or great low-risk reasons to take profit, what is still important to realize is if this is a trend, it still has room to go. The price is still in the narrowest trading range since October 2007. If it has any redeeming qualities as a trend and the narrow range is to be extended, it will break that target level at 1.2931 and move higher.

However, I am back to finding a low-risk trade with defined risk. The difference is I have 165 pips of profit (1.2725 buy, 1.2890 sell), with 16 pips of initial risk.

FINDING CLUES IN THE CONSOLIDATION PHASE

With the well-known resistance at the 1.2915 to 1.2931 level, and other borderline reasons to sell, a consolidation/corrective phase begins. Staying below the topside trend line and the fall below the 100 bar MA (at 1.2871) did find buyers near the 200 bar MA, but the subsequent period was mired with choppy two-way action (see Figure 11.7). The price did manage a break up to the 1.2909 level where sellers against the 1.2915 to 1.2931 level forced the market sharply lower. The level was simply too tempting for scalpers and profit takers on the first real test.

Was the 1.2909 area a good level to sell for me? No and yes (note that I put "no" first). The only caveat is that there are no other reasons to sell. If I were to sell here, my stop would be a break of 1.2915. That's it. I would not want to risk over 21 pips up to 1.2931 and then have to buy on the extension above 1.2931. I would rather be prepared to be an aggressive buyer above the 1.2931 level. I took profit and am comfortable with it. The market is still positive but it is more consolidating rather than trending.

What about consolidating periods? Are there clues to be found in them?

A dynamic of a consolidation after a trend move is that it allows for the moving averages to catch up with the price. In this instance, both the 100 and 200 bar MA on the five-minute chart converged with the price at around the 1.2975 level (see Figure 11.7). When this happens, I term the setup "three's a crowd" (see Chapter 7). The "three's a crowd" setup occurs when the market is nontrending/consolidating. What typically happens is

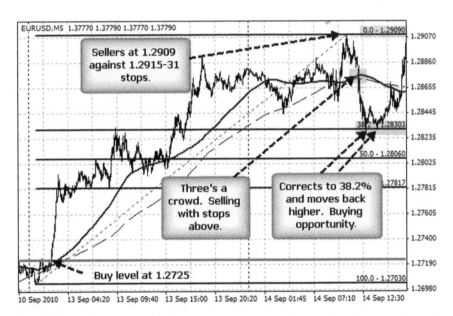

FIGURE 11.7 Correction/Consolidation Finds Support at 38.2 Percent; Minimal Correction Often Leads to a Surge Higher in a Trend Market

that if three is truly a crowd, something has to move away. In the world of charts and financial markets, it is always the price that moves away from the moving averages. Hence my naming of the setup.

This setup on five-minute, hourly, or daily charts is often a low-risk trading opportunity that can transition a nontrending market into a trending market. So pay attention to this setup.

In this case, after the 1.2909 level did find sellers, the price approached the 100 and 200 bar MAs at 1.2875 area and broke through. True to form, the price fell sharply. However, the fall finds support at 1.2830. What is the catalyst for the support? The 38.2 percent Fibonacci retracement stops the slide (see Figure 11.7). A key corrective borderline has been found once again.

A BORDERLINE: ALWAYS A LOW-RISK, UNAMBIGUOUS LEVEL

As we know, any borderline will always be a low-risk trading level.

The tools I use to define a borderline are purposely chosen to give an unambiguous view of the market. That is, if the price is above, it is bullish. If the price is below, it is bearish. With the market a day and a half into a potential trend, the price 79 pips from the high, and the 1.2931 level still looming as the minimal target for the trend move higher, buying against the 38.2 percent retracement is a low-risk dip buying opportunity. It is a borderline level (Figure 11.8).

Note that in this case there is a second chance to buy against the 38.2 percent retracement for the EURUSD (see Figure 11.8). This in my eyes is a free trade. Buying at the level has minimal risk. The initial defined risk would likely be down to 1.2920 (7 to 12 pips) where there were a high and low from the previous day. If, on the other hand, the 38.2 percent retracement holds, the upside potential should increase.

As a general rule, an early trending market that corrects and holds the 38.2 percent retracement is a low-risk buying opportunity. If the level holds, the market will take that as a sign to restart the trend. Risk is 10 to 15 pips on the trade. The profit potential should at least take the price back to and through the old high (i.e., 1.2909). If it does not hold (i.e., you get stopped out), that tells you something too. It could be the end of the trend or at least a period of further consolidation. So watch those early trend corrections to Fibonacci levels, and if they hold, that should be a golden trade opportunity and a clue that the trend has a good chance to restart.

FIGURE 11.8 If You Get a Second Chance, Take It: EURUSD Tests 38.2 Percent Twice

ANOTHER TREND REENTRY

Often on a correction during a trend that holds a 38.2 percent Fibonacci retracement, there is another opportunity to get back on the trend. This is due to the likelihood that the corrective move has breached the 100 bar MA on the five-minute chart (at the least). The second chance comes on a break back above the 100 bar MA.

In Figure 11.8 we saw the EURUSD correct to the 38.2 percent retracement. In Figure 11.9 (bottom left section of the chart), the subsequent move higher sends the price back above the 100 MA at the 1.2861 area, triggering a bullish bias. If a buy was not made at the 38.2 percent, a move above the 100 bar MA is an alternative trade. The stop need only be 10 to 20 pips on the other side of the moving average.

In my new long trade, the bounce off the Fibonacci retracement and the move back above the 100 and 200 bar MA gives me confidence. I have my risk defined (below 1.2820 initially) and am comfortable with that level. I am anticipating the next trend move to the upside. The target on our Bullish Highway would be a breach of the 1.2915 to 1.2931 area. A move above this level opens up many bullish doors.

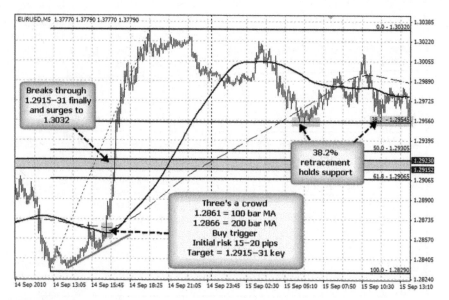

FIGURE 11.9 EURUSD Surges Higher and Breaks above the Target Range Extension Area

Figure 11.9 shows the move. This time, the momentum is directional and fast with little in the way of any correction. The price surges through the 1.2915 level and the 1.2931 old high and does what it is supposed to do. All systems are go for the bullish trend to continue. Lucky once again.

Remember, successful traders make their own luck. When you anticipate trends, trade against key borderlines, and are aware of where buyers and sellers will be, sometimes it makes you appear lucky to others who are not aware and prepared.

The fact is, you *are* lucky. The price does not have to hold the support level. It can go down and stop you out and go the other way. Big deal. That action typically tells me something too. It tells me the market has other ideas about this trend, for the time being at least. It is time to step away.

However, if the price does what it should do, I do consider myself lucky, but what I like to say is, "Successful traders make their own luck." So be glad and feel fortunate that you are "lucky," but understand that your luck was because of your hard work and preparation to attack the currency trend.

Figures 11.9 and 11.10 show the next surge higher. The trend is back on track. The price peaks at 1.3032, nearly 200 pips above the corrective low at 1.2830 and 170 pips above the break of the 100 bar MA at the 1.2861! Trends transition to nontrends, and this move was steep. What I know is

FIGURE 11.10 The Market Will Look for Reasons/Borderline to Sell and Take Profit

that trend moves usually find reasons to slow down. So draw trend lines, follow the Fibonacci retracements, and look for the best borderlines.

Figure 11.10 shows those levels. There are actually two borderlines. One is the continuation of the trend line that was used to exit the first trend move up at 1.2890. That trend line comes in at 1.3040 area. The second trend line is off the high price going back to September 10 and connecting to the 1.2890 high on September 13. That level comes in at 1.3008.

The combination of the two gives a profit-taking option after the steep move higher. The price does move above the first trend line but finds sellers before the next trend line at the 1.3032 level. The five-hour surge took the price from 1.2829 to 1.3030 or 201 pips. With risk defined against the two trend lines, the move does in fact slow, and it is time to take profit. Of note is that once the bottom trend line was broken, the underside of that trend line was used as a borderline. Hint: Undersides of trend lines are low-risk areas to sell against or take profit. Use a stop above the line.

The market consolidates, then corrects back down. Where does the correction find the next support? Would you believe at the 38.2 percent Fibonacci retracement level! Once again I am so lucky!

The pattern is certainly developing and obvious. The 38.2 percent retracement is a nice support level during trends. In this instance, the consolidation extends for two trading days (see Figure 11.11). The price remains supported by the 38.2 percent retracement at the 1.2954 level, which has

FIGURE 11.11 Nontrending, Narrow Range Is a Precursor to a Breakout

been tested three separate times. On the topside is the 1.3032 high. That level was tested three times as well.

The borderline against Fibonacci retracement at 1.2954 has company. That is, there is additional support from the hourly chart. The 50 percent Fibonacci retracement off the hourly chart comes in 5 pips higher at 1.2959 (see Figure 11.12), making the area a key support area from two separate charts with defined risk.

On September 16, the low reaches 1.2975. The high going into the NY open was 1.3034. The 59-pip trading range would likely be extended in the NY session. When the price broke through the ceiling, the market extended back higher to 1.3116 and the trend continued its move higher and higher.

Managing a trend trade as described so far in this chapter is not something that replicates itself each time. All trends have their own fingerprint.

However, what is consistent in trends is the thought process of defining the risk as it progresses and targeting levels ahead. Risk and targets are determined by any one of our tools in any one of our chart periods (i.e., five-minute, hourly, or daily). Exiting is also something that is consistent in all trades. Exiting, like trade entry, should be done for a technical reason. For example, a trade can be exited against a trend line, a moving average, or a Fibonacci level. In my example, I outlined different options for exiting

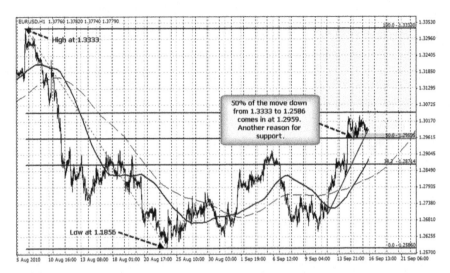

FIGURE 11.12 EURUSD Hourly Chart Is Providing Midpoint Support at the 1.2959 Level

the specific trade and taking profit. The obvious exit was against a trend line at 1.2891.

Our trend trade has taken us to a point where I have outlined what goes into managing the trade as it progresses from one leg of the trend to the next. I hope it allowed you to understand my thought process in a live example. It would be somewhat redundant to continue outlining the trade in this fashion, even though the trend did continue much higher.

However, I do want to fast-forward and look at the trend as it progressed, from the vantage point of the hourly and daily charts. These charts become more important as a trend progresses. They often provide a confirmation of the trend to the trader. The confirmations tend to be more significant in terms of bullishness (or bearishness) than one given on the five-minute chart.

A trend trade will typically have to test key borderlines in the hourly and daily charts along the journey. If the market can pass the borderline tests, it often provides the clues for the next bigger leg of the trend journey.

THE KEY ROLE OF BORDERLINES IN HOURLY AND DAILY CHARTS

The initial preparation for the trend trade outlined in Chapter 10 was reliant on the five-minute chart, the hourly chart, and the daily chart. As the trend progressed early on, many of the clues shown were found off the five-minute chart. In analyzing trend moves—especially multi-day trends like our example—the five-minute chart does play a vital role. The moving averages and Fibonacci retracements are key in tracking the momentum and up and down rhythm of the trending market. The five-minute chart shows that the best.

However, that does not mean I throw the hourly or daily charts out with the bathwater. Both give key confirming and directional clues that define and reinforce the trend, define risk, and provide confidence to the trader that the trend is still strong.

In the next section I will look at the EURUSD hourly chart. Figure 11.13 looks at the EURUSD trend rally through September 21, 2010. Yes, the rally that started at 1.2725 has continued and is up to 1.3271, or over 546 pips! To think it all started by risking 16 pips.

I have added in Figure 11.13 standard trend lines, remembered lines, and the 100 and 200 hour MAs as I would in a real-time trading environment. It is not hard to do. For trend lines, it is simply connecting a line between one low and a higher low. For remembered lines, it is finding those prices that the market uses as a floor, ceiling, or both and drawing a horizontal line across.

FIGURE 11.13 The Hourly Chart Contributes Its Share of Borderline Clues during a Trend Move Too

Fibonacci retracements are a less-useful tool in a sharp trend move because the longer-term corrections typically do not approach the 38.2 percent retracement level. Down the road when the EURUSD trend ends—and there will be clues from trend lines, moving averages, and re-membered lines—the Fibonacci retracements will play a part in defining the profit target for a countertrend selloff (see Chapter 9).

From the start of the trend, the eight days in this hourly chart have produced nine different key borderline levels (see Figure 11.13). I outlined the one at point A. That level was the profit-taking borderline for the second buy trade (see Figure 11.10). In addition to that level, there were four levels that defined low-risk borderline levels to take profit or exit the trend trade (2, 3, 5, and 8). There were also four levels that provided clear signals to reenter the trend (1, 4, 6, and 7). The levels, independent of the five-minute or daily chart, are pretty strong. They are simple (K.I.S.S. principle) but they are *strong*.

For example:

- Buying at the point 1 trend line is a logical low-risk trade with defined risk, which is minimal.
- Selling at the top trend line at point 2 is a logical low-risk trade with defined risk, which is minimal.
- Buying on the first test of the 100 hour MA at point 6 is a logical low-risk trade with defined risk, which is minimal.
- Having the trend line fail at point 7 but having the 100 hour MA pro-vide the support is a logical low-risk trade with defined risk, which is minimal.

Attacking currency trends is about anticipating the trends, defining the risk, and finding those key borderline levels. The hourly chart has its share of key borderline levels to trade the trends. Those borderline clues pave the way for low-risk entry points and clear exit levels that allow you to make the most money with the least amount of risk. That is the mission, isn't it?

Borderlines still play a key role in the daily charts, too. At the begin-ning of this chapter, the macro picture of the daily chart was shown. The trend moved from 1.5144 to the low 1.1876. A countertrend rally took the price to 1.3333, above the 38.2 percent retracement at 1.3124 but below the 50 percent midpoint of that macro move. The EURUSD was in the midst of a nontrending market in a 345-pips trading range. The 100 day MA was tested for four days. On the fourth day, the move below to a low of 1.2643 failed, and the market moved above the 100 day MA at the 1.2657 level. Figure 11.14 shows where the market has gone since that failed break.

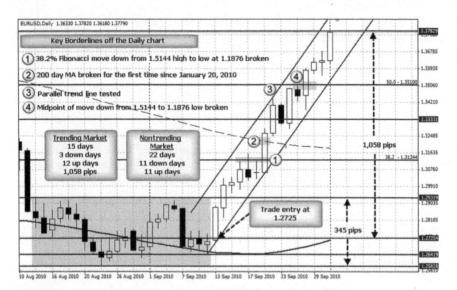

FIGURE 11.14   The Daily Chart Has Surged through Key Bullish Levels along the Trend Move

The trend higher has continued with little in the way of resistance from any bearish clues off the daily chart. The steps from target to target have kept the price firmly on the Bullish Highway.

- On September 13, the price moved above the 100 hour MA borderline, triggering a buy at 1.2725.
- On September 14, the price moved above the 1.2931 range high.
- On September 18, the 38.2 percent retracement was being tested at 1.3124.
- On September 21, the 38.2 percent retracement and 200 day MA was broken (first time since January 20, 2010—SIGNIFICANT).
- Five trading days later, on September 28, the 50 percent retracement of the large macro move down was broken at 1.3510.
- On Friday, October 1, the EURUSD closed 3 pips from the highest level since March 17, 2010, at 1.3779.

The 15-day rally from the trade date traveled 1,058 pips with 12 days up and 3 days down. The preceding 22 days traveled 345 pips, with 11 days up and 11 days down.

Where does that range rank? Figure 11.15 shows the best and worst going back to 2009. Not a bad move. It is getting toward the high range though,

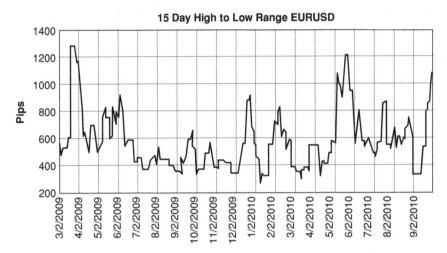

FIGURE 11.15 The 15-Day High-to-Low Range for the EURUSD (March 2009 to October 2010)

between 1200 and 1300 pips. It might be getting closer to that countertrend time. Be aware. Be prepared. But wait for those borderline levels to give the clues.

ATTACK THE CURRENCY TREND

Trends are directional, and they're fast. Trends have a tendency to trade very technically off simple borderline levels. The 100 and 200 bar MA, trend lines, remembered lines, and Fibonacci retracements are all the tools you need. Focus on the five-minute, hourly, and daily charts. Find those levels of significance—those borderlines where the bias is bullish on one side and bearish on the other. Those borderlines become the basis of low-risk trades. They define the risk. With risk defined, fear is dispersed. The borderlines also become targets, or exits along the trend highway. Not surprisingly, they also are your exit points for your trades. The more obvious the level, the better a borderline it is.

Remember that nontrends transition to trends. Train yourself to look for nontrends. Then look to catch the trend early. You will not know if it will work until it gets going, but be patient. Look to invest in your business when it is time to risk *profit* for greater profit. If the market does not do what it is supposed to do, get out. If you do, you should find that even when you lose, your losses can be profits too. When you do have losses, the losses are minimal, and you live to trade another day.

Attack the currency trend. Currency trends will make you money with the least amount of risk and that, traders, is the mission. Believe it, and you might suddenly become the luckiest trader on the face of the earth. God bless and good fortune with your trading.

About the Author

G reg Michalowski is the chief currency and trading analyst for FXDD. He has been with the firm since its inception in 2001. Michalowski's career prior to FXDD included six years at Citibank NY, where he was an assistant vice president and trader in the treasury/funding area; four years as vice president and interest rate derivatives trader at Citibank London; five years at Credit Suisse First Boston NY as a vice president and trader in the bank's funding department; and two years with Tradition NA, where he helped spearhead technology projects for the global inter-bank brokerage firm. Michalowski maintains a daily market commentary and currency analysis web site at http://forex.fxdd.com. His comments on currencies have been quoted by Reuters, Bloomberg, and the *Wall Street Journal*. He has written for various publications, including *eForex*, and is currently the featured Forex Columnist for *Equities* magazine. He speaks regularly at trading conferences and seminars around the world. He is also a featured contributor for www.greenfaucet.com and www.stocktwitsfx.com. His twitter site, http://twitter.com/gregmikefx, was one of thirteen cited by *SmartMoney* magazine as a "go-to" source for making money moves.

Greg lives with his wife of 25 years, Debbie. They have three sons, Matt, Brian, and Bobby.

Index